The History of Barrios Unidos

Healing Community Violence

Frank de Jesús Acosta

Edited by Henry A. J. Ramos
With a Foreword by Luis J. Rodríguez

Arte Público Press
Houston, Texas

This volume is made possible through grants from Barrios Unidos, the Charles Stewart Mott Foundation, the City of Houston through the Houston Arts Alliance, the Exemplar Program, a program of Americans for the Arts in collaboration with the LarsonAllen Public Services Group, funded by the Ford Foundation, the James Irvine Foundation, and the Rockefeller Foundation.

Recovering the past, creating the future

University of Houston
Arte Público Press
452 Cullen Performance Hall
Houston, Texas 77204-2004

Cover design by Exact Type
Cover art by Rene Garcia

Jesús Acosta, Frank de.
    The History of Barrios Unidos: Healing Community Violence / by Frank de Jesús Acosta; foreword by Luis Rodríguez.
      p. cm.
    ISBN 978-1-55885-483-3
      1. Urban violence—California—Santa Cruz—Prevention. 2. Community organization—California—Santa Cruz. 3. Political participation—California—Santa Cruz. 4. Communication in community development—California—Santa Cruz. 5. Santa Cruz (Calif.)—Social conditions. I. Title.
    HN80.S26J47 2007
    303.6'90979471—dc22   2006051751
                                                             CIP

7 8 9 0 1 2 3 4 5 6   10 9 8 7 6 5 4 3 2 1

Dedication

Dedicado a mis padres María de Jesús Acosta y Luis Barrios García and my siblings Carmen, Henry, and Joe for their love and spirit. Para toda mi familia de sangre y de espíritu—beloved nephews and nieces, mis tíos, tías y primos de la familia Fonseca, my twelve godchildren y mis estimados compadres. To my tío José "Chavito" Fonseca, who stepped up to be a father when I needed one. Thanks to Luz Vega-Marquis, Gary Yates, Tom David, Gwen Foster, and Antonio Manning for believing.

Special thanks and blessings go to Henry "Kiki" Ramos and Rubén "Ray" Lizardo, first for their brotherhood and love, second for their critically important contributions to the editing and writing of this book. The love, hope, faith, and humanity of el movimiento remain the cornerstone of our carnalismo. Special thanks to research fellows George Galvis, Claudia De La Rosa, and Venice Williams, the support team of Tawnya Lewis-Mason, Jamie Hilao, Amanda Quintero, Ceylida López, Roberto De La Rosa, Hiranya Brewer, and artists Anthony Rene Garcia and Frankie Alejándrez. Gracias to Luis Rodríguez, Gabriela Baeza Ventura, Dolores Huerta, Harry Belafonte, Connie Rice, Tom Hayden, and Manuel Pastor for their contributions.

Gracias Willie B., Sam Law, Johnjohn P., Ray y Abby, Kiki y Claudia, Primo Oscar, Rolling Stone and Tawnya, Serena M., Mariano y Ruby, Ruben G-2Dogs y Sarah, Sylvia B., Peter N., Bong-Jonah, Stewart K., Cecilia S., Michael-Hootie, Phillip y Jason K., Richard V., Mama Cora and Helen, Boo2, Leonor, Steve y Vannia, Arturo-Congo, Angel Z., Antonio M., Turie V., Roberto L., Waterbug, Sky, Blanca, Bear, Greg-Kudu, Steve-Tiger, Michael L., Brian-Babycakes, Ronnie de la Calle, Ernie G-Wintergardens, Juliamaba, Juliam, Magdalena y Frankie, Fr. Kiki Smolich, Pastor M. Fink, Fr. G-Dog Boyle, L. Rodríguez, Tom-Big Mountain, Wayne S., Anthony C., Irma R., Sandra G., Susan A., Linda B., Susan N., Debbie C., Jai Lee, Linda W., Gwen

F., Fran J., Angela S., Larry A., Paul V., Jaime R., Connie R., Joe H., Gary-Monk, Marisa A., Cindy C., Benny T., Denise F., Gary D., Winston D., Frank G., Skid-Graciela, Tony G., Tim N., Berky N., Victor R., Marlan O., UCLA MEChA, Mike (Nikayla/Trista) Adair, and the JT's gang. Las familias Acosta, García, Fonseca, Palumbo, Bamish, Mason, Lizardo-Rincón, Ramos-Camacho, Díaz, Ruíz, Abaigar, Law, Kobayashi, Nishita, Verches, Kallio, Delgadillo, Balaoing, Shibuya, Chu, Pond, Procello, Jung, Almeida, Ten-Houston, Alejándrez, Quintero, Ayala, Domínguez, Ybarra, Gonzales, Manning, Kim, and Zapata.

Para Nane y Jenny, OT y Sonia, Elder Henry, Walter Firekeeper, Liz, Lulu, Monico, Los Albinos, Vampira, Los Manuels, Rip-Richard, Mitch, Caranina, Shawnalle, Amanda, George, Joaquín, Anthony, Las Teresas, Chemo, Ted, Wayne, Jaime, Yvonne, Roberto, Claudia, Ceylida, Leslie, Manny, Hiranya, Jim, Tío Alberto, Marko, Frank V., Nghia, Magdaleno RA, Dr. Loco, Edward James Olmos, Danny Glover, Hari Dillon, Victor G., Ida H., Patricia P., Len B., and all Peace Warriors and Adelitas of the Barrios Unidos family not mentioned but remembered. To Gaylord, Baba Dodley, Mae, Shed, Venice, Sean, Jerome, Amy, Harvard, Greg, Jcohn, Khalid, Haatim, Kwabena, Brandon, Ernest, Kyle, Steve, Deamon, Busi, Desmond, Regi, Jerod, Tywan, Eddie, Craig, Fonde, Rhatib, C.J., and all of the elders' circles, nation builders-warrior poets, and Simba Nation. *Ashe!*

To Syd Beane and Floyd "Red Crow" Westerman for the blessing of my first sweat lodge. Amor y gracias to my uncle and spiritual guide, Henry Domínguez. To my circle of friends and colleagues who have waited patiently for me to return from this journey—the Watts Century Latino Organization, the Institute for Community Peace, the Los Angeles Multicultural Collaborative, and the Liberty Hill Foundation.

In loving memory of William Acosta, Paula Avalos, Samuel Law, Florence Bamish, Oscar Soto Jr., Fran Díaz, Father Luis Oliveras, Danny Verches, Linda Mitchell, Freddie Ramírez, Carlos Ruíz, Michael Ruíz, Ralph Abascal, Peter Pond, Manuel Martínez Jr., Ted Jefferson, Walter Guzmán, and those most recently departed—Naiche Domínguez, Jr., Rubén Gregorio Maldonado, Frank del Olmo, Ray Gatchalian, Corky Gonzales, Bert Corona, Coretta Scott King, Lalo Delgado, and Marco Firebaugh. To all the homies and innocent souls fallen from or heartbroken by barrio warfare.

Contents

Editor's Note

As a young person growing up in California, I learned early on about the culture of gangs and the institutional inequities that give rise to them. I was comfortably protected from these realities on account of my business-owning, middle-class family's decision to reside on the relatively posh west side of Los Angeles. This largely shielded me from the meaner streets of East Los Angeles and South Central and ensured that I would attend some of the city's better public schools. Nevertheless, I occasionally bumped up against the gang life—*la vida loca* of homeboys and homegirls all around southern California. I found urban gangsters of various kinds by virtue of my interests and my sense of social responsibility, being one of relatively few Chicanos back then who was privileged.

Even on the higher-end west side of L.A. we had Chicano gangs. Those known as "Sotel" in West Los Angeles, the Venice "*13*" gangs, and various overlapping or competing gang families in Santa Monica and Culver City were highly active. Throughout my youth these groups were constant sources of oversight and control by local school authorities and police. They were also periodic threats to my scholarly and sports-centered orientation, which to the gang-bangers I knew seemed to make me both a curiosity and a source of pride. On occasion, they would mock me for being "too white," but they also treated me with a surprising degree of respect for my sense of license and my success in Anglo society. Other than me, they did not know other Chicanos who had been socially and academically successful. Out of deference, they kept their distance from me, notwithstanding occasional signs of disdain for my inclination to play in the *gavacho* world.[1]

---

[1] *Gavacho* is Spanish for one who is "other"; in contemporary Chicano parlance it is typically used as an insulting reference to white European Americans.

When school officials at my elite and largely white high school fell onto problems managing warring gang sets on and near campus, they called upon me to intervene. At a meeting they assembled with Chicano gang students, the hardened Latino youth showed stony stares when asked by the administrators why they would not participate in school academic and social activities, like other students: why they always seemed rather to want to remain on the side or to party and fight. In the deafening silence that ensued, I spoke up. Administration executives, who knew me as a campus leader and model student, were surprised to hear me assert that the school was not creating an inviting environment for Chicano youth. Listing a long line of concerns that I had gleaned from observation and just a few pre-meeting conversations with the Latino students, I implored the school administration and faculty to take greater initiative. I encouraged them to reach out to Chicano students, to become more engaged in the local Latino community, to consider hiring more Latino staff, and to add teaching content to the school curriculum that was relevant to Chicano youth. When the meeting ended, the Chicano gang leaders in attendance came over and quietly thanked me for saying what they felt but could not express.

In my pursuits as a student-athlete, I came to know many communities in the Greater Los Angeles basin, owing to team tours that took me to football games and basketball tournaments in which I competed all around town. My travels exposed me to gangs in virtually every community of color in southern California. The Chicano gangs on the east side of Los Angeles were even more active than the ones where I lived. They were more numerous and more violent too. Their frequent knife and gun battles, and the level of their members' dislocation from mainstream culture, were constantly lamented in local news reports. But, from what I saw firsthand in my travels around the city, the socioeconomic conditions that produced these alienated youths were obviously inequitable. Seeing these conditions up close helped me to understand the gang youths' pent up rage and hopelessness. Asian and African American gangs that I encountered along the way were similarly informed by the harsh living conditions that faced their members and families.

When I went away to college to the University of California at Berkeley in northern California, I became exposed to racial and ethnic gangs across the state. Over and over again, at each encounter with young people living the gang life, I saw similar patterns. Poverty and dislocation were driving factors leading the youth to seek protection and place in gangs. Official reaction and policy was heavily implicated in this. Teachers, police, and social workers—authority figures of all types—were frequently directing these kids toward life's edge, sometimes by design and other times out of sheer ignorance. Too many of the adult figures talked down to the youth rather than with them. Many of the authorities blindly tracked kids into dead-end educational and job programs, often without any diagnostic testing or attention to the young people's interests. Most of the elders misunderstood or disregarded the youths' history and culture. In these ways, the powers that be set up a self-fulfilling prophecy of failure for minority adolescents and teens throughout the system.

The decades following my early exposure to gang culture produced even much harsher realities and outcomes. A combination of disinvestments from state educational and youth recreational programs, economic decline in many inner cities, and massive population increases in the nation's minority communities produced greater gang activity and social dislocation than ever. A disturbing rise in gun- and drug-related violence followed, reaching by the early 1990s unprecedented proportions. Burgeoning incidents of community violence and resulting impacts on emergency and hospital intensive care personnel compelled state authorities to declare the situation a public health crisis. In California, the problems were as bad as anywhere in the United States, and Chicano gangs were heavily involved in the worst of it.

Public reaction was crushing as voters elected a majority of conservative lawmakers who in turn instituted some of the most draconian policy responses imaginable. As a result, the imprisonment of Latino and African American youth and young adults skyrocketed to the point where the prison populations of color began to surpass the populations of these groups in schools and where public investment in new prison construction began to surpass expenditures not only for new school facilities but also for some basic social services and almost all violence prevention programs. Against this backdrop, relatively few grassroots advocates on behalf of affected minority youth had the capacity or the vision to step into the breach and lead a response. The Santa Cruz-based organization known as Barrios Unidos (BU) was one of the few that did. Its subsequent work has helped to model what effective violence prevention and social justice leadership can look like in the modern era.

This book tells Barrios Unidos's compelling story. It underscores the organization's focus on the humanity within even the most hardcore of gang-banging youths, its attention to culture and redemption, and its commitment to faith. It tells of powerful lessons resulting from this work that policy leaders all across the nation can and should learn from. The Barrios Unidos story is one that shows the power of authentic peer support (the organization's founders and principals are former gang members and offenders themselves). It demonstrates the value of understanding history and learning its lessons. Barrios Unidos's story additionally reflects the importance of spiritual and religious practice, discipline, and steadfastness in the face of adversity. Finally, a careful reading of the Barrios Unidos experience enhances appreciation of the potential for multicultural partnership and understanding: BU's impressive evolution has been marked throughout by numerous key collaborations with Native American, African American, European American, and other racial and ethnic leaders. Taken together, these aspects of the Barrios Unidos story should establish the book that follows as mandatory reading for Americans of all backgrounds who wish to learn how to help America succeed as a functioning multicultural society.

During the mid 1990s, Frank de Jesús Acosta, a former youth leader, immigrant advocate, and community organizer, joined The California Wellness Foundation (TCWF) staff to direct its newly established Violence Prevention Initiative (VPI). The VPI was a nearly $75 million, decade-long investment program to which TCWF had committed itself in order to help address the epidemic of gang and gun violence that was devastating youth, families, and communities across the state. One of the new program director's early major decisions was to support Barrios Unidos with $750,000 in multiyear grant funding. BU had only recently established itself as a legal nonprofit corporation, having operated for over a decade as an unincorporated network. Acosta's early investment in Barrios Unidos was one of the most important gifts ever directed to the violence prevention field. His early support and later close affinity with the organization's founding leaders led him to be asked by those leaders years later to write this story. They trusted him to recount the Barrios Unidos experience with a healthy balance of biased love and objective, informed analysis. Acosta's resulting book provides just this delicate balance.

Barrios Unidos's activities over the years, though not without challenges and setbacks, have produced historic gains for Chicano communities facing institutionalized racism, poverty, and violence. Its public policy advocacy leadership has helped to pass important legislation leading to new investments in gang prevention and intervention programs in the state of California. Its particularly strong partnerships with leading Native American and African American social justice leaders have inspired groundbreaking advancements for U.S. multiracial coalition building. Its development of cutting edge cultural economy programs has established new models in grassroots community enterprise strategy. Finally, its innovative work to bring peace to violence-ridden communities while offering new opportunities for gang-affiliated youth has saved countless lives and families.

Until recently, few observers considered BU to be a civil rights or social justice organization, as such. But its body of work, its intellectual/philosophical inclinations, and its wide following of leading American social justice figures reveals its status as a rights and justice anchor institution. The testimonies provided in this book clearly make the point. The commentators Frank Acosta has assembled herein to shed light on the larger significance of BU's work speaks volumes. These are some of progressive America's most revered and accomplished activists and thinkers. Their observations, coupled with the book's caring treatment and thoughtful analysis of an important history and field make this a special publication, indeed. Owing to these considerations, it is an honor for Arte Público Press to have the opportunity to feature Barrios Unidos in our civil rights history series.

Books like this one play a critical informing role in raising public consciousness and encouraging still-needed social justice reforms. Younger readers—both Hispanic and non-Hispanic—who did not directly experience the particularly harsh realities that gave rise to organizations like Barrios Unidos should especially benefit from exposure to this story. By reading Acosta's account, they may take into greater consideration than otherwise the merits of playing a supportive role in combating continuing social and economic injustice. They may contemplate pursuing an activist path in law, education, or community and labor organizing. They may furthermore gain insight into how much commitment, patience, and hard work is often required to forge even the most basic advancements in civil and human rights. Finally, they may gain a deeper appreciation of their own privileges and opportunities in contemporary society and a stronger sense of responsibility therefore to assume some leadership in shaping the social justice history still to be made.

The Arte Público Press Hispanic Civil Rights Series that makes this publication possible seeks to educate, inform, and inspire Americans of all backgrounds—and especially younger Americans—by lifting up the United States Latino community's many important contributions to and struggles for justice in America. With support in recent years from funders, including the James Irvine Foundation, the Charles Stewart Mott Foundation, the Rockefeller Foundation, the Ewing Marion Kauffman Foundation, The California Wellness Foundation, The California Endowment, Carnegie Corporation of New York, and Prudential Financial, the series is producing more than twenty original works by and about many of the leading protagonists of Latino America's post-World War II civil rights history.

Raising awareness about these informing, but still remarkably under-chronicled chapters in U.S. social advancement is more important than ever, as Latinos have emerged to become the nation's new minority of record. With now nearly 40 million individuals comprising the national Hispanic community and a burgeoning youth population that demographers predict will result in fully one in four Americans being of Latino heritage by the year 2050, it is imperative for all citizens and longtime residents of the United States to gain a more evolved comprehension of Hispanic people and for Hispanic Americans themselves (along with their closest friends and allies) to tell the stories of their experiences and social justice contributions over recent decades.

By bringing forward these affirmative stories and the voices of leaders who helped to shape them, Arte Público Press seeks to develop the texture of recorded U.S. history in ways that elevate public recognition of the Hispanic role in defining what it means to be an American. It also hopes to encourage expanded public dialogue about the important continuing social justice work that still needs to be done in Latino and other communities of the United States that confront enduring inequities.

Frank de Jesús Acosta's book, *The History of Barrios Unidos, Healing Community Violence: Cultura Es Cura*, is a truly important addition to our series. The book was largely made possible by a generous grant from the San Francisco-based James Irvine Foundation. We are most indebted to the foundation's president, James E. Canales, for contributing not only to this volume but also to several others that we are currently completing on California Latino and Latina rights leaders. We are additionally grateful to The California Wellness Foundation's Gary Yates for core funding support and to Luz Vega Marquis of the Marguerite Casey Foundation and Stewart Kwoh of the Asian Pacific American Legal Center, whose trustee contributions as board members of The California Wellness Foundation helped to supplement our financial support for this publication. We are also thankful to Gwen Foster and her colleagues at The California Endowment and the David and Lucile Packard Foundation for offering additional supplemental support for the book. Finally, we wish to recognize Hari Dillon and the Vanguard Public Foundation of San Francisco for its support of Frank Acosta's research and project activities that led to this work's ultimate presentation in book form. These partners' assistance provides a shining example of the broad-based collaboration we seek to help us tell the important stories we bring forward through Arte Público Press's work. We are deeply indebted to these and other leaders who have made essential gifts to assist our efforts.

Henry A. J. Ramos
Executive Editor
Hispanic Civil Rights Series

Foreword
Yocoxcayotl: The Movement for Peace and Healing Through Barrios Unidos

Peacemakers are not much valued in our culture. What they do takes time. It takes principles. It takes long-winded, often unproductive meetings and tense dialog. It takes immense patience. People with guns often speak louder. They get heard. They get attention—especially from the prized major media that won't get near a peacemaking process unless blood is shed. Some of those with guns even get paid (many peacemakers I know don't). It's sexier to have an army, to have technologically advanced weaponry to threaten and hurt people. Most armies don't want to fight—but when they do, more gets done than all the talk, meetings, and paperwork that most peace work entails.

War is sweeping, undeniably conclusive, in your face.

And yet, peace happens. It lives. It thrives. Most people in this country are living relatively peaceful lives—most people in the world for that matter. Even in the most violent urban core community, peace gets made. You won't hear about it too often, but there are peacemakers in our families, schools, churches, workplaces, and even among gangs.

Peacemakers among gangs?

¡Claro que si! You simply wouldn't have the great lulls between wars or the fact that most gang youths aren't involved in violence, if this weren't so. Look at the statistics: 250,000 gang members across the land (that's one estimate; it ranges from much lower to much higher). But you still aren't getting 250,000 gang members killing people. Not even a tenth of that. Maybe it's closer to 1 percent (2,500) in a year. Who really knows—statistics on gang violence and murders are far from exact. Law enforcement agencies have yet to decide what

constitutes a gang killing. Los Angeles and Chicago—by far the cities with the highest incidences of gang violence—don't even use the same reporting criteria.

Don't get me wrong: Gangs are a major social problem in this country. When gang members do murder, it destroys families, communities, and our social fabric. It's so tragic because it's usually the young who are dying: people cut down in their prime, intelligent, beautiful, young people who leave behind parents, siblings, and friends. Many times innocent people are taken—babies even. The firepower in the streets is the same as what is used in most civil conflicts around the world: AK-47s, Uzis, and more. In Los Angeles alone, gang violence is believed to have taken around 15,000 lives since 1980. It's also top news. It's on all the television news shows and newspapers. The truth is, any gang killing is one too many.

But yet, even among gang members, there are peacemakers.

Peacemakers, like the individuals that make up Barrios Unidos. The Barrios Unidos organization is on the frontlines of the urban peace movement in this country—it has been for more than a quarter of a century. Barrios Unidos members are about *Yocoxcayotl*—the Mexican Nahuatl word for the path for peace.

The organization—led by the charismatic Daniel "Nane" Alejándrez—includes gang members, former gang members, and non-gang members. It includes youth, children, parents, workers, teachers, the unemployed, spiritual practitioners, and professional organizers. They've been saving lives without much fanfare or accolades for more than twenty-seven years, but they don't stop.

The recognition Barrios Unidos has received is much appreciated. Its multiple sources of funding help to create schools, computer centers, opportunities for cultural expression, employment, housing, and more. But Barrios Unidos members do this work for something much greater: the love of family, community, culture, and tradition.

The love of life.

Nane Alejándrez is a peacemaker—I would venture to say, one of the most self-sacrificing, dedicated, consistent, and humble peacemakers we have ever seen in the United States, if not the world. He's a former Chicano gang member and drug addict. He's a Vietnam War veteran. He bears the scars, tattoos, and the post-traumatic stress syndrome memories. With several of his family members dead and close to thirty family members in prison, you know he's been surrounded by violence and the results of violence his whole life.

Yet, his manner is steady. Gentle. Bright. Compassionate. And intelligent. Nane Alejándrez is proof that you can never write anyone off, no matter how lost they may seem or one believes they are. So much human potential and social capital is wasted in America's predilection to criminalize people and youth of color.

Remember the late Chicano poet Abelardo "Lalo" Delgado's great 1969 masterpiece, "Stupid America," which is a plea to slow down, pay attention, and see below the surface in order to find the Nanes of this world and help prepare a place for them. That's what Barrios Unidos does: its whole mission, approach, and work are summarized in that poem's essential message: Don't write anyone off.

I've known Nane for some ten years. I met him in 1995, at a crucial time in my life—two years into my sobriety (I had finally stopped after twenty-seven years of drugs and alcohol). I got to know well his team of healers and organizers: OT (Otilio Quintero), Liz Ayala, Walter Guzmán, Henry Domínguez, Mary Lou Alejándrez, and the others. I met them shortly after beginning to take seriously my art, including the publication of my 1993 best-selling memoir, *Always Running: La Vida Loca, Gang Days in LA,* and to work among troubled urban youth. In 1994, I helped create Chicago's Youth Struggling for Survival (YSS) to help establish more respectful and meaningful relationships among adult mentors, parents, and at-risk youth. In the many years that have followed, Barrios Unidos has become a touchstone for peace, one of the spiritual and cultural centers of the urban peace movement, our teachers.

Like when my own son, Ramiro, got caught up in the web of the crazy life, Nane and Barrios Unidos invited him, YSS members, and the many other people we worked with in Chicago to conferences, peace summits, and dialog. They saved us. They helped my son, despite his later incarceration, to become more mature, creative, spiritual, and aware—even behind bars.

There are several other reasons why I can testify from firsthand experience to the power of healing and reconciliation behind Nane's and Barrios Unidos's intensive peace work. I've been a peace warrior and activist for more than thirty years—even as a teenage gang-banger and drug user in the streets of my East L.A. area barrio, I eventually found a political and social consciousness in the Chicano Movement that propelled me into trying to end barrio warfare. Prior to that, I had walked out of my middle school during the 1968 East L.A. "Blow-outs" in which thousands of students walked out of public schools to demand better education. I took part in and got arrested during the 1970 Chicano Moratorium against the Vietnam War. I painted murals, helped organize Chicano students, learned Mexican indigenous dances, and helped develop a truce between my barrio and our main enemy barrio.

I left the gang life and drugs soon after committing to revolutionary social, economic, and cultural change. In my mid-twenties I began to lead poetry workshops in prisons, juvenile facilities, schools, and various L.A. barrios through the Barrio Writers Workshops of the L.A. Latino Writers Association.

When I moved to Chicago in 1985, I became active in the vast poetry scene there and lived among hip-hop dancers, MCs, and graffiti artists. I did workshops in homeless shelters, juvenile halls, schools, and prisons. Despite my own battles with alcohol and negative impulses, I kept struggling for more healing, more knowledge, more connections.

In 1993, *Always Running* got published, and everything escalated for me. I gained the opportunity to sit on the national stage and to convey what I had learned all those years (now sober and in a better frame of mind and spirit) to important new audiences. My connection to Nane Alejándrez and Barrios Unidos was vital in keeping me grounded as a person and as an activist.

It was their example, after Barrios elder Magdaleno Rose-Avila ended up working with L.A. gang youth deported to El Salvador, that sparked my efforts to help create Homies Unidos, an international gang peace movement focused primarily on engaging Salvadoran youth across the United States and Central America in healing and transformation work.

Years later, after I had moved back to Los Angeles, Nane and Barrios Unidos attended the opening of Tía Chucha's Cafe Cultural, the Chicano-oriented bookstore, cafe, art gallery, performance space, cyber cafe, and workshop center that I helped to establish in the Northeast San Fernando Valley section of the city—the "Mexican" side of the Valley. Nane came with prayers and eagle feathers, presenting me with one in a magical moment captured by a PBS-TV production crew.

I'm honored to have known and worked with Nane and his Barrios Unidos staff and supporters. I thank the Creator that I'm part of such a vital and crucial peace movement.

Sadly, as Nane and the Barrios Unidos family know all too well, being a peace champion is not sexy. It's not lucrative. It's often heartbreaking and traumatic. But peace, even just a little bit, even for just a little while, is worth it all. The hope is that the work of healing and transforming ailing lives and broken communities will call to everyone.

¡Órale pues! That's the brand of thinking and spirit that guides Barrios Unidos's warriors, organizers, teachers, healers, thinkers, and doers. Their work is successful because Barrios Unidos is fundamentally informed by a righteous legacy complementing strategies, traditions, values, talents, and prayers—because they understand the deepest truth: that the arts and the heart are the greatest paths to peace.

Yocoxcayotl.

May the Creator bless them, protect them, and guide them for as long as they're needed, for as long as any of our youth and families are caught up in the madness, dying just to die, with little or nothing to live for, little or nothing to dream, with our communities broken and at each other's throats. For as long as we have war and uncertainty, that's how long the truth and beauty of Barrios Unidos should grace our lives with hope, vision, connectedness, and meaning.

Luis J. Rodríguez

C/S

Author's Note and Acknowledgments

When I was first asked by the leadership of Santa Cruz Barrios Unidos (hereafter Barrios Unidos, or BU) to be the scribe and messenger of their story, I was both deeply honored and overwhelmed by the daunting nature of the task. There I was, freshly departed and recovering from the singularly most gratifying yet taxing position of my professional career, having served as the senior program officer of The California Wellness Foundation's (TCWF) Violence Prevention Initiative (VPI) for five years. My tenure with the Foundation had allowed me to bring my collective experiences as a professional and advocate in human services, youth development, race relations, immigrant and refugee rights, and community development work to a new focus. More importantly, it took me into local, state, and national arenas that connected me to some of the most diverse, creative, intelligent, capable, compassionate, and committed people that I have ever encountered in my life.

The VPI is considered by some community advocates to be one of the most cutting-edge philanthropic ventures ever undertaken to focus on at-risk youth and promote community empowerment. Providing $70 million in grants over ten years to support community peace projects, develop new youth and antiviolence leaders, establish new bodies of multidisciplinary research, and promote more constructive social policy, the VPI was a significant and groundbreaking effort by any measure. The imaginative VPI public health approach brought together an incredibly diverse cross-section of fields and disciplines. By design and by necessity, the VPI focused on issues of poverty, justice, equity, and discrimination as root causes of violence.

The VPI umbrella created unprecedented neutral space for an unusual mix of players to collaborate, including homeboys and home-

xxiii

girls* straight out of the barrios and ghettos of the state, grassroots nonprofit leaders, health and human services professionals, religious groups, law enforcement officials, researchers, educators, lawyers, and policy wonks. The sheer diversity of these various stakeholders created real challenges to building trust, communication, common vision, and a culture of cooperation. But an underlying shared commitment to alter the landscape that had produced epidemic rates of violence and loss across California in recent years prevailed; our unwieldy cohort of violence prevention advocates produced substantial collaboration and public benefits throughout the Initiative's lifespan. Barrios Unidos was a critically important element and leader of this work. This is one of the major reasons why I gained interest in writing the organization's history and accomplishments as a logical follow-up to my tenure heading up the Wellness Foundation's Violence Prevention efforts.

Foundation staff that directly supported the VPI included my esteemed colleagues Gary Yates, Tom David, Michael Balaoing, Crystal Hayling, Tawnya Lewis, Susan Bozeman, and Magdalena Beltrán Del Olmo. National experts from various fields, such as Larry Cohen, Rubén Gonzales, Susan Cameron, Ray Gatchalian, Rene Wilson-Brewer, Gary Delgado, Ralph Abascal, Ken Kizer, Jonathan Fielding, Sheldon Margen, Darnell Hawkins, Douglas Patiño, Luz Vega-Marquis, Loretta Middleton, Andrew Maguire, Liz McLaughlin, Alice Lytle, Peggy Saika, Greg Berg, Jack Calhoun, Mark Rosenberg, Jim Mercy, Barbara Staggers, Larry Wallach, Linda Wong, and Debra Prothrow-Stith, also advised the Foundation. Several other private foundations provided vital financial support as partners of the Initiative. A few foundation representatives involved themselves quite deeply, with notable contributions coming from Mariano Díaz, Jai Lee Wong, and Gwen Foster of The California Endowment. VPI grantees spread across the state and nation are ultimately responsible for the VPI's many successes and a legacy of helping to create and legitimate a new field of inquiry. I would encourage everyone interested in learning

---

*Homeboys and homegirls are vernacular references to local youth or relations who share grassroots neighborhood experiences, often in connection with street gangs.

more about this historical effort to prevent youth and community violence to visit The California Wellness Foundation's website
(www.tcwf.org) in order to access its rich documentation of the VPI's
work and lessons.

I believe that my ending up at the Foundation, working to prevent
youth violence, came as divine intervention that enabled me to gain a
measure of redemption for deeds past. I was born in the heart of the
barrio in East Los Angeles, raised with two siblings, Henry and Carmen, in a single-parent household headed by a loving Mexican immigrant mother, Maria de Jesús Acosta. My mother worked herself to the
point of disability after years of toiling in multiple menial jobs.
Despite her best efforts, those long hours at work meant that I spent
much of my formative years on the streets. My father was out of the
house due to alcoholism by the time I turned five years old, and
although he lived in the neighborhood, he wasn't much of a positive
parental influence because of the advanced stages of his disease.

My mother would remarry when I was in high school to Luis García, and together they birthed my youngest brother, Joe. But for the
undying love, sacrifice, and prayers of my mother, along with her
example of devotion to familia, there is no doubt I'd be dead or in the
belly of the beast. Her prayers must have summoned an angel or two
at critical crossroads in our lives, because my older brother Henry and
I stretched the boundaries of our mother's protective faith and God's
grace through frequent engagement with gangs, violence, drugs, alcohol, and juvenile criminal activity. In so many ways my story is not
unlike many of those who the Wellness Foundation was hoping to
serve and support through the VPI. I was fortunate to survive my
youth as I look back upon things now through the mature eyes of
adulthood. All of my academic, professional, and civic involvements
of the past thirty years have sought in some small way to repay this
debt. Working in philanthropy to promote violence prevention offered
a special opportunity to honor my mother's admonitions to face life
and death alike, with enduring gratitude, integrity, and humility. So
each morning with a spirit of gratitude I walked into my Wellness
Foundation corner office on the seventeenth floor in Woodland Hills

reminding myself, "This is a long way from East L.A. Boy, don't let them down!"

The first time I set eyes on Barrios Unidos principals Nane Alejándrez and Otilio Quintero was at a VPI annual conference in 1995. In seeing Nane's gray fedora hat, Pendleton shirt, and black Ray Ban sunglasses, I was taken back to another time and place. Watching these two homeboys command the attention and respect of an audience of more than five-hundred people took me back to a political rally at a park in East L.A. that occurred when I was barely twelve years old. My boyhood friend Ernie Gonzales, also one of the neighborhood *cholitos* (street youth), and I had gone with some older *vatos* (guys) from the neighborhood to a rally organized to support the Chicano Moratorium, a protest effort of Mexican Americans and antiwar activists to halt U.S. military intervention in Vietnam. Of course, being *mocosos* (snot-nosed punks growing up way too fast), we went for all the wrong reasons, that is to cause trouble, meet girls, and get stoned. Along the way, though, Ernie and I somehow got pressured into holding a banner that read *"Raza Sí! Guerra No!"* Although I had heard slogans such as "Chicano Power" and *"Que Viva La Raza!"* (Power to Latino People) before, they quite honestly had never moved me. But as one speaker after another came to the podium, talking about justice and the lack of it in U.S. culture for Chicanos, these words and slogans took on meaning. The experience at the rally, my love of family, and an occasional nudge by a few good people along my subsequent path proved to be just enough to keep me from the abyss.

Now, more than half a lifetime later, as I watched Nane speak to the VPI audience, I remembered the first time I heard the term *barrios unidos* (united neighborhoods) and learned about the Coalition to End Barrio Warfare. It was many years after I had changed my own life, but I remember wishing that my friends Freddie, Blackie, Leo, José, Rudy, Jesse, and many other homeboys I knew who had lost their lives to gang violence, could have been enlightened and spared as I had been. I wish that they had been able to meet peace warriors, such as Nane, OT, Gus Frías, Blinkie Rodríguez, Mike Ortiz, Father Greg Boyle, Alex Sánchez, Luis Rodríguez, Piri Thomas, Liz Ayala, Marylou Alejándrez, Rubén Gonzales, Sylvia Beltrán, Albino García, Julia Sabori, Maggie Escobedo-Steele, George Galvís, Vampira Gallardo, María Texiera, Gilbert Sánchez, Bill Martínez, and Yvonne and Claudia de la Cruz—guardian spirits of the barrio.

After taking the job at the Wellness Foundation and meeting Nane, Otilio, and my adopted brother Rubén Gonzales, I knew I had found an extraordinary home base from which to learn and serve. In order to expand the VPI's prospects for success, I built a strong multicultural base of external support, including such people as Rubén Lizardo, Cecilia Sandoval, Henry A. J. Ramos, Syd Beane, John Castillo, Stewart Kwoh, Debbie Ching, Bong Hwan Kim, Linda Wong, Connie Rice, Antonio Manning, Karen Bass, Denise Fairchild, Gynethia Hayes, Joe Hicks, Larry Aubrey, Gary Phillips, Cindy Choi, Torie Osborne, Paul Vandeventer, Arturo Ybarra, and Angel Zapata. My path of prior community-based experience as a student activist at U.C.L.A, university advisor, nonprofit executive, and advocate with the United Methodist Downtown Social Service Center, Downtown Immigrants Advocates, the Coalition for Humane Immigrant Rights of Los Angeles (CHIRLA), and the Center for Community Change had all prepared me to effectively facilitate the vision and aspirations of leaders like Nane Alejándrez and groups like Barrios Unidos.

I was unabashed in my efforts to serve as a bridge between youth, grassroots leaders, community groups, and more mainstream institutional sectors. Fear of failing the communities I cared about proved to be the motivation I needed to succeed. Too often for people in our community the highway from the barrio to the boardroom turns into a one-way ticket for one passenger rather than a new pathway of access for many. My experience being a barrio Chicano with a serious activist bent, serving in a high-level mainstream institution, and trying to deliver on both ends while maintaining my integrity amounted to frequent struggle. I leave it for God and history to judge my success. But there can be no doubt that my years with the VPI involved more than just doing a job and collecting a paycheck.

By the summer of 2000, after serving five years at the VPI's helm, I was on the brink of exhaustion. I resigned from TCWF set on taking some time off to restore my physical and spiritual health. My hope was to work on a few select consulting projects and explore an independent full-time sabbatical arrangement that would allow me to write about the field of violence prevention and the community peace movement. I began to take monthly trips to Santa Cruz to heal and find my spiritual center by learning more about indigenous ceremony with Barrios Unidos elder Henry Domínguez, Nane, and others. One of these spiritual retreats dramatically changed my plans and my life. On that occasion, following a very beautiful and particularly powerful sweat lodge and pipe ceremony, the Barrios Unidos leadership circle prayed with me and asked if I would consider telling their story. They wanted, they said, to produce a book that would chronicle their journey since the organization's inception, and they wanted me to write it. It was an incredible honor to be entrusted with such a responsibility. Although I felt ill-equipped and in many ways unworthy, not being a journalist or published author, the only answer I could give to my brothers and sisters was yes. The journey between that moment of decision and the writing and publication of this book has been a long and winding road filled with challenges, serious setbacks, and tests of faith.

Only a few months after beginning to explore our publishing and financial support options, Marylou Alejándrez of the Barrios Unidos leadership circle suffered a terrible accident that almost took her life and that of her spouse. Shortly thereafter, Nane was diagnosed with an intestinal cancer that required surgery and a regime of chemotherapy and indigenous healing ceremonies over the course of a year. Marylou's full recovery and the complete remission of the cancer in Nane are among the most beautiful parts of the story behind the scenes that informed this publication. If all these challenges were not enough to derail us, my newborn nephew, John (Little John of God), would then be called to fight for his life for several months in the intensive care unit of the Whittier Presbyterian and Children's Hospitals. I offer two poems at the conclusion of this publication—*A Prayer for Nane* and *Of a Child and Mother*—that were born of these periods of struggle. All of these experiences were emotionally and spiritually taxing, and they naturally slowed completion of the book that follows here.

Other logistical and personal factors would further complicate and delay the project's completion. Even after receiving generous project support from The California Wellness Foundation, The California Endowment, and the Washington Mutual Bank for planning, research, and development, it would take until the summer of 2003 before I could move to Santa Cruz to begin a fourteen-month residency at Barrios Unidos. Becoming a part of the daily life of the organization and family would enable me to write the book through a process of true immersion and participatory research. Taking in the pain, beauty, hard work, and continuous nature of the struggle, as well as the depth of love and spirit that is Barrios Unidos, meant opening my heart and rolling up my sleeves. The organization and its history cannot be fully experienced any other way. In the end, the time in Santa Cruz thus gave me back my heart and soul. But approaching the book this way also took more time than any of us had anticipated.

After returning to Los Angeles for the final stages of the book's completion, we hit a couple more bumps in the road. A serious leg injury kept me bed- and home-ridden for months, all while the organization fought through its worst financial crisis since the establishment of its nonprofit arm. And, just in the past month, we also lost longtime Barrios Unidos resident artist and founding circle member Rubén Molina.

The many challenges and delays that marked the development of this work helped us all to find new wisdom, hope, and faith. During the entire period of Nane's conventional western medical treatments, we gathered in the *temascali* (sweat lodge) at the Barrios Unidos retreat site every weekend to pray, sing, drum, and give thanks to *Tata Dios*. Nane also received traditional medicine and healing ceremonies from indigenous elders who came to Barrios Unidos or whom he traveled to see. Through Nane's trials, and those of other BU family members, we developed multiracial ecumenical prayer chains involving leaders of the Simba Circle in Chicago, Columbus, Milwaukee, and Strawberry Point, as well as the Survival Camp Sundance at Big Mountain, the Watts Century Latino Organization of South Central Los Angeles and the Washington, DC-based Institute for Community Peace.

The relentless staying power of those closest to this work who suffered setbacks as it was being completed offers an apt metaphor for the Barrios Unidos organization's resilience. Nane's healing has been truly miraculous. He has been given a clean bill of health and remains cancer-free in a manner that has baffled his physicians. Elder Henry Domínguez, who has nurtured Barrios Unidos and seen us through so much, has suffered through bad health, the loss of a son to prison, and the passing of his young grandson Naiche. Still he walks on for his family and stands proudly for Barrios Unidos. Marylou is well and moving forward. Little John spent nearly a year in the hospital after his premature birth but now smiles, jumps, and dances (despite lingering health challenges) to the everyday delight of his family. It is important to report that the Barrios Unidos organization learned valuable lessons from its recent fiscal crisis, made some critical adjustments, and is now a stronger and more viable nonprofit than ever as it moves forward with exciting new development plans.

This is a story of redemption and humanity, of liberation and purpose for the young ones in the barrios of America. The prayers and unyielding support of our families, the perseverance of the Barrios Unidos leadership circle and our institutional partners, and the abiding faith of our project underwriters have made this long road worthwhile. Special thanks and gratitude belong to Henry A.J. Ramos and Nicolás Kanellos of Arte Público Press, who never gave up on me. Their editorial support, substantive suggestions, and allied advice, along with contributions from California Tomorrow capacity building director Rubén Lizardo, were essential elements of the book's successful publication. Simply stated, without the role played by these partners, particularly Henry and Rubén, this book would have never been finished and made public.

Henry Ramos opened the door for the book to be produced at the University of Houston by Arte Público, the nation's premier Latino-focused publisher, as part of its civil rights series. As my book editor, he also played a major role in making this work not just an interesting story about BU, but also an important contribution to the literature in the fields of Chicano history and violence prevention. He fundamentally strengthened my initial manuscript through formidable editorial work and analytical insights that contributed mightily all along the way. Rubén Lizardo provided early editorial guidance that included his own gems of insight and analysis, as well as unbending moral support throughout.

There has been a long period between our announcement of the project and its completion. Early on, I promised Barrios Unidos supporters Danny Glover, Hari Dillon, and Harry Belafonte that it would be done in their lifetimes. We can now say to them and the many others who contributed, participated, and believed in the telling of this story that we kept our promise.

Originally, our idea was to make this book an equal treatment of both Barrios Unidos and the Simba Circle (Rescue, Release and Restore, Inc.) movements. The Simba Circle is a model Afrocentric rites of passage program for young men, which like Barrios Unidos centers on culture and spirituality. In fact, I spent two summer sessions in Strawberry Point, Iowa, as witness to the transformative power of the Simba Circle. The Simba Circle youth, elders, army of nation builders, and warrior poets embraced me as a brother of Africa. They remain represented in this book but deserve their own. However, when the opportunity arose to make this book part of the Arte Público Press Hispanic Civil Rights Series, it made perfect sense to lift up the Barrios Unidos story in that context. So, with the blessings of our brothers and sisters at Simba, we changed course. This book remains a testimony to our collective work and partnership as Latinos and African Americans, working together to preserve and advance the history and common destiny of our people. Sharing our message of solidarity in common struggle and purpose with others in our respective communities must continue.

As I used to tell the Simba Circle's founder, Gaylord Thomas, it is no coincidence that both of our ancestors built pyramids and great civilizations yet continue to stand tall in the midst of great suffering, pain, injustice, and oppression today. To all our African American brothers and sisters, I say here that your middle passage is our trail of tears, and your *Sankofa* is our return to *Aztlán*. By taking our children and communities on an intellectual and spiritual pilgrimage to their ancestry and history, our people find healing, identity, commonality, and higher purpose in the world. The destiny and future of our people is inextricably interwoven, from the motherland of our ancestors to the spaces on Mother Earth that we now share. My brothers and sisters of Simba—I prayed for you, and you prayed for me, now we are one. One love, one struggle, one Creator! *Ashe!**

The leadership of BU wanted this story to be told by a family member and not a professional writer, and for choosing me I am eternally grateful to them. Nane Alejándrez especially believed that there would be power in a *barrio* brother from the south (me) and a barrio brother from the north (him) sharing in the telling of this story of higher love and solidarity. I pray that this exercise in faith was not wasted. The book is equal parts storytelling, literature, history, journalism, poetry, and feeble attempts by this author to use any other means available to capture the kind of beauty, truth, heart, spirit, and power that the Barrios Unidos organization embodies. Without a doubt, sharing in this journey has been one of the most transformative experiences of my life. We pray that in the final judgment it will be well worth the struggle of the journey. It is dedicated to all those who live, work, and sacrifice for love, justice, compassion, and peace anywhere in the world. The struggle continues! And in the words of my elder and hero, Dolores Huerta, *¡Sí, Se Puede!*

---

*Ashe is a statement of affirmation frequently used at the Simba Circle. It means "Let it be so!"

Introduction
The Power of Culture and Spirituality:
*Cultura Es Cura**

Culture is the mother of vision. Developing people need to rediscover the life-preserving, life-enhancing values and insights of their own traditional experience. They need to understand [historically] what happened to them as a people—what forces and changes made the world the way it is today. Every culture within it contains pathways for seeking new visions of human possibility . . . these must be vigorously and systematically pursued . . . articulated and connected to the hearts and minds of the people.

Michael Bopp and Phil Lane Jr.

The story of the Barrios Unidos community peace movement and the organization known today as Santa Cruz Barrios Unidos now spans some thirty years. It is a story of individual struggle and redemption by its early pioneers who discovered a way out of the street gang warfare, addiction, and poverty that grips the barrios of America. It is also the story of an evolving grassroots mobilization originating in the Mexican American (or Chicano) civil rights and antiwar movements of the 1960s and 1970s, which focused on collective efforts to bring unity and peace to fractured, violence-ridden Latino communities in California and other states.

Over the course of a quarter-century, BU's work has grown and evolved. That work has engaged thousands of people, saved untold scores of lives, developed leaders, and instilled hope that has helped to transform neighborhoods across the country. This book tells the

---

*Cultura Es Cura is Spanish for "Culture is the cure." Also referred to as "La cultura cura."

story of how Barrios Unidos and its leadership circle harnessed the power of culture and spirituality to rescue and restore imperiled young lives, provide avenues to quell gang warfare, and offer a promising model for building healthy and vibrant multicultural communities.

BU's founding is inextricably tied to Daniel "Nane" Alejándrez, its executive director. A child of the violent, squalid migrant farm-worker camps and the drug-infested barrio of Fresno's Westside, Alejándrez overcame heroin addiction and entrapment in gang warfare to become one of the most influential social justice and community peace activists to emerge from the late 1970s. He came to believe that internecine fights between Chicanos only served to distract them from uniting to fight their true enemies: discrimination and injustice. Rather than fighting and killing each other, he believed Chicanos needed to develop a positive sense of their cultural identity and use that to promote their rights. By the 1980s Alejándrez was promoting cultural politics as a potent aspect of personal growth, solidarity within the broader Chicano community, and expanded social and economic equity.* As Alejándrez reflected at Barrios Unidos's twenty-fifth anniversary celebration on October 26, 2002:

> We are at a cultural and spiritual crossroads where we must reclaim the truth and traditions of our heritage as we move forward toward the promise of our future. As we have learned to know and respect ourselves, we have learned to honor and respect the dignity of others. We need to practice nonviolence and embrace old and new partnerships with those that share our vision for equal social and economic justice for all people. This is the true and only path to peace.

To be sure, violence remains a persistent problem in contemporary American culture. There is an ongoing war that plays itself out daily in the homes, streets, schools, and workplaces of this nation. Far too many people, from all walks of life, lose their lives to violence every day in America as a result. The United States supports one of the highest rates of violence, homicide, and incarceration in the indus-

---

*See Daniel Alejándrez and Aaron Gallegos, *Peace Warrior, Survival and Transformation in the Madness of the Barrio* (Unpublished manuscript, 1998), in the Barrios Unidos archives.

trialized world. According to the National Center for Injury Prevention and Control, youth violence is a leading cause of death and injury in the United States among individuals 15 to 24 years of age.

These alarming statistics, particularly pertaining to youth, have not and will not be changed as a result of quick-fix, "super predator" myths leading to policies that try youth in our courts as adults or incarcerate unprecedented numbers of young people. Michael Males, author of *The Scapegoat Generation*, points out the hypocrisy of blaming youth for social conditions that they did not create. Males, like other experts from various fields and disciplines, believes that the roots of violence are to be found in the expanding reach of poverty, racism, inadequate housing and education, unemployment, and other indices of human suffering. Such reflections of socioeconomic imbalance, in turn, are perennial sources of antidemocratic policy and practice across the planet and the span of history. Each generation's struggle for justice is framed against the backdrop of chronic inequality. Thus, perhaps, the most accurate bellwether for the vitality of American democracy today is the welfare of our children and the degree to which poverty and violence permeate the fabric of our society.

Dr. Robert M. Franklin of the Interdenominational Theological Center, speaking before an Institute for Community Peace conference in 1999, used a passage from Mary Shelley's classic novel *Frankenstein* to illustrate metaphorically the dimensions of youth violence in our time. The passage captures the dramatic high point of Shelley's story: Dr. Victor Frankenstein coming face to face with the disgruntled monster he had stitched together from the stolen remains of corpses to create a "perfect" human specimen. The words uttered by the benighted creature to his creator bear a haunting resemblance to the mind-set and mood of young people today, who in so many instances have been abandoned by America's increasingly tattered assemblage of adults, communities, and institutions:

> I am malicious because I am miserable. Am I not shunned and hated by all mankind? All around me I see bliss from which I alone am irrevocably excluded. You, my creator, would tear me to pieces. Consider that and tell me why I should pity man more than he pities me? If I cannot inspire love, I will cause

fear. I was virtuous, misery made me a fiend. Make me happy, and again I shall be good.

In the process of neglecting and abandoning, then criminalizing and demonizing contemporary youth, we are mass-producing such sentiments among those who are relegated to the far fringes of society. The imaginative use of Mary Shelley's book by Dr. Franklin does not apply solely to poor young people of color. He has also aptly connected the sentiments of Dr. Frankenstein's monster to outbreaks of violence among young people reared in comfortable homes and communities where a profound inner emptiness, alienation, and misery often equally reside. According to Dr. Franklin, a growing array of factors account for our society's expanding incidence of youth violence: a general sense among young people of spiritual crisis, a deep aimlessness, a lack of noble purpose, and isolation from family and community. These sensibilities, which transcend race, class, and culture, speak to a creeping detachment from higher universal values or "moral literacy" and seem to characterize too much of what is happening in our society today. The moral literacy of which Dr. Franklin speaks requires us to model and teach enduring virtues—justice, truth, goodness, compassion, and magnanimity—that flow from the humanity of all cultures and that can be distilled from history's most redemptive lessons.

In his brilliant and incisive book, *Hearts and Hands, Creating Community in Violent Times*, writer and youth advocate Luis Rodríguez calls for a radical realignment of societal and personal priorities that coincide with the imperative to re-create a communal environment in America, one that fosters our children and youth to the fullest expression of their humanity. An essential part of his message is that healthy children, strong families, and nurturing communal structures are prerequisites for ameliorating youth violence in society. "A violent and fractured community," he contends, "will produce violent and lost children."

Since its inception, Barrios Unidos and the community nonviolence movement has been driven by the hope of rebuilding society's human and institutional fabric to sustain healthy children, youths, and families. To this end, it has used a wide variety of organizational strategies extending beyond services to address the broad-ranging needs of its constituents. In this regard, Barrios Unidos is not a traditional youth service organization; rather, it is a hybrid social enterprise that works in a holistic fashion with youths, families, and institutions to build human and community capital that inspires practical social change.

The unfathomable violence and inhumanity that occurred on September 11, 2001, makes it incumbent on all of us to reaffirm what is good and just in the United States. Though several years removed, the trauma of that fateful morning lingers. As individuals, it is only natural to do whatever it takes to recapture a sense of security and justice, recalibrate our moral compass, and lean on the regenerative powers of the human spirit to make sense of the madness. But as our government officials, private institutions, civic leaders, and the international global community focus outwardly on issues of international terrorism, the war in Iraq, disarmament, and spreading democracy and human rights, we must not neglect the ongoing challenges that face our nation within its own borders. There remain far too many American families and children that live without the bare necessities of life. Poverty and its attendant social dysfunctions pose a real threat to individual health and welfare, as well as community and democracy here at home.

This book is not a science-based evaluation of the efficacy of Barrios Unidos's programs and community-based strategies to build community and prevent youth violence. The organization and the communities it serves have been the focus of many studies and evaluations over the years.* Neither is the book another exhaustive history of gangs, an etiological study of gang culture, a collection of gang survivor biographies, or even a social commentary on the impact of gang violence on communities; other authors, poets, social commentators, and academicians, from Jimmy Santiago Baca and Sister Sha'Keyah

---

*As participants in a landmark grant-making program of The California Wellness Foundation's ten-year, $70 million Violence Prevention Initiative, for example, Barrios Unidos and sixteen other innovative community-based violence prevention programs were the subject of a multimillion dollar evaluation designed by capable professionals at RAND, Johns Hopkins University, Stanford University, Portland State University, and the Children's Hospital of Los Angeles. Visit the Foundation's website at www.tcwf.org.

to Tom Hayden, James Diego Vigil, Malcolm Klein, and Joan Moore, have covered that terrain well.

Instead, what follows here is a chronicle of the Barrios Unidos movement—a movement committed to redeeming and giving back the dignity and identity of children, youths, and adults who have experienced the unfathomable pain and despair of living in exile from their own humanity. This book is written as a compilation of stories—much in the way of indigenous storytelling—about key individuals in the movement and the times in which they have lived and worked to achieve justice.

A core objective of the book is to place the origins of the Barrios Unidos movement in the context of the nation's civil rights struggle, past and present. As BU's story unfolds, the connection between the community peace movement and the larger struggle for civil rights in this nation becomes apparent. This story needs to be told. It is a central part of the broader history of Mexican Americans in the second half of the twentieth century. It is also a story that has thus far been sadly marginalized. Our hope here is to correct this omission of our history in America.

THE BU MOVEMENT: HISTORY AND EARLY INFLUENCES

As the Vietnam War raged overseas during the 1960s and 1970s, another war was taking shape in the poorest communities of this country. On the streets of the barrios across California and the Southwest, a growing portion of the Chicano community—and the younger generation in particular—became increasingly alienated from a mainstream society that held little regard for Chicano culture and heritage or the notion of extending equal opportunity to Mexican Americans. Grinding poverty and imposition of the dominant culture had broken down the social fabric that historically bound families and communities together. A sad byproduct of communal disintegration was the rise of destructive gang-related activity and violence that pitted participating Chicano (and other minority) youths against one another in territorial warfare. The need to unite warring neighborhoods in the struggle for justice, equality, and peace gave birth to the concept of *barrios unidos*. The term *barrios unidos* literally means united neighborhoods (or communities), and it was drawn on as a deliberate philosophical statement that sought to use common culture and human experience to create a new collective consciousness. Its underlying belief was that the individual and collective empowerment of Chicanos and Latinos in America was rooted in reclaiming and restoring their cultural pride.

Prior to the emergence of a definable Chicano movement, American injustice was mostly cast in a black/white paradigm, even among emerging Chicano activists. The language, themes, icons, heroes, and historical benchmarks of the Chicano movement were, accordingly, drawn largely from the African American experience. According to Henry Domínguez, a longtime Barrios Unidos elder and spiritual leader, African Americans developed the building blocks of liberation and unity for those seeking to bring peace to poor minority neighborhoods. Latinos built on these landmarks in search of self-esteem, common identity, and the restoration of communal values in Chicano *cultura* and traditions.

The resulting sense of collective cultural identity stimulated students and young people, who were drawn to the movement's emphasis on dignity, self-worth, pride, and a feeling of rebirth. A new culturally-based solidarity marked the development of community members identifying themselves as Chicanos before any other political or personal distinction. Chicano scholar Juan Gómez-Quiñones points out that this new ideology was amplified by the seminal Chicano civil rights groups of the era: the United Farm Workers Union, the Crusade for Justice, *Alianza Federal de las Mercedes*, and the La Raza Unida Party. Moreover, activist Chicano groups, such as the Brown and Black Berets, the Chicano Student Organizing Committee, and the Chicano Moratorium, forged sophisticated and well-articulated, culturally-based organizing platforms that remain benchmarks for Latino youth activism and community building today.

Drawing on this history, Barrios Unidos and allied social activists engaged early on with the emerging field of Chicano Studies at the academy, ultimately forming a core mission and pedagogy for the BU César Chávez School for Social Change. A common ingredient across BU's academic, general education, and leadership programs remains teaching young people to be critical thinkers and astute observers of history and contemporary events in a way that informs their activism and service to the community.

Many important civil and human rights leaders contributed significantly to the Chicano civil rights legacy. But three of them—César Chávez of the United Farm Workers (UFW) union, Rodolfo "Corky" Gonzales of the Crusade for Justice, and Reies López Tijerina of the Alianza Federal de las Mercedes—were particularly important in the development of Barrios Unidos. What made their leadership distinctive to BU principals was their dual application of *cultura* and spirituality, not only as it pertains to political and social theory, but also relative to effective organizing and institution-building. During the 1960s, Tijerina and Corky Gonzales helped to coin the term (and concept of) "Indio-Hispano," a reference that openly explored the dual identity of Chicanos as Amerindian and Spanish for the first time in an important political way.* Tijerina's indigenous rights organization, Alianza, laid claim to ancestral lands in New Mexico usurped by the United States in violation of the Treaty of Guadalupe Hidalgo. Tijerina articulated the philosophical basis for cultural consciousness and political action among Latinos/Hispanics in America and surfaced their connection to an indigenous past. Reflecting on his youth, Tijerina wrote in his recently published memoir, *They Called Me "King Tiger,"* "I felt like a stranger on this great planet. I did not know the history of my people, much less the world. I had to learn many things so that I could understand the rights of my people and how to help [them]."

Tijerina was among the first in the movement to articulate the parallel struggle of Chicanos, African Americans, and Native Americans, building alliances among all three groups. He was also one of the first to voice publicly special historical connections between Chicanos and Native Americans, based on their common cultural and legal relationship to the land. Alianza's work in New Mexico was crucially important to connecting Chicanos to a newfound appreciation of their land,

---

*It should be noted for the record that at least one Barrios Unidos interviewee with whom I spoke in the preparation of this publication recalled Corky Gonzales articulating serious ambivalence about the term *Hispano* during a visit to the organization in the late 1990s.

their culture, and their collective history of struggle—all of which helped significantly to bridge gaps between urban and rural Mexican Americans and between the Chicano and the broader civil rights movement. By acknowledging common elements of struggle across racial lines, Tijerina helped to articulate the particular interests of Chicanos in the vernacular of the civil rights movement, serving as the first Chicano chairperson of Martin Luther King, Jr.'s Poor Peoples Campaign.

Like Tijerina, the late Corky Gonzales was a source of many of the radical cultural polemics of the Chicano movement. Gonzales was among the first social activists to draw a straight line of cause and effect between loss of cultural identity and the frustrations, anger, and breakdown of the communal fabric that led to gang and family violence. He saw the need to build community-based institutional structures as supports for organizing and social cohesion. The Crusade for Justice, the organization he founded during the late 1960s, was among the first full-fledged, multipurpose, Chicano-oriented, activist organizations in the United States.

The Crusade for Justice Center, located in Denver, Colorado, served as a social, cultural, and political base for the community. It sponsored critically important events and offered a unique space for community-building among Chicano activists. Its activities included theater, dance, and art shows designed to promote Chicano unity and pride; strategy meetings to address and resolve important issues affecting the community; and civic gatherings intended to foster strength, inspiration, purpose, collective mobilization, and political will. The Crusade also established La Escuela y Colegio Tlatelolco, a primary, secondary, and undergraduate school that provided a culturally-based educational curriculum focused on preparing future community leaders. Gonzales was fiercely committed to involving youth in the leadership of the movement. The Crusade sponsored three National Chicano Youth Liberation Conferences that helped to galvanize direction and solidarity around broad movement goals. More than any organization established during this period, the Crusade for Justice provided the institutional and strategic organizing framework for Barrios Unidos.

The third and perhaps most important civil rights figure that profoundly influenced the philosophy, values, and principles that guide Barrios Unidos was César Chávez. The late leader of the farmworker struggle for justice and dignity was instrumental in creating a moral and spiritual framework for Chicanos and Latinos in America in much the same way that Martin Luther King, Jr. did for African Americans. The moral authority and spiritual dimension that César Chávez brought to the movement inspired a new generation of activists and broadly exposed the conditions of the Latino poor to the American public, engendering widespread support for change in a way other efforts in the Chicano civil rights movement had not. Chávez offered a set of values, principles, and practices that honored the most revered elements of Chicano cultural identity, while building a national political movement committed to achieving justice, equality, peace, and reconciliation among all people.

Much like Martin Luther King, Jr., Chávez described the desolate conditions of the poor and articulated their aspirations in a manner that appealed to the highest, most universal beliefs of humanity and democracy. And he embraced the principles of nonviolence and nonviolent organized resistance. In these ways, Chávez effectively transcended his status as a Mexican-American leader to achieve a far-reaching multicultural leadership standing. But the farmworker organizer was firmly rooted in his core constituency's essential make-up and needs. He fundamentally understood that, for Chicanos, culture, spirituality, community, and socioeconomic progress were inextricably tied together. The *Virgen de Guadalupe*, for example, the indigenous apparition of the Virgin Mary—and, for many Chicanos, the patron saint of the poor—served as the galvanizing symbol of organizational and political unity for Chávez's union, the UFW.

These three activists—Tijerina, Gonzales, and Chávez—exerted a profound influence on Nane Alejándrez and on his early conceptualization of Barrios Unidos. The first years of BU's work, beginning in 1977, can be traced to the grassroots organizing work of Alejándrez in the poorest communities of West Fresno, California, and at the University of California, Santa Cruz. Already working under the banner of Barrios Unidos in a growing number of northern cities, including

Fresno, Santa Cruz, and Watsonville, Alejándrez met Gus Frías, the founder of the Coalition to End Barrio Warfare during a trip to Los Angeles. Concerned Chicanos and Latinos, also referred to as *Raza*, started the End Barrio Warfare (EBW) movement in the violent streets of East Los Angeles to alleviate the senseless killing of brother by brother. Frías writes in his book, *Barrio Warriors, Homeboys of Peace*, that the EBW movement brought together gang organizers, street workers, and other interested parties from throughout California to find creative solutions to the problem of gang and community violence. From the late 1970s through the early 1990s, Barrios Unidos worked with the California Coalition to End Barrio Warfare as the Coalition's organizing arm in the northern part of the state, promoting nonviolence values and strategies. Together, they broke new ground by developing workshops and school presentations, a network of trained gang workers across California, and a series of highly visible peace summits and conferences. This fruitful partnership helped to forge many of Barrios Unidos's subsequent organizing and mobilization strategies.

During these early years in the development of Barrios Unidos, community organizers were volunteers. Most were either students or young adults holding down entry-level or part-time jobs to pay their bills. Alejándrez, for example, was a student at the University of California, Santa Cruz at this time. Nane was known around the communities in which he worked as the gang worker who used the trunk of a 1964 Chevy as his office. There, Alejándrez would carry the tools of his trade: educational and outreach materials, T-shirts that he would silk-screen in the living room of his home, and poster boards filled with photographs and Chicano art. In this traveling caravan of peace, Alejándrez would pull up to street corners, local parks, schools, churches, community organizations, and wherever people would gather and listen to him, to recruit young people. The original Barrios volunteers were supported in this work by small donations that paid for lunch and gasoline.

BUILDING AN ORGANIZATION, SUSTAINING A MOVEMENT

The period between 1989 and 1993 can be characterized as a period of institution-building for Barrios Unidos and a reaffirmation of its own, and the community peace movement's, core values. By the mid-1980s, BU leaders had made spiritual expression and indigenous ceremony centerpieces of their theory of change. To them it had become evident that standard conventional interventions alone, emphasizing either constructive alternatives to violence and crime or official criminal sanctions, could not be relied upon to solve the problems of Latino or other youth involved in gang and related antisocial activities. Instead, as they saw it, cultural awakening, awareness, and respect were the essential keys to progress. As a result, *Cultura Es Cura* (Culture is the Cure) came to be known as BU's guiding philosophical tenet, and a wide array of alternative healing and consciousness-raising practices came to anchor the organization's efforts. This was considered groundbreaking, faith-based work aimed at ending the cycle of violence in communities across America. Much of BU's development in this direction was inspired by indigenous Native American traditions and influences, including those extending back to the origins of tribal civilizations throughout the Americas. As Aaron Gallegos wrote in *Sojourner* Magazine (January-February 1996):

> Latinos in the United States who are conscious of their indigenous roots are joining American Indians in sustaining their faith through prayers in the sweat lodge, purification with sage, the sacred pipe and sun dance ceremonies. Called *Cultura Cura*, or healing culture, it includes ceremony, rituals and art that can be used to help many Latinos overcome the multi-generational pain that surrounds them and can lead to death and destruction [via involvement in gangs, counterculture, and/or other antisocial behavior]. Its healing flows through the expressions of communal traditions and life through art, music, poetry and *danza* of the vibrant Latino culture of *Aztlán*. The indigenous people of Mesoamerica saw no distinction between art and religion. *La Cultura Cura* can be a catalyst for the spiritual healing and renewal of the Latino community.

The movement toward spirituality and ritual ultimately distinguished Barrios Unidos in ways that spoke increasingly to young Latino gang members and at-risk youth. This cultural approach, combined with disturbing increases in California youth violence and the urban unrest that culminated in the 1992 Los Angeles riots, elevated BU to a key position in the national youth violence prevention field. Significant foundation grant support and new opportunities to expand followed.

As the organization grew to become a multimillion-dollar social enterprise between 1993 and 2004, the challenges of growth proved to be many, but so did the rewards. The past decade has produced rapid institutional growth for BU through the expansion of its program services, staff, funding sources, local and statewide partnerships, and property assets. Growth can also be marked in the form of Barrios Unidos's affiliate chapters; over the eleven-year period dating back to 1993, close to thirty BU affiliate chapters were established in cities across the nation. Moreover, during that time frame, Santa Cruz Barrios Unidos became affiliated with The California Wellness Foundation's massive network of grassroots and civic leaders, policy centers, universities, medical institutions, multi-sector civic organizations, and public officials interested in working together to prevent violence against youth.

The 1993 National Urban Peace and Justice Summit in Kansas City, Missouri, catapulted BU into the national spotlight. In the aftermath of the 1992 civil unrest in Los Angeles, a truce that began between the primarily African-American gangs known as the Crips and the Bloods in that city began to spread to other black gangs in cities across the country. Parallel truce efforts led by Barrios Unidos and the Coalition to End Barrio Warfare in Latino communities across California created a natural alliance. Working with lead summit organizer Carl Upchurch, Nane Alejándrez and Fred Williams from Los Angeles served, respectively, as the Latino and African-American cochairs of the historic gathering in Kansas City. There had never before been an organized effort to bring together Latino and African-American leaders of the community peace movement in a venue of this magnitude.

Significant organizational growth and enhanced standing in the national field pushed Barrios Unidos to evolve. So too did changing circumstances. As a result, the Barrios Unidos theory of change has evolved over time and continues to evolve. Because the organization's change orientation is at the core of its work, it is an important focus of the story here. Key aspects of several chapters that follow examine how cultural and spiritual considerations served to make BU's theory of change more explicitly value-driven than many nonprofit community organizations over time. Exploring the recollections of "elders" and "founders" about the early days and pivotal moments in the organization's development provides rich insights on this last point. Subsequent chapters provide program descriptions and an in-depth presentation of BU's "Model in Action" in ways that show how Barrios Unidos's work and thinking have actually helped to advance the community youth development and gang violence prevention fields.

An important focus of BU's community change strategy is informing and promoting the development of creative social and economic policies to address the root causes of violence. In large measure, the organization pursues this work programmatically and in ways that are comprehensive. Thus, a full chapter is dedicated here to exploring the related dimensions of Barrios Unidos's education and skills-building projects, including the organization's enterprise arm: BU Productions and its recent land acquisition program. In addition to this work, the organization has been involved in seminal policy education and advocacy activities that challenge counterproductive juvenile and criminal justice practices, lax liquor and firearms sales and licensing policies, and draconian immigration- and race-focused measures (such as California Propositions 187 and 209), which have substantially diminished the quality of life in the state during recent years, particularly for Latinos and other poor minority populations.

During the late 1990s, the organization's policy education and advocacy efforts were particularly instrumental in helping to inform the passage and implementation of Assembly Bill (AB) 963. Known as the California Gang, Crime and Violence Prevention Partnership Program, AB 963 has substantially increased public grant resources directed to grassroots organizations with demonstrated competence in promoting violence prevention. This legislation's passage established a milestone rewarding years of hard organizing, skills development in policy advocacy, and coalition-building among multicultural leaders in California who see alternative public investments, rather than incarceration and harder sentencing, as the solutions to community crime and violence.*

CONTENT OF THE BOOK

The chapters that follow are intended to chronicle the essential elements and distinctions of the Barrios Unidos organization. The presentation is organized in five interrelated parts. Parts I and II track BU's formative influences and the early stages of its institutional development. Part III explores the guiding principles, values, and action strategies of the BU organizational model; it also examines the social justice dimensions of the organization's inter-cultural learning and exchange work. Importantly, this chapter illustrates how Barrios Unidos has historically collaborated with other organizations on strategy and programming and, most importantly, on efforts to build solidarity between Latinos and other racial/ethnic groups within the national community peace movement. In Part III, these issues are particularly a point of concentration in relation to BU's work with African American leaders and groups. Part IV of the book offers commentaries by several leading civil rights activists on the relevance of BU's work in relation to the ongoing struggle for justice in America: Dolores Huerta, Harry Belafonte, Tom Hayden, Connie Rice, and Manuel Pastor.

Finally, Part V seeks to synthesize major milestones, lessons learned, and associated recommendations for those interested in building further on the work and legacy of the Barrios Unidos movement. This concluding section offers some basic insights on possible future directions for BU and the fields of violence prevention, criminal and juvenile justice, youth development, and community-building.

---

*The Gang, Crime and Violence Prevention Partnership Act (penal code sections 13825.1-13825.6) was passed in 1997 and is administered by the California Department of Justice. The ensuing law has funded community-based violence prevention programs to apply a public health model for the prevention of youth violence in designated locations throughout the state of California.

An Appendix closes the book with various poems that speak to the *corazón* (heart) of the barrio and our indigenous Latino culture—the spirit of Barrios Unidos. In addition to featuring my own words and sentiments and those of other BU adherents, the Appendix includes the voices of selected African-American family members of the Simba Circle organization, one of BU's most important strategic allies outside of the Latino community.

Research for the book is built primarily on first-person stakeholder interviews and written testimonies, supplemented by related news media archives, organizational documents and reports, evaluations, and violence prevention field studies. Ultimately, I am responsible for any contents herein that may fall short of my aim to shed new light on the continuing struggle for civil and human rights in America, using the lens of creative organizational responses to the epidemic of violence such as have been developed by BU and comparable groups. My hope now is that this work will find a special place among the survivors of those who have lost their lives to gang warfare and violence, those who have found new lives through the transformational power of culture, and those who have dedicated their lives to the quest for peace and justice.

Part I
Barrios Unidos: The Formative Years

Introduction

Barrios Unidos's foundational work—its early formation, the development of its leadership, its implementation of effective core strategies, and its more recent institution-building efforts—now spans nearly thirty years. This is a blink of an eye in the vast history of Chicanos in America, whose ancestral roots extend into the past thousands of years to the indigenous civilizations of Mexico and Central America. Delving into antiquity, dating back at least five-hundred years to the Spanish conquest of the Americas, is critical to shedding light on the dynamics that have shaped contemporary Chicano life and the community organizations that have emerged to give voice and direction to Chicanos in America. Barrios Unidos is one of many such organizations. The magic of the Barrios Unidos (BU) story is that its founders and leaders have effectively and consistently drawn on collective history and wisdom to connect the distal corners of the past and present to the many people and communities the organization serves.

All social movements that have marked human history have been defined by the experiences, vision, values, and purpose of the men and women who have participated in and led them along the way. The story of the Barrios Unidos community peace movement is no different. It is the story of forward-thinking men and women who brought the BU movement—and later the organization—into existence. Because these visionary, purposeful, and committed people dared to empower and strengthen their families and peers along the way, it is also a story about how a community is defined, nurtured, and transformed.

The retelling of BU's early history requires exploration both of the particular circumstances that shaped its founders' approach to personal and community transformation, as well as the larger context in which their vision and leadership took root. This first part of this book thus examines both the personal and the contextual factors that informed the organization's founding, amplifying as much as possible the organizational founders' first-person accounts of the circumstances that brought them together and ultimately solidified their partnership in a movement dedicated to creating peace and social change.

THE HISTORICAL CONTEXT

Throughout the 1960s and 1970s the Chicano community of the United States waged a continuous struggle to achieve political and economic justice. Simultaneously, Chicanos pursued an equally important battle to achieve expanded cultural rights and autonomy by affirming the integrity and power of Chicano heritage and traditions. The issues of greatest community concern during this tumultuous period included achieving equity in education, politics, health, and economics; addressing the most blatant effects of institutionalized racism in police-community relations, urban ecology and land title disputes; and improving the status of Chicanos in key professional fields, ranging from law and medicine to media and the cultural arts. Although struggles in each of these domains achieved a degree of real success, a more sober review of the accomplishments of these times reveals relatively modest gains. These included basic reforms in social policy, somewhat improved representation in politics and civil society, and slight increases in upward mobility for Chicanos and other poor people of color in America.

At the same time, the Chicano movement that advanced these efforts for change inspired an awakening of community pride, self-determination, and activism. Scholars and community activists alike point to this amazing period in history as an unprecedented watershed moment. It was a time of cultural renaissance that unleashed new consciousness, energy, and spirit; it also fostered unprecedented Latino community civic engagement and expression. It is clear that the Chicano community's spirited and sustained activism during these years resulted in the opening of doors previously closed to Latinos in the political, educational, and social arenas. For these reasons, the Chicano movement is widely credited with helping many in the broader Latino community to achieve gains that had previously been reserved for only a privileged few.

Unfortunately, many of these gains would be re-contested by conservative forces beginning in the late 1970s. Among the array of successful retrenchment efforts organized by conservative forces to counter Latino and other minority gains of the 1960s and early 1970s were California's Proposition 13, the Supreme Court's *Bakke* decision, constant federal and local attacks on humane immigration policy, the development of the English-Only Movement, a host of draconian law enforcement and criminal justice measures targeted at black and Latino males; and "Reaganomics" (which fundamentally swung the political pendulum back in favor of protecting corporate wealth and privilege at the expense of the poor).

In the midst of this reactionary assault, the populist and grassroots efforts that had informed the successful Chicano student walkouts, the UFW-led grape boycotts, and the rise of the La Raza Unida Party began to give way to more mainstream and conformist Latino community leadership approaches.

Pulled into conformity by the purse strings of private and public funding, as well as the politics of maintaining a seat at the bargaining table, many movement leaders and organizations settled into roles as social brokers or defenders of gains that had been made, rather than continuing in their previous roles as catalysts for more fundamental change. It is precisely this social and political context that influenced and motivated the pioneers of the community peace movement to forge an alternative vision. Barrios Unidos's founders were squarely in this camp by the mid-1970s, when the first major wave of reaction to Latino gains in civil rights began to emerge.

SOCIOLOGICAL FACTORS

Although Barrios Unidos's founders drew heavily on the experiences and lessons of the civil rights and Chicano movements, they also concentrated on indigenous barrio culture in ways that those other leading movements did not. A major distinction for BU in this connection was the group's informing focus on at-risk youth and families and their marginalization and abandonment by mainstream society.

The process of social dislocation affecting these forgotten Americans has created, for many decades now, large intergenerational groups of abandoned young men and women who dwell in their own barrio subculture across the American Southwest. Over time, these groups have woven themselves deeply into the consciousness and social fabric of the Chicano community.

Some social commentators and scholars have characterized the development of this subculture as a statement of social defiance and cultural resistance; others have labeled the phenomenon more clinically as maladaptive socialization, deviance, or self-hatred. Still others view the development of barrio youth gangs as a survival strategy in an oppressive society. For some Chicano youths, street subculture clearly establishes a sense of identity, status, and belonging while providing a vehicle for expression; for others, it serves as a family and communal structure that those caught up in the gang way of life could not find elsewhere. These relatively positive responses to the significant hardships most Chicano gang members confront is a testament to such youths' innate resilience and need for community.

But just as clearly, there are real negatives associated with involvement in the Chicano youth gang culture. For most who have become involved, the street subculture, filled with the frustrations of poverty and alienation, has become a potent vehicle for directing their sights to racism, sexism, substance abuse, violence, and crime. The more negative values and norms of the street along these lines quickly breed self-destruction, fratricide, and community warfare. Dreams are dashed and lost forever in the rough-and-tumble world of gang warfare. The rules of gang life and of the streets are often cruel, resolute, and unforgiving. Individual identities become blurred and are eventually lost, along with lives, in the communal trenches of gangland and barrio life. Over time, the young men and women in this danger zone come to be known by many names other than their own, including *cholo/a*, *pachuco/a*, homeboy/girl, and gangster—all designations that have been embraced by those who have lived, died, or survived by the accords of the street.

Young men and women like these, seemingly lost but ultimately redeemed, have been the focus and engine of Barrios Unidos's powerful body of work, from the organization's founding right up through the present time. By developing a safe and authentic space for peer-to-peer support and evolution that lifts Chicano gang members to new levels of possibility, Barrios Unidos has filled an essential need that key social institutions—families, churches, youth clubs, for instance—once fulfilled for American youth, though sadly less and less so today.

According to many leading thinkers in youth development, the social, economic, and cultural dislocation of recent decades has dismantled the civic fabric that is needed to properly nurture and rear Chicano and other socioeconomically disadvantaged children. They point out that across rural and urban settings in America, the attention of poor people (adults, parents, elders, and youth) is mainly on mere survival—on scratching out a living to attain the most basic necessities of life. The stresses of modern industrial society on families and neighborhoods are not balanced by supportive communal structures in most U.S. communities today. Children and youth are thus left to be reared by over-crowded schools, under-resourced community service organizations, and institutions of social control, such as juvenile detention facilities. When these alternatives are unavailable or inadequate, young people typically find their way to the streets. The lack of cultural fluency in public schools, where young people spend most of their formative years, is a key factor in the failure of our society to properly socialize Chicano/Latino youth, particularly those who come from impoverished circumstances in the home.

In addition, the tendency of correctional institutions to focus on retribution rather than rehabilitation exacerbates the problem. As activist-author Luis Rodríguez has observed, schools and law enforcement are poor substitutes for a healthy family life and nurturing communal structures. With so many parents focused on the economic survival of their families or, as is increasingly the case, with so many children growing up without the steady presence of a parent or caring circle of adults, the various rites of passage that connect healthy childhood to responsible adulthood have broken down in most communities. In effect, the rituals of initiation that flow from the street and gang subculture have too often replaced traditional pathways.

BU's cornerstone tenet is *Cultura Es Cura*—culture cures. Implicit in this core organizational principle is the notion that restoring cultural traditions and values to the people is the essential medicine needed to begin healing what ails the youth of America's barrios. As their powerful stories show, many of the architects of the Barrios Unidos movement walk today as living testaments to the power of *Cultura Es Cura*. In the rediscovery of their true culture, each has found restoration, identity, dignity, and purpose. Much like the children and families that they serve, the early leaders of Barrios Unidos have themselves come from poor communities, lived in public housing projects, stood in welfare lines with parents, felt the disorientation of drug and alcohol abuse, served time incarcerated, and felt the deep pain of senseless violence in their homes and streets. Against all odds, through the trials of poverty, racism, addiction, broken homes, gangs, and community violence, each has found healing and redemption. The power of culture and spiritual transformation has been the source of their survival and success. Their stories profoundly evidence the Barrios Unidos movement's steadfast commitment to personal, family, and community empowerment.

THE FOUNDING CIRCLE OF BU: PEACE WARRIORS

Although BU's work has always been described by its founders as a collective endeavor—one that could not have been successful without the energy, commitment, and spirit of many men and women—the organization's foundational achievements have resulted principally from the vision and efforts of a few early leaders: Daniel "Nane" Alejándrez, Henry Domínguez, Walter Guzmán, Otilio "OT" Quintero, and, more recently, peace warrior Liz Ayala. The focus of this book, therefore, is on these principals, though clearly they were surrounded and supported by other organizational figures, such as Raquel Mariscal, Barbara García, Marylou Alejándrez, Billy Zaragosa, Manuel Martínez, Manuel Aparicio, Rubén Molina, and Cruz Zamarón. Still other second- and third-generation leaders have also played important roles in BU's development over the years. Because the story of Barrios Unidos is also their story, portions of this book include references to these individuals, as well as occasional mentions of other contributing personalities. However, the major focus of the text is on the organization's most prominent and informative founding leaders, most of whom completed detailed first-person interviews with the author in the preparation of this volume. (Sadly, Walter Guzmán, BU's founding board president, died in early 2000 before formal interviews with him could be conducted.)

This "first voice" approach to telling the story of Barrios Unidos's formative years provides invaluable insights into how its vision and core strategies were developed, why cultural and spiritual traditions became a central aspect of its work, and what factors moved early BU founders and other pioneers of the community peace movement in California to develop an organization that could sustain a statewide social change agenda over the long haul. Accordingly, much of the story that follows is about the journeys, relationships, and decisions of a few key principals within BU's founding circle of peace warriors. Without comprehending who these founders were and what motivated them to organize for peace, it is not possible to fully understand the Barrios Unidos organization or movement.

DANIEL "NANE" ALEJÁNDREZ, BARRIOS UNIDOS FOUNDER

Since the beginning, a key guiding force for Barrios Unidos has been its founder and executive director Daniel "Nane" Alejándrez. In so many ways, the story of this movement and organization is a reflection of Nane's journey from a child of the barrio to a purposeful and visionary leader for peace and justice. Born into the hard life of a migrant farmworker family and raised in the poorest neighborhood of Fresno's Westside, Nane's testimony to young people always underscores his early experiences contending with the disorienting effects of drug addiction and surviving the madness of gang warfare. As Nane puts it, "These dark forces of *La vida loca* had enveloped my family."

Nane recounts how his formative years were spent following the harvests from state to state with his family, as they struggled to eke out a meager living working as migrant laborers in fields across the country. From his birthplace in Merigold, Mississippi, to shantytowns in Idaho, Wyoming, Kansas, Minnesota, Oklahoma, New Mexico, Arizona, Texas, and finally California, Nane's earliest image of "home" was a run-down house or tent in the labor camps. Traveling with his father, mother, siblings, uncles, aunts, and cousins as they caravanned together across the country, it was not until his family settled in Fresno, California, that Nane learned what it felt like to live outside of a labor camp environment. He was fifteen years old when his family settled in Fresno.

It was through the migrant experience, says Nane, that he got a first sense of the two sides of life that would shape his future. Though they were in rural areas, the labor camps that Nane's family lived in were not immune to the ills of poverty and cultural dislocation that plagued Chicano families in America's urban barrios. According to Nane, widespread alcohol and drug abuse, violence and many forms of discrimination plagued the labor camps. The pachuco culture, which had seeped in from the urban neighborhoods to rural communities and labor camps, took firm root in Nane's family. "My father and several others in my family embraced la pachucada, paving the way for us younger ones to follow in the years to come."

Although the labor camps would bring Nane and his family into contact with many negative influences, it was also in this place of great pain and hardship that the Barrios Unidos founder would be exposed to significant life-giving forces. Chief among these were the commitment, will, and courage to take life's challenges head on, relying on creativity and constructive instincts as survival tools. It was also in the fields and labor camps that Nane gained his first exposure to a powerful messenger of social change, a man who would inspire his sense of purpose and possibilities.

At age sixteen, Nane was introduced to César Chávez's powerful message about the fundamental importance of peace and social justice to America's democratic integrity. Chávez's vision and life example would spark in Nane a lifetime commitment to promote peace and social justice. "I was only sixteen," says Nane, "but the spirit of the movement had found a central place in my heart." Standing in solidarity during a wage strike with a group of young farmworker organizers who were spreading the message of Chávez's then-emerging United Farm Workers (UFW) union, Nane's first organizing experience occurred in the melon fields of Mendota, California.

Nane was drafted to serve in the Army in 1968 and then sent into combat in Vietnam during 1970-71. The experience of fighting in a war he did not understand, against an enemy he did not hate, raised many questions for Nane. "Flying bullets, cries of anguish, and being surrounded by death have a way of giving fuel to epiphany," Nane warily recounts. "This war made as little sense to me as the war raging on the streets of the barrios back home." At the time, Nane decided that upon his return home he would dedicate himself to ending the madness raging on the streets by promoting peace.

Unfortunately, after his tour of duty in Vietnam was completed in 1971, Nane, like hundreds of other young soldiers, returned to America strung out on heroin—an addiction that he would have to battle for many years. So strong was the hold on him that, although he answered the call to fight for social justice and peace, as Nane puts it, "I continued to walk in two worlds through my first decade of activism."

Nane's return home to Fresno was fraught with other challenges. Within days of his return, he could see that his family had become deeply immersed in the local drug trade and street madness. Despite a powerful desire to become a peace warrior, Nane was thus drawn daily into the drug and violent street culture that had continued to grow in his absence. In the midst of this madness, he found employment and sanctuary in a place called Tomás Fashions. Tomás Bachicha, a former *pachuco* and local activist in Fresno, had turned his small clothing enterprise into a cultural and political gathering place in the community, supporting the work of the UFW, the La Raza Unida Party, and the Brown Berets. Nane's employment at Tomás Fashions offered the positive influences and social involvement that staved off a complete lapse back into the negativity surrounding him. Nane describes these years "as a time when the darkness that had wounded every lost *vato* in the barrios fought against the beauty and birthrights of his heritage for control of his soul." Over the next years, Nane battled drug addiction and the pain of violence all around him.

In 1975, after eleven members of his immediate family received long-term prison sentences, Nane vowed to make profound changes in his own life. He had become weary of the daily onslaught of pain and fear that accompanied living by the rules of the street. Apart from the disabling effects of his addiction, Nane, like others in his family, lived with the constant threat of street violence as well as fear of confrontation with local authorities. Ultimately, the fear of incarceration loomed large. In a very short period of time, more than thirty members of Nanc's family were incarcerated (a number of them remain in prison). These terrible circumstances solidified Nane's resolve to change.

While still struggling to disengage himself from the street life, Nane enrolled at Fresno City College and earned an Associate Arts degree. Then, in 1977, he transferred to the University of California at Santa Cruz and began to engage in Chicano civil rights organizing and the first stages of his community peace work. Nane concentrated his early efforts on work in Fresno, Santa Cruz, Watsonville, San Jose, and other northern California cities.

It was also at this time that Nane began to incorporate the power of indigenous culture and spirituality into his own recovery and discovery process (to overcome his addiction and direct his vision). In his own surrender to the healing power of culture, Nane found a prescription for community healing and transformation.

Nane Alejándrez's story of personal transformation and his related journey to establish Barrios Unidos winds through some of the darkest corners of America's barrios. It is a deeply personal tale of victory and achievement and of the tenacity and heart that he has poured into thirty years of social activism as an organizer, youth advocate, and standard bearer for a new civil rights agenda. Nane nevertheless insists that the story of Barrios Unidos "is much bigger than one man's salvation and singular achievements." As he sees it, the work of civil rights is far from complete because many thousands of women, men, and young people have yet to take up the fight to change conditions for the poor that remain remarkably unchanged forty years after America's War on Poverty. As Nane puts it, "I believe the work that this nation faces to end gang and community violence is inextricably linked to the work it must undertake to end poverty; in essence, achieving peace within poor communities and realizing the unfulfilled dreams of the civil rights movement are one and the same."

ORGANIZING IN THE EARLY DAYS

By the late 1970s the number of intentional injuries and homicides attributed to gang and street violence was reaching unprecedented levels in black and brown communities across the state of California. Concurrently, within the California Youth Authority (CYA) and the state's penitentiary system there was a schism forming between incarcerated Latino gang members from the north —Norteños—and those from the south—Sureños. According to BU founder Nane Alejándrez, "this trend would eventually galvanize a division of the state between north and south among Raza gangs and between the Bloods and the Crips in the African-American community." Leadership and power issues at the neighborhood level were determined by this complex network, with constantly changing alliances, subsets, and crews—all loosely connected to one or another of these major gang networks.

Responding to the alarming rise in violence and homicides, Nane's early peace work focused on organizing local events and reaching out to other peace workers across the state. He was looking for partners and allies who wanted to focus their ideas and energy on the growing dilemma of gang-related interpersonal violence. Alejándrez's early organizing efforts largely tracked and sought to mitigate the emergence of competing regional *clicas* (clicks or gang subsets) among Mexican and Chicano gangs up and down the state. Being from the north, he could clearly see the elements of a dangerous intracommunity conflict brewing as shifts in population and territorial concentration brought Norteños and Sureños into closer proximity and increasingly frequent contact during these years.

The Sureños, who were originally from Southern California, were quickly becoming strong throughout Northern California, in a territory that was until then controlled by Norteños. For many years, gangs in the north had identified with the Nuestra Familia, a major prison gang founded in 1965 in Soledad penitentiary. The gangs in the south identified with and were similarly assumed to be associated with La Eme, also known as the Mexican Mafia, the oldest and largest prison gang in the United States. Within each major gang and its subsets, tensions also existed between Mexicano immigrants and U.S.-born Chicanos. This complex set of fault lines created significant challenges for other organizations that sought to heal divided communities and build lasting alliances on both a local and statewide level.

To respond to these complex dynamics, Alejándrez and other BU leaders turned to a potent and inherently unifying concept: Barrios Unidos! The term *barrios unidos*, which connotes community unity, was drawn on as an affirmative aspiration that could serve simultaneously as a rallying cry, a strategy, and a vision for change. BU elder Henry Domínguez recalls first hearing the term at the Chicano Moratorium march in Los Angeles in 1970. As Henry recalls, *Barrios unidos!* was both a "*grito de esperanza* (cry of hope) and a call to recreate community." Because the term *barrios unidos* literally means united neighborhoods (or communities), the BU founders could invoke it as a compelling tool to inspire harmony and collective consciousness among poor grassroots Latinos of all backgrounds. A key premise of the concept of *barrios unidos* was the belief that individual and group empowerment of Chicanos and other Latinos in America was rooted in their shared efforts to reclaim and restore lost cultural pride.

As veterans of the Chicano movement, Nane, Henry, and others had witnessed the use of powerful symbols and themes to galvanize oppressed peoples. Almost immediately, they recognized that they could use the term *barrios unidos* and its deeper symbolic (cultural) meaning to effectively communicate their vision of a community peace movement capable of providing a powerful alternative to the pull of gangs. Although using powerful symbols to foment and amplify cultural solidarity was a strategy used by virtually all of the seminal Chicano civil rights groups of the 1960s and 1970s, Henry points out that it was the Brown Berets organization, a paramilitary youth group, that was first in the movement specifically to target hardcore homeboys and homegirls from the barrios and involve them in the struggle for justice. These efforts were highly influential to Barrios Unidos's early founders.

Even more influential to BU founders was César Chávez because of his dual use of *cultura* and spirituality as practical tools for building and sustaining a poor people's movement. "More so than other leaders in the movement," Nane says, "Chávez forged a direct link between the social movement to achieve justice and dignity for his people and their struggle to regain cultural and spiritual traditions of the past. Chávez believed the universal tenets of indigenous and other spiritual traditions provided a bridge between contemporary people that no political manifesto could."

Virtually everyone involved in providing leadership in the early stages of BU's work to end barrio warfare was both a child of gang madness and a product of the Chicano movement. Many of the earliest pioneers of the community peace movement in the north, such as Richard "Chocolate" Santana, Francisco Chávez, Rodrick Serrano, Willie López, Billy Zaragosa, Mike Chávez, Guillermo Aranda, Otilio Quintero, Bob Campos, Liz Ayala, Mary Lou Alejándrez, Janet Flores, Barbara García, and Raquel Mariscal, came from various fronts of the civil rights movement. Similarly, pioneers in the south, such as seminal leader Gus Frías, Johnny García, Ronnie Martínez, Henry "Topper" Toscano, David Sánchez, Mike García, David Plaza, and Charlie Durán, all had activist roots. Homeboys and homegirls straight out of the barrio, these early leaders were activists, organizers, educators, academics, counselors, attorneys, artists, actors, musicians, laborers, and students. According to Alejándrez, "The community peace movement needs and draws on people from all walks of life. . . . The common denominator is their understanding and *corazón* for the struggle of the barrio."

Nane describes early BU organizing work as an innovative enterprise that challenged peace activists to draw on a combination of street wisdom and their experiences in the Chicano movement to fashion dynamic messages and tactics that could attract youth involved in or influenced by gang or street culture. "My early organizing approach included stumping and preaching peace while I was working at the *cultura*-focused company Tomás Fashions. That job enabled me to plan community cultural events in partnership with such local groups as the UFW, the Brown Berets, La Raza Unida Party, MEChA, Teatro de la Tierra, Teatro del Barrio, and Mi Chante Café." Indeed, the job provided Nane with a base to find unfettered visibility before hundreds and even thousands of young gang members and potential allies at countless gatherings throughout the state of California. Focusing on issues such as police abuse, poor community resources, failing schools, and other long-standing social justice problems, Nane took his message of community peace to holiday fiestas, Chicano art and music festivals, and political rallies and conferences. Invariably, his talks and presentations invoked Chicano history and culture, art and *teatro*, music and *danza* to make his case for barrio unity. Through these various interactions he gradually found a large audience sympathetic to the cause of ending community warfare and fratricide.

Before long, Alejándrez set out to establish relationships with other like-minded men and women he encountered at *charlas* (informal discussions and workshops); he began to organize at schools, churches, parks, and other community venues. A common denominator among the early BU pioneers was the hunger to explore viable strategies to address escalating violence among youth in the streets and in the schools. Nane made his way through different territories and communities in ways that ensured he could always connect directly with each neighborhood's leaders of young people. As he would later recall, "I would go any place there was a willing audience of young people and potential organizers, including living rooms, street corners, school yards, and jail cells." Alejándrez describes the method he used at this time as "organizing through personal testimony, one-on-one mentoring, street outreach, movement education, and sheer perseverance."

Like the growing number of community allies he encountered, Nane volunteered his time to the budding movement for community peace. "We all had to earn a living in other areas—as teachers, counselors, service workers, or in another profession—taking time off from work or using evenings and weekends to come together around the issue of gang and street violence." Conducting the work as a side job did not slow the BU founder's productivity or impact. In a short time, he became well known in the neighborhoods and communities where he was active.

In addition to his riveting message and inspiring personal story, Alejándrez came to be distinguished early on for using the trunk of his 1964 Chevy as a combined filing cabinet and business office. Lacking a real business address or home base for the work, Nane used his car trunk creatively to stock a mobile office chock-full of the tools of his trade. These included T-shirts and posters with iconographic photographs and donated Chicano art (which Alejándrez silk-screened in the living room of his home) to get young folk's attention, as well as educational materials to feed their minds. Like any organizer in the movement, Nane concentrated his energy on the task of building a base among his core constituency, young homeboys and homegirls, while also working diligently to build collaborative relationships with other grassroots leaders, including other youth organizers, movement activists, teachers, academics, artists, and clergy.

In these formative years, "low-rider" car shows were particularly popular among barrio youth and adults in neighborhoods and communities across the Southwest. The low-rider cars themselves were a unique form of cultural expression, adorned with chrome, lights, custom paint jobs, and even beautiful depictions of Chicano artwork. "Because the car shows were very much a part of the cultural landscape in the Chicano community at this time," says Nane, "low-rider car clubs became another means for youth and adults to find identity, cultural pride, and fraternity." Although the car shows were not political, these events became ideal venues for Chicanos to celebrate and share their culture. The car show events often included art exhibits, community information booths, music, and guest speakers. As a result, car shows became a favored venue for Alejándrez and other community peace workers to reach youth and potential organizers. According to Nane, "Plugging into such events was part of the Barrios Unidos philosophy of meeting young people where they lived."

In 1978, while attending a car show in Los Angeles, Nane met Gus Frías, founder of the Coalition to End Barrio Warfare, then a fledgling community peace effort in Southern California. Nane was at the Los Angeles car show filming a documentary for a college project on the popular Chicano music group Little Joe y La Familia. Little Joe had given Gus, a young community organizer, a platform to spread his message of peace and unity among warring gangs before hundreds of Chicano music fans and car show attendees.

The meeting of these two pioneers of the barrio peace movement, Nane and Gus, marked the beginning of a powerful union of forces that ultimately helped galvanize significant violence prevention work in northern and southern California. The two leaders immediately made a connection and forged a collaboration intended to promote peace among warring Latino gangs across the state. Nane and Gus quickly and correctly recognized that an alliance between community peace workers in the north and south would create an unprecedented opportunity to spread the message of unity and peace among rival gang sets in the two regions.

Barrios Unidos's early inclination to collaborate with the Frías-led Coalition would be the first of several groundbreaking partnerships and borrowings that would mark the organization's eventual development. In areas ranging from the arts to civil rights and from education to human rights activism, BU developed a quick predisposition to work with other groups and/or draw from other traditions in order to advance its aims. Indeed, collaboration and adaptation became distinguishing features of BU's institutional culture and vision.

ORGANIZATIONAL PARTNERS AND INFLUENCES: FORGING THE BU VISION

COALITION TO END BARRIO WARFARE

Moving on a track similar to BU's leadership in the north, Gus Frías and others concerned with escalating gang violence in Southern California began to envision a plan to deal with the self-destruction of youth in the barrios of East Los Angeles. In 1977, Frías and his fellow activists established the Coalition to End Barrio Warfare as a means to support collective unity and peace efforts in the barrios. Like Barrios Unidos, the Coalition sought to build on the powerful lessons, messages, and strategies of the Chicano civil rights movement by supporting community education and organizing activities. Key elements of the Coalition's work and vision thus initially included working across competing neighborhoods to educate gang-affiliated homeboys about Mexican-American culture and history, build their organizational skills to work constructively with their peers, and motivate them to excel in school. A broader coinciding goal of the Coalition was to build an army of Barrio Warriors—gang organizers, street workers, and other interested parties across Southern California—that could help to promote policy solutions to the problem of gang violence. The Coalition's eventual alliance with BU extended this work to a statewide stage in California.

The formal coming together of the Frías-led Coalition with Nane Alejándrez and early leaders of Barrios Unidos in the California Coalition to End Barrio Warfare led to many remarkable achievements. As the partnership took root, statewide organizing in communities was strengthened through workshops and school presentations, the development of a growing network of trained gang workers with an emphasis on peer learning, and a series of well-attended peace summits and conferences. Over the course of fifteen years of effective collaboration between Barrios Unidos as lead organizers in the north and Frías and others in the south, the California Coalition to End Barrio Warfare sponsored activities reaching many thousands of people and organizations across the Golden State. At one point there were upwards of ten strong and active chapters of the Coalition scattered across California. These were exciting times for the fledgling movement in which people who had worked in isolation so much of the time were finally able to benefit from solid regional solidarity and support.

Frías and other members of the Coalition produced some of the most cutting-edge educational materials and street organizer curricula that were developed anywhere during this period (and into the mid 1990s). In addition, Coalition organizers were prolific in disseminating social commentary, analysis, and allied information on gang and community violence to important policy and community stakeholders. "These kinds of resources—such as forums for advancing field thinking, policy formation efforts and collective organizing strategies to end community violence," Alejándrez would later comment, "did not readily exist at such a level before this time." Increasingly, Coalition leaders and guest speakers focused on the root causes of community violence. As they saw it, these root causes included poverty and inequity and discrimination in education, employment, criminal justice, health, and other fields. The Coalition's social and political agenda to end barrio warfare and achieve long-term community peace was thus directly linked to ending discrimination, inequality, and injustice.

By advancing these aims and pioneering new approaches in the fields of gang intervention and community-based violence prevention, Coalition members rightfully earned their place in the history of this country's peace and justice movement. For BU leaders the partnership with the Coalition created a strategic opportunity to experiment with new approaches and, at the same time, to develop and refine the organization's own unique methodology. Multiple influences from the fields of social psychology, nonviolent political protest, and indigenous spirituality were combining to inspire BU's founders. Conveniently, the organization's involvement with the California Coalition to End Barrio Warfare presented ample opportunities to explore work and ideas drawn from each of these arenas.

In fact, the statewide Coalition framework offered its leading entities considerable room to experiment with regionally distinctive approaches to the work; and leaders in both the north and the south did just that. Alejándrez and other BU leaders used their symbiotic relationship with the Coalition to build their own vision and strategies for change. As a result, many of the California Coalition's localized efforts in such places as Santa Cruz, Watsonville, Fresno, San Jose, Salinas, and Stockton took on a distinctively Barrios Unidos flavor in comparison to activities led by their Frías-led Coalition partners in the southern part of the state. According to Nane, "the conferences and workshops cosponsored by Barrios Unidos featured content similar to that of the L.A.-based Coalition, but the placement of the arts and indigenous ceremony as mediums for political organizing, education, healing, and expression came to be especially prominent at BU activities and events."

During this period, peace conferences organized by BU and their Southern California counterpart organizations in the Coalition were typically billed under the collective sponsorship of the California

Coalition to End Barrio Warfare—whatever their differences in content and regardless of whether they were organized in the north or the south, in order to engender statewide solidarity within the larger movement.

ARTS AND CULTURE

The arts in their various forms remain for Barrios Unidos today a potent means of expressing *cultura*, communicating experience, developing political awareness, underscoring themes of evolving identity, and promoting popular education. Art, poetry, music, dance, and creative writing have provided Barrios Unidos and its adherents a way to share experiences and ideas that have been historically denied to Chicanos through mainstream media and education. Barrios Unidos art exhibits at various gatherings have consistently brought together styles and expressions from the streets, prisons, and religious institutions reflecting various Latino or indigenous traditions, Mexican mural influences, Chicano and African iconography, tattoo art, and other creative genres. The central place of the arts in BU's work has included featuring a broad range of performance, writing, folkloric and film arts traditions as well, including Aztec *danza*, *ballet folklórico*, break, and hip-hop, as well as poetry and creative writing, craft making, and other expressive mediums, such as film documentary and photojournalism. Convinced about culture's essential role in organizing and education work that seeks to bridge intergenerational, communal, and intercultural divides, BU founders have historically drawn deeply on artistic expression to promote peace work among community youth.

THE CIVIL RIGHTS MOVEMENT AND SPIRITUALITY

Steeped in the politics of self-determination and resistance to oppression, the Chicano civil rights movement of the 1960s and 1970s included a decided strain of revolutionary militancy. The icons, culture, and organization of many activist youth groups, such as the Brown and Black Berets as well as MEChA, flowed from revolutionary liberation movements in Latin America (and elsewhere), as well as the Black Power movement in America. More established Chicano movement leaders, such as Corky Gonzales and Reies López Tijerina, contributed to this dynamic through their militant style and fiery rhetoric. Over time, however, for Nane and other BU leaders, an exclusive focus on confrontational tactics and militant culture began to seem counterintuitive to their aspirations to develop an alternative framework that could challenge the violence-oriented ethos of barrio warfare. As a result of their collective interrogation of this dilemma, within the BU leadership circle there emerged a belief that for those who had been caught up in the madness of the streets, gangs, or drug addiction, emphasizing militancy would be irresponsible and unwise.

Nane recalls that in those days he and other BU founders struggled for ways to integrate concepts relating to nonviolence, multiculturalism, and spirituality in order to position affirmative reform at the center of their powerful and urgent message. To do so, Nane and the BU leadership turned to the nonviolence tenets of revolutionary leaders such as César Chávez, Dr. Martin Luther King, Jr., and Mahatma Gandhi. In the process, Barrios Unidos activities began to gravitate more and more toward a full embrace of indigenous healing culture and spirituality as medicines for self-hatred, alienation, and neo-tribal warfare in the barrio. By the mid-1980s, Barrios Unidos's leadership had decided to make ancient indigenous spiritual expression and universal humanism the touchstones of their community peace work. They were convinced that the practice of universalistic cultural values and ecumenical spiritualism brought to BU's work a level of healing, reconciliation, interconnectedness, and communal purpose that racialized politics simply could not. To some within the mainstream religious establishment, this was considered groundbreaking: the use of faith-based work to help end the cycle of violence in poor communities across the country.

D-Q University and the Connection to Native Groups

Barrios Unidos's relationship to indigenous community culture and concepts has been strong and particularly influential in its development over the years. This should not be surprising, since Native American blood and culture have been a part of Latinos since the time of European colonization of the Americas. The Chicano and American Indian people share many parallels in terms of historical experience and cultural development. The processes of migration, settlement, conquest, and natural human interchange between the people that settled the northern reaches of New Spain/Mexico (especially before 1846) and the indigenous nations of the Southwest resulted in substantial inter-marriage and cultural intermingling. Despite this reality, and efforts among such Chicano activists as Reies López Tijerina and Corky Gonzales to make connections to native groups around issues including land and cultural rights, for many reasons early efforts in the civil rights movement to build political alliances between Chicanos and Native Americans failed to take hold.

Gratefully, in time, Latino and native community ties were developed through the efforts of a handful of enlightened individuals who turned to the collective study and exchange of their people's history and culture as a strategy to build the groundwork for more meaningful collaboration. Such leaders as Jorge Cevedo, a Chicano Studies professor at Deganawidah-Quetzalcoatl (D-Q) University; Dennis Banks of the American Indian Movement (AIM); Tony González of the International Indian Treaty Council; and Barrios Unidos elder Henry Domínguez worked effectively in broad coalitions to build solidarity between these communities—culturally, spiritually, and politically. The organizational impact of this coming together of cultures involving early Barrios Unidos leaders was significant.

Barrios Unidos leaders, and especially Henry Domínguez, wholeheartedly embraced the convergence of cultural, spiritual, and political bonds between Chicanos and Native Americans. Ultimately, this led to one of BU's most significant collaborative engagements: a spiritual and strategic alliance with D-Q University in Yolo County, California. The school's name was drawn from Iroquois traditions of the north (Deganawidah) and Aztec/*Mexica* traditions of the south (Quetzalcoatl). Organized around the goal of preserving, advancing, and integrating indigenous cultural heritages in strategic efforts to support movements for self-determination, D-Q University was established as an accredited two-year institution of higher learning for people of indigenous descent. D-Q University faculty was comprised of scholars and activists from various tribal nations who dedicated themselves to collaborative efforts to preserve and strengthen traditional values through spiritual ceremony, scholarship in community self-help strategies, and support of movement work.

In the early 1970s, Henry Domínguez enrolled at D-Q in order to expand his possibilities of encouraging social change. Henry entered D-Q as a recent member of the Black Berets, a paramilitary group of Chicano youth activists. He left D-Q a changed man, fundamentally committed to nonviolent protest and improved intergroup harmony. Domínguez's journey, a long one by any conceptual measure, was fundamentally made possible by D-Q's unique institutional mission and culture. For its founders and students, D-Q University offered sacred ground, a home for traditional Indian ceremonies and intertribal or ecumenical rituals. A life-affirming interchange of northern and southern tribal traditions played out daily in this unique and powerful place. Among the many ritualistic impulses to the spirit offered by D-Q were *Danza Azteca* and the Plains sun dance; the sweat lodge and the *Mexica Temascali* (a traditional prayer, cleansing and healing ceremony); the vision quest (a spiritual passage that requires days of fasting and prayer in total seclusion); the sacred pipe ceremony; and various drum and song regimens. Also featured were the sharing of creation myths and beliefs, including sacred stories about revered figures such as the White Buffalo Calf Women and the apparition of the Virgin Mary to Saint Juan Diego.

Once exposed to these activities and the historic significance of their meaning, BU leaders became devoted practitioners and champions of spiritualism and ritual. They became, along with their Native American counterparts at D-Q University, much more closely connected as a result. As one Barrios Unidos activist has described it, "In the rising smoke of burning tobacco, sage, and *copal* during ecumenical and indigenous prayer ceremonies, a new solidarity was formed."

Along the way, BU leaders were particularly impressed by D-Q University's role as a planning base for significant native organizing efforts, such as "The Longest Walk" (which began in California and terminated in Washington, DC) and "The 500-Mile Indian Marathon." Over the years, D-Q University has served as a leading staging ground for many such political mobilizations focused on bringing attention to indigenous rights issues. The university has produced hundreds of influential movement activists and scholars versed in traditional knowledge, who have been transformed by the practice of spiritual ceremony. Many of D-Q's graduates and beneficiaries over the decades have been Barrios Unidos leaders and family members.

D-Q University's influence relative to BU's growth and direction has expanded to the point at which, presently, the two organizations' philosophies and directions have become fundamentally connected. Indeed, the approach and work BU hopes to realize in its next stage of growth through the development of a BU Institute (an envisioned multiplex of Chicano learning and political activism discussed more fully later in this book) is a direct outgrowth of its long-standing ties to D-Q University. As Nane Alejándrez puts it, "Understanding our historical relationship to D-Q University and our own *indigenismo* as Chicanos who are tied to other Native American experiences is critical to understanding the institutional priorities that guide Barrios Unidos today."

HENRY DOMÍNGUEZ, BU ELDER AND SPIRITUAL LEADER

The activist journey that enabled Henry Domínguez to become the spiritual elder of Barrios Unidos originated in the barrios of San Jose. Having gone through the gauntlet of street violence, substance abuse, and incarceration as a young man, Henry credits his community movement engagements as the source of eventual change in his orientation to life. More specifically, he talks of consciousness-raising and cutting his political teeth as a member of the Black Berets in San Jose during the peak of the Chicano movement. Working under the leadership of Sal "Chemo" Candelaria, he remembers being fully committed to the militant ethos of the time and doing whatever was called for to deal with the blatant discrimination and mistreatment of Latinos by police authorities and other civic institutions. "Many of us believed that armed resistance, if needed to protect the dignity and rights of our people, was a reasonable and viable option," recalls Henry. "This was the romantic notion of revolution that guided many of us coming out of the 1960s." Like Henry, Chemo and his wife Teresa would later become part of the circle of Barrios Unidos elders and spiritual leaders transformed by la cura cultural and the philosophy of nonviolence.

A bellwether moment in Domínguez's leadership development was a Black Beret-supported organizing campaign to challenge racist public celebrations sponsored by the City of San Jose. As Henry recounts, "The struggle revolved around an annual, city-sponsored parade called La Fiesta de las Rosas. The event commemorated the conquest of Mexico by Spain in terms that were offensive to many of the city's Chicano residents. The conquest remains a particularly painful historical period that many Chicanos view as the beginning of a long struggle with colonialism. The parade included a famous Western actor of the times dressed in the style of the *gachupines* (Spanish-born ranchers), riding on a white horse as he pulled along a Mexican campesino seated on a small donkey. In 1971, after many years of enduring this public humiliation, Black Berets active in Northern California, including Domínguez, organized effective protests that eventually helped to end this outrageous act of public-sponsored social irresponsibility.

Like the Brown Berets in the South of the state, the Black Berets advocated justice, challenged racist institutional policies, and played an important role in providing a buffer between Chicano communities and abusive police authorities. Domínguez believed in the Black Berets and was a committed participant in their efforts to address all manifestations of anti-Chicano racism, like the La Fiesta de las Rosas. In time, however, he became concerned that he might not be doing as much as possible for the movement or his family by failing to pursue a higher education degree. These factors led him to enroll at D-Q University.

While at the university, Henry immersed himself in learning more about the traditions of his mixed cultural heritage as a Chicano and a Chiracawa Apache Indian. He also continued to deepen his skills as an organizer, becoming part of the AIM and serving as a coordinator and participant in "The Longest Walk" and "The 500-Mile Indian Marathon." Along the way, Domínguez fully dedicated himself to learning the healing power of Aztec ceremony, melding other northern indigenous traditions, such as the sweat lodge and vision quest, into his spiritual practice. Under the sponsorship of Dennis Banks,

Henry was among the first Chicanos at D-Q to participate in the Lakota-Plains sun dance ceremony.

Henry describes Banks as a mentor and guide in helping him to reconcile his mixed heritage. Having been reared in the Catholic Church, Domínguez was staunchly devoted to his Christian faith and saw the Virgen de Guadalupe as his guardian spirit. It was during his vision quest ceremony that Henry chose the path of peace over violent political militancy. He tearfully describes the revelation of his vision quest experience as follows: "My spirit guide made me choose. I had to put down my gun and pick up the sacred pipe and my rosary as the tools of a peace warrior."

Henry's decision to abandon the militancy and ethos of armed resistance he had embraced as a member of the Black Berets and a staunch supporter of AIM manifested a poignant and profound transformation. It was a transformation he would later seek to bring to other Latino and Latina street warriors through the Barrios Unidos movement.

When Domínguez was called back home to assist efforts to bring peace to the barrio, street violence had reached unprecedented proportions in San Jose. Upon his return home, Henry was committed to build on the lessons of his life-changing revelations at D-Q University. He made a vow to himself that he later recalled in these terms: "I decided that as a carrier of the sacred pipe, I would make spiritual ceremony the center of all my activism as a peacemaker in the barrio."

In 1979, Henry Domínguez organized an historic spiritual walk through the streets of San Jose in an effort to unite its warring barrios. He also organized the first Barrios Unidos Conference at Lincoln High School, incorporating the best elements of Coalition to End Barrio Warfare conferences, such as *teatro*, arts, culture, and motivational speakers. This time, however, he organized these activities with a more visible spiritual message and presence. Since the mid-1980s and into the present, Domínguez has served as an organizing partner, elder, and spiritual guide for Nane Alejándrez and Barrios Unidos. Henry's personal transformation and embrace of the nonviolent approach to organizing thus marked a critically important moment in BU's development—the positioning of spiritual ceremony and traditional healing as a centerpiece in the Barrios Unidos peace movement.

THE LATE 1980S: SOLIDIFYING THE BASE AND ESTABLISHING NEW PARTNERSHIPS

At the close of the 1980s, BU's emerging leadership was mainly consumed by the need to focus on consolidating the organization's base. At the same time, however, BU leaders continued to pursue and grow from strategic alliances with other important groups. In 1989, Alejándrez took on a volunteer position with the Veteran's Peace Action Team (VPAT). Veterans dedicated to nonviolence formed VPAT to promote humanitarian international policies and self-determination on behalf of such sovereign countries as Nicaragua, El Salvador, and Guatemala. "These were exciting times when I was putting together my experiences as a poor migrant worker, homeboy, Viet Nam veteran, street organizer, and activist," Nane would later recall. "More than ever, I realized at the time, this work helped me to understand that the responsibility of a true peace warrior stretches from the barrio to any other place in the world where there exists a struggle for justice."

Contemporaneously, Alejándrez became more deeply involved with Tony González of the International Indian Treaty Council in both domestic and global efforts to promote intertribal unity on indigenous rights issues, joining international peace delegations to several nations, including Nicaragua and Switzerland. In 1990, VPAT leaders decided to actively support the self-determination of the Navajo (or Dineh, as they call themselves) and Hopi peoples. Both nations were engaged in resisting forced relocations from Big Mountain, Arizona. VPAT organized a massive humanitarian aid and education project in response to the U.S. government-driven relocations. The project was dubbed the "Veterans Peace Convoy." The VPAT effort significantly mobilized Barrios Unidos leaders and constituents in solidarity with the Dineh and Hopi peoples' cause.

BIG MOUNTAIN, ARIZONA: THE RESISTANCE MOVEMENT

During early 1990, the U.S. government enacted PL 93-531, a law ostensibly intended to end a land dispute between the Dineh and Hopi tribes living within what was called a Joint Use Area (JUA). Both tribes had many long-settled families living in a cooperative spirit on the affected land. After multinational energy companies discovered the land was rich in coal, natural gas, and uranium, federal authorities, working in cooperation with a co-opted Tribal Council and the Peabody Corporation, orchestrated passage of a new policy to relocate families under the pretense of an intertribal land dispute (See *The VPATSA Newsletter*, 1/3 [December 1989]). Traditional tribal elders from both the Dineh and Hopi nations refuted the existence of any dispute and opposed desecration by mining companies of holy lands that were home to generations-old native burial grounds and sacred ceremonial sites. The federal policy partitioned the JUA in a way that would egregiously displace the Dineh peoples. In an act of civil disobedience, Dineh tribal elders and families living on the land refused to move, thus initiating the Big Mountain Resistance Movement aimed at rescinding PL 93-531.

The resistance was based on fundamental notions of native identity and culture. As Dineh elder Pauline Whitesinger observed at the time, "In our tongue there is no word for relocation. To move away is to disappear and be seen no more." The indigenous elders called on civil, human, and indigenous rights organizations, the religious community, and concerned people of goodwill to support their resistance. Nane Alejándrez and activist Pam Escarcega served as VPAT national coordinators of the western states for the Veterans Peace Convoy and brought in Barrios Unidos elder Henry Domínguez, also a member of the American Indian Movement, to serve as a liaison to Dineh and Hopi resistance leaders.

The Veterans Peace Convoy to Big Mountain consisted of 150 people traveling from fifty-two cities in sixty-three vehicles to deliver twenty-five tons of food and medical supplies to affected Dineh families and their Hopi supporters. The food lasted only a few short months, but the attention and support relationships the convoy generated endure to this day. On the road to Big Mountain, the convoy stopped for an overnight stay at the home of César Chávez in La Paz, California. Chávez addressed participants in the convoy, expressing his support for the resistance movement and the self-determination of Native Americans. He also reaffirmed the solidarity and common destiny of Latinos and other people of indigenous descent in America. According to Domínguez, "The role of Barrios Unidos in the convoy embodied a convergence of progressive policy positions, interrelationships and spiritual dimensions that were developed through the civil-rights, indigenous-rights, and community-peace movements during the first thirteen years of our work."

During these years, cooperative and solidarity-based efforts such as the convoy, the development of D-Q University, and "The Longest Walk" significantly strengthened the bonds between indigenous peoples of the north and California Chicanos, who were in many cases themselves descendents of Aztec-Mexica, Taramaru, Maya, Yaqui, Apache, and other sacred Indian nations. The sharing of traditions and spiritual ceremonies was central to all of these endeavors. Several individuals in the Barrios Unidos leadership circle who have shared these experiences are now primary functionaries and participants at sweat lodge and other indigenous ceremonies. Such leaders as Albino García and his son Albino Jr. are Sun Dancers at Big Mountain Survival Camp, the site of ongoing resistance among the members of the Dineh nation. Still to this day, the García family carries the Barrios Unidos message in ceremony and in barrio peace work in Albuquerque, New Mexico, and across the country.

FUTURE PLANNING AND ESTABLISHING AN ORGANIZATIONAL CULTURE

During the late 1980s and into the early 1990s, BU founder Nane Alejándrez continued to work as the northern coordinator of the California Coalition to End Barrio Warfare, while at the same time advancing the work of Barrios Unidos. Over these several years, Nane also began to work more closely with a circle of people in the north that would come to form the founding board of directors, core staff, and volunteers of the BU movement's nonprofit headquarters corporation, Santa Cruz Barrios Unidos. The story of Barrios Unidos's successful development as a nonprofit community organization is finally a reflection of the vision and leadership of these men and women. The specific individuals comprising this core leadership group included

Walter Guzmán, Otilio Quintero, Raquel Mariscal, Barbara García, Steve Vigil, Manuel Martínez, Marylou Alejándrez, and Liz Ayala.

WALTER GUZMÁN (1954–2000), 1ST BOARD PRESIDENT

The late Walter Guzmán was born and raised in Los Angeles and spent much of his formative years growing up on the mean streets of various eastside Los Angeles-area barrios. Like so many of the young men and women Walter served over his decades of activism and leadership, he fell into the life of gangs and drug addiction early in his journey, before he found his way. The streets had a firm hold on Walter, and it took many years before his intermittent involvements with various programs aimed at preventing violence and substance abuse took root to facilitate his ultimate sobriety. In search of his own personal healing, Walter found his life's calling as a substance abuse and youth counselor. Always a student and pioneer, he relished exploring and testing best practices and contemporary approaches in youth development and substance abuse recovery.

Walter's path would eventually land him in Northern California as director of Youth Services at Santa Cruz Community Counseling Services, Inc. In this capacity Walter worked with Latino youth, families, and community members to develop program approaches that were more culturally relevant, especially with regard to recovery and prevention approaches for Latino/a juvenile offenders. By developing partnerships with community residents, other nonprofit organizations, and juvenile justice officials, Walter helped found the model Grow Program, an intensive home supervision intervention for first-time drug offenders. Through his work in Youth Services, Walter actively explored alternatives to incarceration for young people. He established an intensive support and community reentry program for teens in the local juvenile justice and detention systems. While Walter was a man deeply committed to a multicultural vision and values, he felt particularly driven to fill the void in culturally competent recovery programs for Latinos.

In 1991, Walter cofounded and became the first director of ¡Sí, Se Puede!, a culturally centered residential substance abuse recovery program for Latino men in Watsonville. A profoundly spiritual man, he quickly incorporated cultura and indigenous spiritual traditions into the healing and recovery curricula at ¡Sí, Se Puede! A few years earlier, Walter, a long-standing acquaintance of Nane Alejándrez, had re-entered Nane's life and become familiar with BU's evolving model of indigenous healing and spiritual practice. During this time, he served Nane as both a professional anchor and confidante. His influence became an essential source of grounding for the BU founder. Indeed, it is Walter who Nane credits with "teaching me to draw on the power of my spiritual walk, to fortify my recovery and a lasting sobriety." In time, Walter and ¡Sí, Se Puede! became invaluable resources to Barrios Unidos, directly serving and supporting many of the young people BU was trying to reach as they fought through the ramifications of substance abuse in their personal lives and in the community.

The close partnership and bond between Walter and Nane flourished and was particularly instrumental as the Santa Cruz Barrios Unidos nonprofit corporation was being formed. Walter became the founding chairperson of the organization's board of directors in 1992. Nane is quick to point out that from the outset of his involvement, Walter was the guiding spirit behind BU's evolution. Just prior to his passing, Walter had visited Canada to participate in a ceremony at the longhouse of the Mohawk Oneida Nation, where he received the spiritual name "Keeper of the Knowledge." Walter was also known as "Fire keeper" because he humbly held the responsibility of tending the sacred fire during sweat lodge ceremonies. Walter's guidance, boundless energy, vision, and love allowed him to serve as an important spiritual leader in the community peace movement for many years.

Walter Guzmán's wife of many years, Caranina, and his children and family members, in blood and spirit, survive Walter. This great, early BU elder's life and passing, however, are remembered by still many more each year at an annual ceremony held at Santa Cruz Barrios Unidos, and his spirit lives on daily in the hearts and actions of everyone he touched. At the first year commemoration of Walter's passing, the feathers of a sacred red-tailed hawk were given to members of his immediate family and others in attendance to guide their prayers. Every year since, the ceremony has been repeated—a red-tailed hawk flying vigilantly over participants, offering from the spirit-world Walter's blessing and protection.

OTILIO "OT" QUINTERO, CO-ARCHITECT OF THE BU COMMUNITY ORGANIZATION

Among BU's early adherents, Otilio "OT" Quintero would emerge to play a particularly significant, long-term leadership role in the movement's and organization's development. In effect, Quintero, presently Barrios Unidos's assistant director, would join Nane Alejándrez as the soon-to-be incorporated organization's co-architect. The path that ultimately brought these two leaders together was a somewhat logical one, based on the substantial reputations they had developed on separate but closely related tracks in the Santa Cruz region prior to their formal meeting. OT, who was working in public schools to advocate reforms on behalf of at-risk Latino youth, had heard of Nane's efforts to organize the community around peace and justice. Nane had also heard of OT's work to address cultural and equity issues in schools. In a short period, the two began to consolidate their work, capitalizing on Otilio's position within the school system and Nane's cache at the neighborhood level, to effect policy change in local schools that led to improvements for Chicano students. As their association and partnership grew, the two naturally began to discuss with other members of the organization's leadership circle the incipient concepts that ultimately formed Santa Cruz Barrios Unidos's institutional development.

Growing up in the San Joaquin Valley and living in various labor camps as his family followed the seasonal crops, Otilio Quintero's identity and worldview was deeply affected by the migrant farmworker experience. Eventually, his family settled in Three Rocks, an impoverished federal housing area for migrant families located just 45 miles west of Fresno, California. Like youth in so many other migrant settlements, young men in Three Rocks had assimilated manifestations of the *pachuco*, gang, and drug culture with all the attendant conflicts between neighboring clans—the rural equivalent of urban barrio warfare. Quintero commonly known by his nickname, OT, was significantly shaped by this reality.

As a young man, OT was also profoundly influenced by the Chicano peoples' long history of resistance in the San Joaquin Valley. The people of Three Rocks and surrounding migrant settlements took great pride in having provided refuge and care to Joaquín Murrieta during his flight of rebellion from U.S. and Mexican authorities during the mid-nineteenth century. As Quintero puts it, "Murrieta was to the Chicano *Indio* in the San Joaquin Valley what Geronimo was to the Apache nation, a symbol of the right to cultural integrity and the right to freedom. This spirit of conviction was handed down to me by my elders." Like Nane, OT was also heavily influenced by the power of César Chávez's message and skills as the leader of the United Farm Workers union. Curiously, despite these early political influences, OT's early years did not find him heavily engaged in politics or activism. This would change, however, during his early adult years.

Moving out of Three Rocks at age seventeen to attend college, OT began a transition leading him to become a lifelong community activist and organizer. While a student earning his undergraduate and masters degrees in education counseling at the University of California, Santa Cruz and San Jose State University, respectively, he immersed himself in a wide range of educational reform and equity battles. He soon became adept at organizing Latino students and parents in Santa Cruz and Watsonville to challenge local schools to better meet community cultural and educational needs. Working as a substitute teacher and counselor in these communities, OT began organizing cultural events at selected middle schools and high schools, providing topical workshops addressing matters such as violence and substance abuse, and teaching Chicano history.

Always, in these efforts, Quintero partnered with other local activists to plan community support interventions and organize campaigns designed to promote equitable changes in schools. These activities would almost get him fired on more than one occasion. It was not long before Nane Alejándrez became aware of OT's leadership efforts, and the two joined forces. The coming together of these two visionary and committed leaders would usher in a new phase of development for the Barrios Unidos movement, one that would result in the building of a strong organizational infrastructure to further and sustain the movement's core strategies.

RESPONDING TO CRISIS, FORMALIZING A STRUCTURE, BROADENING THE LEADERSHIP CORPS

Throughout the early 1990s, BU leaders worked to develop the organization and its programs on an unpaid, volunteer basis. Like other BU leaders, Nane Alejándrez made ends meet by working at varying jobs in the nonprofit and private sectors. It was not until the mid-1990s that Nane began to solicit the initial planning grants to support the establishment of a nonprofit organizational base for Santa Cruz Barrios Unidos. The inclination to formalize BU's work was in part a byproduct of establishing a critical mass of Barrio warriors to advance its philosophy and advocacy agenda. But institutionalizing BU was also a response to growing gang and street violence in California on the cusp of the new millennium.

During these years California experienced a marked rise in interpersonal and community violence involving youth. The northern communities of California where Barrios Unidos worked were particularly affected by this trend. By the early 1990s, violence-related crime rates had reached epidemic proportions, becoming the second leading cause of death for minority youth. Public health officials and allied networks of social workers, educators, and foundation leaders began to warn policy makers, media executives, and the general public that youth violence, particularly among poor minorities, was becoming a serious national problem. The involvement of these influential professional groups in the field stimulated a broader multi-sector discussion in America on the problem of community violence and the linkages of its root causes to persistent poverty and injustice. The resulting formation of a professional violence prevention advocacy network would have tremendous implications for Barrios Unidos. In effect, this development established a parallel organizing capacity among elite societal groups and important grassroots community peace advocates. Eventually, BU and similar community-based peace groups would directly benefit from alliances with institutional leaders and professionals committed to community violence prevention.

As these developments unfolded, Alejándrez and Quintero accelerated BU's use of community convenings and unity summits to help mobilize then-budding violence prevention coalitions. Initially this work focused solely on BU's immediate Northern California region, targeting first Watsonville and Santa Cruz. But before long, BU's leadership in the arena would take on national proportions.

BU conferences consistently drew between 100 and 200 participants from local host communities. Typically, these gatherings included at-risk youth, key community leaders, and interested adults from within and outside of violence-ridden Latino neighborhoods. At each meeting, efforts would be made to establish consensus around advocacy strategy using deeply spiritual practices and ceremony. The approach proved remarkably compelling to BU convening participants, many of whom were seeking healing and connection. Barrios Unidos gatherings dramatically strengthened the organization's following and encouraged its evolution in directions not entirely consistent with other groups and networks in the field. Barrios Unidos Unity Conferences held at EA Hall and Veterans Hall in Watsonville and Santa Cruz, respectively, in 1989 and 1990, mark the beginning of the organization's decision to move more intentionally toward sponsoring its own conferences, meetings, and other organizing activities, independent of the California Coalition to End Barrio Warfare. BU's evolving approach proved especially costly relative to its involvement in the California Coalition to End Barrio Warfare. As Nane Alejándrez remembers it,

> BU's particularly strong reliance on unconventional mobilization strategies was not without its tensions between organizers in the north and those in the south. Growing disagreements on strategies, tactics, the access and allocation of resources, and the nature of alliances had spurred the need to embark on a planning process that would lead to the incorporation of Santa Cruz Barrios Unidos, Inc. Although at times relationships became contentious and there were disagreements, even personal in nature, we recognized that the partnership prepared BU for the future. We always acknowledge the contributions of our partners in the south to our success and are even more grateful to them with the passage of time.

In many respects, Barrios Unidos conferences continued to build on core change strategies that the organization had developed or adopted over the previous decade. They included trainings for street organizers and youth workers, topical workshops on prevention, and education on community issues. Personal testimonies of former gang members and violence alternative vignettes by satirical *teatro* groups, such as Teatro de Las Cucarachas, continued as mainstay educational strategies. These activities served to impart *cultura*, stimulate critical thinking by youth participants, communicate strategies for personal change, and promote barrio unity.

Peace activist Richard "Chocolate" Santana fashioned a particularly powerful role-play exercise to breakdown stereotypes and nihilism among gang-affiliated or other at-risk Chicano youth that was frequently featured at BU gatherings. Chocolate would begin his presentation dressed in *pachuco* attire and talk in street vernacular about the madness of the street culture, its rules of honor and belonging, the falsehoods of identity it created from within the community, and the stereotypes and discrimination it engendered from without. As he spoke of the difficulty of breaking out of the madness and changing paths, he would literally transform his appearance, shedding his *cholo*-wear to reveal a dress shirt and tie underneath. "I never knew I could go to college and get an education," Santana would tell his audience. "I thought I'd die a gang-banger." He would go on to encourage participating youth to find their true culture and identity through education and service to the community. Invariably, such convening elements had a large impact on the target youth participants, and BU leaders made sure to retain them over the years.

But the tensions over approach that ultimately separated BU and the Coalition to End Barrio Warfare compelled Barrios Unidos leaders to seek independent space and resources to fashion an additional set of change strategies around their own evolving vision and values. While Barrios Unidos would remain committed to building a broader state and national community peace movement, its founders also committed the organization to building a broader grassroots constituency, developing new youth-led initiatives, and forging new organizational alliances at the local and regional levels. In each of these endeavors,

Barrios Unidos leaders additionally committed themselves to developing a model for change that placed indigenous culture and traditional spiritual ceremony even more at the center of their movement and their organization. BU founders decided at this time to use community conferences initially organized in conjunction with the Coalition to End Barrio Warfare as a platform to further consensus-building and support for a more freestanding and culture-driven Barrios Unidos organization. Community conferences thus became critical benchmarks in the Barrios Unidos story. The conferences brought together like-minded individuals around a nascent vision to build a strong organization in support of culturally and spiritually based efforts to promote community peace. Numerous community activists supported Barrios Unidos and contributed in different ways as it undertook this formative process. These included Guillermo Aranda, Marciano "Chango" Cruz, Chemo and Teresa Candelaria, Teresa Juárez, Tino Esparza, Eduardo Carrillo, Lorenza Ramírez, Armando "Bear," Robert Castro, Bob Campos, Roberto Maestas, Chris Matthews, Richard "Chocolate" Santana, and Kali Mabula.

Liz Ayala recalls the intensity and sense of purpose that permeated these early convenings. As a young student during the early 1980s, Liz attended her first Coalition to End Barrio Warfare conference in Watsonville, where she met Nane for the first time. A subsequent conference convened in Santa Cruz a decade later was particularly important to Ayala, who had nearly lost her brother to street violence the day the event began. "I made my decision then," Ayala observed in retrospect, "to dedicate myself to working with Nane to establish Barrios Unidos and to become a part of the community peace movement." Ayala has been a particularly important fixture in the Barrios Unidos leadership circle and community peace movement in America ever since.

Throughout the mid-1980s, Nane, Walter, Liz, and others found themselves collaborating professionally on several projects through Fenix Services, a Watsonville youth service organization. The resulting shared exposure to community-based organizational life and the possibility of similarly institutionalizing BU's evolving work model galvanized their resolve to make a Barrios Unidos organization a reality. These individuals and others thus began meeting regularly to plan and develop the core strategies, programs, and community-building activities required to establish the nonprofit organization Barrios leaders envisioned. What they had in mind from the beginning, however, was not merely a conventional nonprofit service and advocacy group, but rather a far-reaching, ongoing campaign that would transform lives and communities that were being destroyed by violence.

Over the course of BU's first thirteen years, its founders drew on powerful experiences that defined their own lives and development as peace warriors to shape a coherent and durable organizational vision. In its next stage of development BU's leaders would formalize their association with an eye to advancing a national movement for change with enduring potential for impact. Through this formative period of activism, discovery, and learning, BU's founders struggled to identify exemplary organizational models to draw on in formulating a road map for building the movement they envisioned. But they quickly realized that such a template did not exist.

BU principles fundamentally sought to change the world, as they knew it. They wanted to expand community and public engagement on violence prevention matters and also to improve the lives of individuals, families, and neighborhoods that were being overtaken by violent conflict. But they wanted to pursue and achieve these objectives in a way that broadly engaged affected community members themselves and especially at-risk youth.

All of this had a significant bearing on BU's institutional evolution. Early leadership discussions centered first on broad-scale social-change outcomes rather than the minutia of program design and development. Research, while valued as a learning tool, was secondary to action on the hierarchy of organizational priorities. Finally, increased civic leadership, democratic participation, and community development came to be viewed as strategies and outcomes at once. In effect, BU's early leaders wanted the budding organization they sought to champion into reality to do more than just promote community peace and heal affected constituencies; even more than that, BU's founders wanted to inspire a broad-based movement for peace, democracy, and social justice in America.

TAKING STOCK, REFLECTING ON BU'S LEGACY

In its still very brief fourteen-year history as a nonprofit community organization, Barrios Unidos has succeeded in pioneering a visionary model for change that is restoring the lives of troubled youths while redefining contemporary notions of community-building based on spiritual and multicultural values. Through its many programs and organizational endeavors, BU has helped thousands of at-risk youth and families to connect cultural and spiritual consciousness to political action. It has helped to promote increased community self-reliance and economic development, to forge important interracial alliances and coalitions, and to galvanize nonviolent efforts intended to bring about needed change in this country and other parts of the world. While BU has not yet succeeded in changing the world as such, it has informed important social gains that do make a large difference. By focusing on recapturing the cultural and spiritual traditions of the people, teaching understanding of and respect for the dignity of others, and encouraging community responsibility and action, BU's programs and activities have surely made a meaningful contribution to the lives of many.

The instinct to formalize BU's efforts through legal incorporation and institutional capacity-building has accounted for a significant degree of the organization's effectiveness in recent years. Accordingly, it is important to treat in greater detail in the next section just how BU consolidated its institutional base during the late 1980s and early 1990s.

Part II
Building an Organization,
Sustaining a Movement

Introduction

When I think of Barrios Unidos, I first think of a beautiful and creative social movement versus an organization or a set of programs. The underlying tenets of the Barrios Unidos approach are equal parts the recapturing of cultural traditions, cultural evolution, and cultural revolution. It represents the intensive process of cultural healing and reconciliation with oneself, one's community, and the many diverse people that make up American society. Barrios supports work that will make the communities it serves and the society we live in a better place for everyone to co-exist in mutual respect, equality, dignity, and peace.

Ray Gatchalian

After a thirteen-year journey of working for peace and justice in the barrio, the founders of Barrios Unidos had come to a moment of truth. The sum total of their life experiences, social-change activism, and convictions had convinced them of the need to establish a formal organization to support the movement. Now, historical circumstances and trends well beyond their powers of control converged to provide a window of opportunity to fulfill their shared dream of establishing an anchor institution to support community peace organizing and advocacy. All across the state of California and the nation, a marked spike in rates of interpersonal violence, including intentional killings, random murders, and hate crimes, manifested itself during the early-to-mid-1990s. Indeed, the availability of cheap, high-powered firearms had made interpersonal violence more lethal than ever in the nation's history.

While America had always arguably been a nation of violence, something different characterized the escalation in transgressions witnessed during this period. The difference had to do mainly with the relative youth of both America's newfound victims and perpetrators of this violence. More and more across the nation, young people were becoming the primary actors on the stage of American violence. Whether through gang- and drug-related activities, peer-based conflicts, or alienation-driven rage, young people across the United States came to constitute a new ground zero for injury and death by violence.

Along with African-American youth, Latino adolescents and teens became centrally featured actors on the stage of America's growing spate of violent activities during this period. Pressed by poverty and institutionalized racism, including especially repressive police tactics targeted at black and brown youth in many U.S. cities, Latino and other minority young people came to be increasingly implicated in violent incidents. This set of circumstances created a unique space and standing for groups like BU to step in and offer needed interventions and solutions.

In California, three important developments especially opened the window of opportunity, and the imperative, for Barrios Unidos to establish a nonprofit organization that could effectively intervene at both the grassroots and governance levels. First, the reactionary development of increasingly punitive social and criminal justice policies aimed at minorities and the poor were unwittingly exacerbating community violence. Among these policy developments were efforts to deny non-U.S. citizens essential public services, to prohibit state agencies from using affirmative action tools to expand minority workforce participation and upward mobility, and to establish harsher sentencing requirements for youthful and other criminal offenders (with young people often being tried as adults for more serious offenses). A second, and closely related, development that influenced BU's growing centrality to the issues was the 1992 civil unrest in Los Angeles, which opened a new civic dialogue on the need for more meaningful responses to intractable social problems. A third and final aspect of the dynamic in California that accelerated BU's organizational development during this period was the growing interest of public health professionals in violence prevention and allied investments in community peace work by leading philanthropic organizations, such as The California Wellness Foundation—factors that greatly helped to legitimate community peace work in the state and nationally.* Each of these factors simultaneously enabled and pushed BU leaders to formalize the organization's structure and programs during the early-to-mid-1990s.

BROADER SOCIOPOLITICAL CONTEXT (1990–1993)

Entering the 1990s, the economic, social, and political circumstances of most poor minorities remained relatively dire. The Carter-Reagan-Bush-Clinton years had generated some "trickle down" benefits to the middle class, but by and large the divide between the haves and have-nots of society had widened despite three decades of minority struggle to achieve civil rights equality. For Latinos in the barrios of California and the Southwest, indices of poverty and victimization from various forms of violence all well-exceeded national averages. Institutionalized racial discrimination, oppression, cultural alienation, and inequality in many Latino communities fueled much of the problem.

Sociologist and historian Darnell Hawkins has pointed out that in the post-War on Poverty and post-Civil Rights eras, American social policy did little to advance structural change or further governmental initiatives to eradicate the nation's last remnants of de jure racism. To the contrary, by the late 1970s the pendulum had swung so dramatically to the political right that many American policy makers began to question or completely abandon the core principles and goals of the civil rights movement.

In California, voter approval of Proposition 13 in 1978 served as a touchstone event, precipitating a gutting of funding for public schools, social programs, and essential infrastructure in poor communities that had historically helped to build resiliency against delinquency, crime, and violence. Passage of Proposition 13 in California

---

*Other leading California private foundations that informed this direction in social policy and investment included The California Endowment, The James Irvine Foundation, Sierra Healthcare Foundation, Alliance Healthcare, the S.H. Cowell Foundation, the Crail Johnson Foundation, and the David & Lucile Packard Foundation. All of these funders ultimately partnered with The California Wellness Foundation in support of its flagship program intervention in the field, known as the California Violence Prevention Initiative.

served as the harbinger of anti-poor legislation and voter ballot measures across the nation, which would take hold for the better part of a generation. By the late 1980s, high rates of crime and violence came to be preferred targets of the draconian policy created by leaders increasingly prone to frame solutions solely in terms of punishment and social control, rather than with an eye to addressing the root causes of public problems.

In mainstream public discourse, youth of color came to be demonized as a looming generation of "super-predators" fueling voter fears across numerous states. In California, the nation's first "three strikes" sentencing law was passed, followed soon thereafter by a state-approved initiative to try and sentence youthful criminal offenders—most of them Latinos and African Americans—as adults, in a significant number of cases. Subsequent actions building on these policy changes denied essential public services to immigrant families in California and substantially undercut state affirmative action programs benefiting youth and poor communities of color. California's policy direction along these lines influenced many other states to adopt similar repressive measures. Collectively, these developments increased incarceration and sentences to levels unprecedented in the civilized world, denied essential health and human services to poor immigrant families, and reversed hard-fought minority civil rights gains.

There can be no doubt that these developments had an unmistakable, disproportionate, and negative impact on poor communities of color. Witness the effect of the "three strikes" sentencing policy on the incarceration of African American and Latino young men and adults: the U.S. Department of Justice, Bureau of Justice Statistics, for example, reported in March 1994, that African Americans were being incarcerated at a rate more than six times that of whites, with comparable numbers for poor Latinos.

On April 29, 1992, a watershed event swept away any pretense that the desperate conditions of America's poor were being remedied. On a warm Southern California afternoon, in the aftermath of a dubious court exoneration of Los Angeles police officers accused of wrongdoing in an internationally televised suspect beating, the mounting frustrations of poor African Americans and Latinos exploded onto the streets of Los Angeles. The L.A. uprising became a metaphor for everything that was still wrong with America twenty-seven years after the Watts Riots and twenty-two years after a Chicano Moratorium demonstration erupted into major violence in unincorporated East Los Angeles. For the leaders of Barrios Unidos and others involved in social justice work, the Los Angeles riots became a lightening rod for augmenting mobilization and advocacy efforts intended to address the root causes of community violence.

Even prior to the L.A. unrest, efforts involving BU and comparable groups had begun to bring peace to the streets in communities across California. For instance, a gang truce initiated by leaders of the rival street gangs known as the Crips and the Bloods called an unprecedented halt to hostilities in order to end the devastation that fratricide was wrecking on African American families and communities. Seizing the limelight created by the riots, organizers of the nascent truce began to garner media attention and support from churches and more established leaders, such as community organizer Carl Upchurch, celebrity-activist Jim Brown, and civil rights attorney Connie Rice. Truce leaders began to fashion a community change platform to bring jobs, economic investment, improved educational opportunities, job skills training, and leadership development programs to their neighborhoods while advocating for more humane law enforcement and criminal justice practices for their fellow young black men and women. The truce movement paralleled peace-building efforts within the Latino community by the Coalition to End Barrio Warfare and Barrios Unidos across California and the Southwest. These efforts, which would eventually converge at an historic African American/Latino peace summit in Kansas City, underscored the growing sense among gang members themselves that community violence in America was spinning out of control.

The epidemic level of violence affecting America at the outset of the 1990s was chronicled in a startling report released by the National Center for Health Statistics. The report estimated that, on an average day in the United States, sixty-five people were dying from interpersonal violence. More than an additional 6,000 people were being physically injured. The proliferation of firearms in inner-city settings had increased the lethality of violence as never before. During the 1980s, victimization from violence claimed the lives of 48,000 youth between the ages of twelve and twenty-four. According to a 1980–89 report by the Federal Bureau of Investigation, homicide had become the second leading cause of death for this age group. These trends prompted pioneering U.S. Surgeon General C. Everett Koop to convene a Workshop on Violence and Public Health, officially signaling the entry of public health professionals into the field of violence prevention. The formation of the National Center for Injury Prevention and Control in 1991 as part of the Centers for Disease Control and Prevention (CDC) underscores this development by virtue of the new center's inclusion of community violence as a central aspect of its institutional mission and focus.

Ultimately, these seminal developments came together to stimulate a new openness among institutional and political leaders to address the various systemic issues that underlie social problems like youth and community violence. Many private foundations and corporate entities began to reexamine their investments in community in order to increase their strategic impacts on violence prevention issues. One such philanthropic institution, newly created at the time, was The California Wellness Foundation (i.e., Wellness Foundation or TCWF). Endowed with a $300 million corpus by HealthNet, Inc. after its conversion from a nonprofit to a for-profit health care provider, the foundation chose youth violence prevention as its first grant-making venture, investing $70 million over a ten-year period to support model intervention programs in multiple regions of the state. The foundation's decision to invest significant resources in preventing youth violence would provide an unprecedented boost to organizations involved in serving youth, organizing to end violence, reforming juvenile justice approaches, building community, and other related efforts to promote well-being, peace, and justice in California.

DEVELOPMENTS IN NORTHERN CALIFORNIA—SEIZING THE DAY

At the community level where Barrios Unidos focused its organizing work, the conflict between the gang elements known as "Norteños" and "Sureños" that began in the California prison system had matured, spreading to communities across the state. The line between north and south was no longer confined to the distal regions of California where prison gangs held influence, but was now driving a wedge within neighborhoods in cities like Oxnard, Bakersfield, Santa Cruz, Watsonville, Fresno, San Jose, Salinas, and San Francisco. Divisions and tensions that had incubated in the state's juvenile and adult correctional detention facilities were literally bleeding out into urban and rural barrios of Northern California, exacerbating gang, neighborhood, and school-based violence in ways never before seen. The rifts between *norteño* and *sureño* allegiances had in fact taken on a life of their own in most communities, having little to do with their origins within the prison system. These conflicts were fomenting increasingly violent gang entanglements in adjoining neighborhoods, in public schools among native and foreign-born youth, and even within immediate extended families. The divisions were fed by growing profitability within the underground drug trade and the creation of territories corresponding to evolving gang sets, making community peace organizing more difficult than ever.

For the most part, the developmental needs of those involved in these conflicts, principally young people perceived as "hard core" and unredeemable, were going unmet by public schools, youth programs, health care organizations, and conventional social service agencies. Through the 1980s the policy environment faced by advocates for these troubled youths was one characterized intermittently by neglect, suspicion, and hostility. The gulf of mistrust was especially profound between mainstream leaders and grassroots street organizers. Underfunded community agencies continued to offer traditional services and recreational activities to at-risk youth, but thanks to the gutting of the tax base that once supported them, demand for these interventions far outstretched resources in the poorest and most violent neighborhoods. A common dilemma in these neglected areas was that no one organization provided the necessary range of comprehensive service strategies to make a lasting mark. In addition, there was a profound absence of coordinating infrastructure for groups seeking to address mounting violence either in schools or in the community. Finally, the lion's share of youth services and advocacy being offered at the time lacked innovation and cultural relevance sufficient to sustain meaningful participation among those most in need of alternatives to gang-related violence. Barrios Unidos emerged in this context as an important new player in the field, whose perspective and approach could help to address these issues.

According to BU founder Nane Alejándrez, the organization's entry onto the scene, and its institution-building work over time, helped to provide an unprecedented foundation for at-risk Latino youth to connect to society and to themselves in ways that were authentic and natural to them. According to Alejándrez,

> It's not that agencies and schools completely failed to offer some quality or well-intentioned programs and services. The problem was that too few had the experience or the needed *confianza* (trust or street credibility) to reach into the back streets, alleyways, detention centers, and homes of the most troubled young people with tough love and affinity; we came at them with firsthand experience in the madness of *la vida loca* and our scars exposed, offering them new knowledge and the full healing power of *la cultura*, a different way to see themselves and to understand the world, a way that could make them whole again.

At the very moment that Barrios Unidos founders were developing a nonprofit organization to fuel their innovative grassroots movement work, leaders in other disciplines concerned with preventing violence were also exploring new approaches to social policy and programs. Chief among these were experts in the somewhat unlikely field of public health. Visionary leaders in public health, observing the growing incidence of violence across America, its increasing consumption of young people, and its interaction with a broad range of social pathologies, began at this time to equate community violence to a social disease. Such leaders began to make credible in key leadership circles the notion that community violence was an outward manifestation of multiple factors, especially institutionalized racism, class inequity, media bias, and corporate greed. The placement of community violence in the larger context of U.S. political and economic policy and practice was unprecedented and naturally complemented BU's well-formed but nonscientific analysis and response. The connection of BU's work to that of public health experts across the nation was immensely validating and significant. Otilio Quintero has described it this way:

It was as if the community peace movement and public health were two pieces of a puzzle waiting to find each other to become stronger and more complete. Unlike the tunnel vision in other fields, the public health framework for preventing violence emphasized interdisciplinary approaches with multiple strategies, including education, outreach, leadership development, organizing, advocacy, collaboration, research, and the potent element of healing. More importantly, the public health approach acknowledged the relationship between the individual manifestations of violence and the social conditions that caused these behaviors. The framework offered hope that violence was preventable simply by identifying the cause of the illness and providing the medicine to heal both the individual and the society. These were things we already practiced in many different ways.

The coincidence of BU's formalization with the public health field's progressive take on the issues played a large role in helping policy, media, and foundation leaders to consider the possibility that groups like Barrios Unidos might not only be helpful but also arguably essential partners in efforts against the growing tide of community violence. Barrios founders gathered accordingly to seize the opportunity to build on their collective dream.

GATHERING THE FOUNDERS

BU's founding leaders had been meeting intermittently to advance the formal nonprofit infrastructure since 1989. Planning meetings took place in several venues in Watsonville and Santa Cruz, including Youth Services, ¡Sí, Se Puede!, the University of California at Santa Cruz, and the Veteran's Peace Action Team (where Nane Alejándrez continued to serve as a coordinator). Barrios leaders would eventually inherit office space in Santa Cruz from Veteran's Peace Action on Center Street, establishing BU's first official headquarters. At this time, Otilio Quintero was still teaching in local area high schools and at Cabrillo College. Liz Ayala and Billy Zaragosa were working as youth advocates at Fenix Services. Barbara García was serving as executive director at Salud Para La Gente, a local health services agency. Raquel Mariscal was director of the Criminal Justice Council of Santa Cruz. Walter Guzmán was organizing the ¡Sí, Se Puede! substance abuse recovery program. Marylou Alejándrez was a part-time student working in the private sector, and Manuel Martínez was working for the department of social services and as a volunteer coordinator for a recreational center at the Villa Housing Complex. While each of these leaders remained effectively engaged in their day jobs and attendant responsibilities, BU's growing institutionalization requirements came to take up more and more of their time during this period. They remained committed to the organization's development throughout, however, and sought whenever possible to piggyback BU meetings on other activities or community events in which they were involved, such as community workshops, school gatherings, local cultural events, or conferences at the University of California at Santa Cruz.

As one founder recalls, "These meetings didn't always have set agendas nor were they highly structured. Rather, the group usually used the time to touch base, talk about the escalating problems on the street and in juvenile hall, share resources and discuss collaboration opportunities, while allowing plenty of space to dream out loud about what Barrios Unidos could become and what it would take to get there." Otilio Quintero has characterized the modest goals that came out of these early meetings as "baby steps" that would build momentum leading to BU's first planning grants.

This period of dreaming was tempered by genuine soul-searching about the prospects of building a nonprofit "arm" to sustain a BU movement that would not succumb to convention or routine. Barrios Unidos founders universally wanted to remain a community-relevant and progressive entity. According to Raquel Mariscal, an early BU principal,

> We shared a strong notion of what we wanted to create and what we did not want to create. . . . It seemed that far too many community nonprofits were becoming more and more specialized, politically moderate, and service-focused in their mission. We were collectively committed to resisting that trend.

The challenge of raising funds to formalize BU's work posed several new dilemmas for its leaders. As organizers and activists working in voluntary coalition and with virtually no organizational management experience in their ranks, the founding members had so far been largely spared the array of issues associated with garnering and administering large sums of money. Now they faced a steep learning curve to gain practical knowledge about nonprofit management best practices they would need to employ in order to raise funds. They also faced new dilemmas about reconciling the principles of struggle and activism with the basic workings of a professionalized organization. The notion of establishing a nonprofit corporation to support the organizing work of the Barrios Unidos movement forced BU's founders to confront the possibility of compromises to the movement's "purity" as they had known it to date. As Nane Alejándrez recalls:

> For the most part we had earned our bread in jobs that paid us, and then when we were done working, we organized in the streets for free. In those days there was still some stigma in the streets with gang organizers who were getting paid for their activism or community work. These were real questions and concerns for the founders of Santa Cruz Barrios Unidos. How true could Barrios Unidos, the nonprofit organization, remain to the values and principles that guided Barrios Unidos, the movement. It was clear that finding a way to bring a core leadership that believed in the vision of Barrios Unidos under one roof to work together was important and made practical sense, but at what cost to our credibility on the streets?

As BU elder and leader Henry Domínguez put it, "Although many of its leaders had gone professional, the community peace movement at its core, remained fueled by the sweat equity of its grassroots leaders. There was still a purity and nobility because it was mostly volunteer activism. There was something inherently pure about designing and selling T-shirts, posters, and coloring books or being supported by the small donations of schools and churches where you delivered your message of healing and peace to youth. Not to be overly dramatic, but it was akin to ancient warriors, teachers, and healers being fed by the people and community they served."

All of BU's founders had been around long enough to see once strong and relevant community advocacy groups become nonprofit institutions only to lose focus in relation to their purpose, becoming effective service agencies while losing their edge as agents of social change. Clearly, they did not want to follow that path. At the same time, it was clear to most BU principals that undertaking social-change work on a big stage called for stronger organization. Long-time experience in community-based work had shown them that the only groups positioned to capture the resources needed to do larger-scale community work were nonprofit corporations. Whenever a new source of public or private funding became available, these were the groups receiving grant support and sponsorships. "It was frustrating at times," according to Nane Alejándrez. Too often, BU leaders would see larger nonprofits be awarded grants for work less formalized groups like theirs could arguably do better. Indeed, many times these larger groups would acknowledge this reality by turning to Barrios Unidos for help. As Alejándrez recalls, "There were some nonprofits claiming to do what we did that were receiving grants, then coming to contract with us to do the work." Such arrangements made clear that BU was gaining currency among regional independent-sector executives for its budding innovations and uniquely strong grassroots knowledge and ties. But playing second fiddle to more established organizations simply on the basis of size and legal status did not sit well with BU leaders.

BU's resistance to doing the bidding of larger, more established organizations was somewhat remarkable. Many other grassroots groups and leaders would have been logically seduced by the sort of largesse and opportunity for affiliation BU was increasingly being met with. In fact, several leading mainstream youth services nonprofits now approached Barrios Unidos to come under their roof. Offers ranged from operating as a project of the larger organization to establishing a fiscal sponsorship relationship. Having worked with many of these organizations in the past providing contract services or collaborating on community projects, Barrios Unidos founders knew and respected their commitment to the issues but intuitively felt that the core strategies and approaches BU sought to pursue would ultimately not fit the mold of their proposed hosts. They believed BU's strong focus on *cultura* and spirituality, along with its commitment to building activist leaders among the youth and community members, would substantially test the aspiring sponsor groups and quickly result in an outlasted welcome.

In the end, the early BU leaders decided to create a new organization that could be fashioned around their particular vision for change. Once this decision was made, Alejándrez and Quintero were charged with moving the project forward. The two began to prepare themselves by studying the organizational models of early movement leaders, as well as more contemporary advocacy organizations they knew of and respected. Among these organizations were Youth Services, Inc. in New Mexico, the Real Alternatives Program in San Francisco, the National Council of La Raza, and the International Indian Treaty Council. The more they investigated and explored leading nonprofit models, the more BU's founding leaders realized they would be charting new ground through their efforts to place traditions of *la cultura* and movement-building at the heart of their work.

Mindful of the need to maximize their prospects for organizational success through close adherence to nonprofit management best practices, Nane Alejándrez and Otilio Quintero approached the Santa Cruz Community Foundation for technical assistance. The aspiring nonprofit leaders knew little about the mechanics of actually starting, managing, and growing a nonprofit organization. Under the tutelage of senior foundation staff, over the course of several months, Nane and Otilio immersed themselves in an intensive crash course in nonprofit organization. As OT recalls,

> We were introduced in an intensive way to the many facets and principles of nonprofit management and community development in a caring and challenging environment at the foundation. We were being taught from *"caldo to cacahuates"* (soup to nuts) in the conventional methods and practices of nonprofits.

As Nane and OT presented preliminary drafts of BU's organizational plans and structural proposals for the new nonprofit organization they aspired to incorporate, the community foundation staff challenged their thinking and assumptions at every turn, but ultimately in ways that were supportive and facilitative of BU's ultimate success. OT has described the exchange and its outcomes in the following way:

> We would put forward our best thinking about what we wanted to create for Barrios Unidos and how we proposed getting there. The foundation staff would pose incisive and critical questions, give us some instruction and homework, and we would then return to the community and go at it again to design a better plan. The learning curve was very challenging as we moved back and forth between meetings with the Barrios Unidos founding group and the foundation staff, to sharpen our thinking and the plan. The program included basic instruction in organizational and financial management. What we left this relationship with was not only the ability to articulate the vision and theory of work for Barrios Unidos with greater effectiveness, but we were also much more prepared with practical skills to make it happen. The investment of these in-kind resources by the community foundation made the avalanche of this intensive organizational planning somewhat bearable as we continued to work our regular jobs and do the ongoing street organizing work of Barrios.

In a very short period, the Barrios Unidos leadership had learned a great deal about what it took to establish an effective nonprofit organization from the community foundation's informed and caring leadership. However, even with the foundation staff's practical guidance and support, much work remained still to be done to inform BU's qualitative direction as a grassroots, value-driven organization; this work could only ultimately be dealt with by its leadership circle operating largely in the absence of clear direction. As OT would later say,

> Going from working as an all-volunteer organizing effort guided by *cultura* and spiritual ceremony to working in a more formalized nonprofit culture required all of us to go through a paradigm shift. There were some historical examples of movement organizations we could draw on/and some

contemporary groups that we learned from, but there was no real road map for us to follow.

Founding elder Raquel Mariscal recalls this salient moment in BU's development this way:

> The conversations we had were centered as much on principles of organizing as they were on organizational structures and program models. The old cliché of form following function applied to our discussions as we set out to put down on paper the definitions of the who, what, why, and how that would define and drive the work of Barrios Unidos far into the future. Taking the best of our collective experiences, and the trust between us, we all held each other accountable to the agreement of being true to the movement and keeping the values of *cultura* and the *movimiento* front and center on the table, while translating them into an understandable "organization speak."

In 1992, as Barrios Unidos leaders finalized their preparations to incorporate and pursue funded programming, they were presented with a large unanticipated opportunity to secure major start-up grant support. The California Wellness Foundation (TCWF) had begun to hold grant information meetings in various regions across the state to inform potential grant seekers about the structure and application requirements of its newly formed $70 million Violence Prevention Initiative. The new private investment program was designed in large part to address gang- and gun-related violence affecting at-risk youth populations in California—issues that were naturally at the core of BU's work. In an effort to promote innovative approaches, moreover, the foundation was reaching out beyond traditional institutional partners to engage an unprecedented array of gang organizers, violence prevention practitioner organizations, grassroots community groups, public health agencies, youth service centers, academic and research institutions, policy centers, and allied stakeholders in law enforcement, public media, and schools. The foundation was especially interested in supporting local initiatives involving collaborations among multiple nonprofits, public institutions, grassroots constituencies, and other local stakeholders. An informational meeting on this evolving work sponsored by the Santa Cruz County Office of Education established a key turning point for Barrios Unidos leadership. The office of education had invited various community organizations, including Barrios Unidos, to be part of a partnership under its sponsorship to apply for Wellness Foundation funding. After careful deliberation, BU founders decided to pursue the foundation's support with Barrios Unidos acting as the lead organization in the context of its own local project collaboration. Although the BU movement had never sought a major grant, its founders believed the TCWF funding program offered a rare opportunity to take their movement to the next level. TCWF's decision to support partnerships intended to attack the root causes of youth and community violence, moreover, was a natural fit with the BU founders' vision of developing a nonprofit organization that would be a catalyst for community change and societal transformation.

Because Barrios Unidos still lacked legal nonprofit status pending the dispensation of its application for tax-exempt designations by federal and state authorities, its leaders turned to several trusted area charitable organizations to facilitate their interest in competing for Wellness Foundation and other private funding. Some of the organizations that BU approached were unable to extend themselves or did not fit as ideal partners for a variety of reasons. Fenix Services of Watsonville and the Vanguard Public Foundation of San Francisco, however, both enthusiastically offered to serve as the initial sponsor and fiscal agent for Barrios Unidos's application to TCWF. The backing of these organizations, along with continuing technical support from the Santa Cruz Community Foundation, helped Barrios Unidos leaders immensely, both in their continuing quest for nonprofit accreditation as well as in their efforts to partner with TCWF and other important private funders. The support of these more established institutions furthermore helped BU to galvanize the interest of other grassroots and regional leaders, who now became increasingly willing partners in the effort to build a compelling nonviolence campaign that could gain major funders' interest.

In 1992, Santa Cruz Barrios Unidos, Inc. finally became a legal nonprofit entity. Shortly thereafter, the organization was awarded a

$175,000 planning grant by the Wellness Foundation. Years later, Otilio Quintero would describe the significance of these developments in the following words:

> The timing of the Wellness grant application process pushed us to step forward to establish the nonprofit organization that we had been dreaming of for so long. We knew that it would stretch us all beyond anything we could possibly imagine and require a lot of time and personal sacrifice, but history had provided us an opportunity and we were going to answer the call.

The decision reached by Barrios Unidos to pursue major funding and associated leadership commitments involving other groups and institutional interests was an exceptional one, to be sure. For years, BU's founders had resisted external engagements or decisions that might compromise their budding movement's integrity and independence. Even the California Coalition to End Barrio Warfare—the early collaborative effort with Southern California Chicano nonviolence leaders—had not finally proven entirely workable for Barrios Unidos principals. Now, BU was actually preparing to take on greater encumbrances than ever. But the fact that BU founders and their agenda would drive this work proved decisive and irresistible.

The staff recommendation by Gary Yates and Crystal Hayling to support BU's work reflected a unique vision by the The California Wellness Foundation as well. Given the nascent status of the organization at the time, TCWF's decision to award a major grant to Santa Cruz Barrios Unidos represented a tremendous leap of faith by a mainstream grant-making institution. The Violence Prevention Initiative was the largest and most comprehensive private funding venture addressing youth violence ever undertaken in the history of the United States. Over the course of the VPI's life span, the program would produce over three quarters of a million dollars in foundation grant support for Barrios Unidos (along with still millions more targeted to eighteen other participating community organizations across California). Still today, BU leaders acknowledge with deep appreciation the faith and support demonstrated by Fenix Services, the Vanguard Public Foundation, and the Santa Cruz Community Foundation, which helped to make Barrios Unidos a grant-worthy partner for TCWF and other major foundations that supported this work. "Without the efforts of these early institutional partners, despite seeing the potential and power of our work," says Nane Alejándrez, "The California Wellness Foundation might not have been willing or able to make the initial planning grant that put us on the map."

BU's successful efforts to develop a values-driven nonprofit organization and to secure major grant support from The California Wellness Foundation marked a new era in the life of the Barrios Unidos community peace movement. TCWF's initial grant was ultimately extended to include ten years of core operating support. Within this critical developmental period, BU would also come to receive essential investments from The California Endowment, the David and Lucile Packard Foundation, and the S.H. Cowell Foundation. This major funding in turn would give Santa Cruz Barrios Unidos leaders the rare opportunity to simultaneously establish a strong organizational infrastructure while launching and refining many of the strategies for effecting change they had fashioned from their movement experiences on a scale they had only dreamed about. TCWF's significant investment and subsequent allied support received from other important philanthropic, public, and civic groups gave the leaders and staff of the new organization nearly unbridled opportunities to take risks and experiment with new program approaches. BU leaders responded in turn with seminal thinking and action that helped to inform new organizing and policy interventions related to minority and youth violence, both in California and other states across the nation.

BU's GUIDING VISION, VALUES, AND PRINCIPLES

From the beginning, Barrios Unidos leaders have periodically taken time to engage in organizational dialogue to clarify and affirm the organization's vision, values, and principles. As these institutional templates are refined and strengthened, they are shared with BU stakeholders and incorporated into all aspects of the organization's work. Below is a current version of BU's core organizational commitments.

The Barrios Unidos Vision

From its inception, the focus of Santa Cruz Barrios Unidos, Inc. has been to build a culturally and spiritually based organization in support of a broad grassroots community peace movement. The organization's long-term vision is to establish a Barrios Unidos Institute for Peace and Development based in Santa Cruz, California. The Institute will be dedicated to healing youth and families, preparing new leaders, and advancing the study and application of new methods of peace- and justice-oriented education, organizing, civic engagement, and youth and community empowerment. The geographical focal points of this work will be selected barrios throughout California, the United States, and the world.

Guiding Values and Principles

Cultural Identity and Tradition—We believe that the expression of cultural and spiritual traditions are central to the humanity, health, and well-being of people of Chicano, Latino, and indigenous descent. The highest expressions of our humanity, family, and communal values flow from the understanding and practice of our traditions.

Organizational Integrity—We shall seek to apply the highest values of *cultura* to all aspects of our core strategies, organizational endeavors, and community life. The staff and volunteers share the responsibility to preserve the integrity of the organization and apply its guiding values across all aspects of our work.

Cultural Integrity and Respect—We believe that respecting the cultural integrity and dignity of people of all backgrounds is central to the well-being of our community and of society as a whole. We value intercultural exchange and mutual learning for societal benefit and advancement. We recognize the critical importance of developing a high level of cultural fluency among our people and of working to promote pluralism and respect across diverse populations and the social, public, and private institutions that make up society.

Collaboration and Partnership—We believe that central to our mission is working to create peaceful and healthy communities through solidarity, partnership, collaboration, and coalition-building with other culturally diverse communities, institutions, organizations, and movements that are dedicated to achieving social justice, broad democratic participation, and economic equity.

Economic Self-Reliance and Empowerment—We believe that community-centered economics begins with developing human potential, creating equitable opportunity, and maintaining the responsibility for good stewardship of the land and its resources. All of our economic development enterprises, including the attainment and management of our assets, are socially responsible, serving broad community benefit and promoting self-reliance through access to quality education, training, labor markets, and business opportunities.

Civic and Political Empowerment—We believe that central to our mission is promoting and supporting informed involvement in democratic and civic life by all community residents: youth, parents, and elders acting as stakeholders in society. All of our leadership development, education, organizing, community mobilization, and political action must be guided by the values of democratic pluralism and nonviolent principles for positive social change.

Part III
The Barrios Unidos Theory of Change and Strategies in Action

A Living Theory of Change

You must be the change you seek to make in this world.
Mahatma Gandhi

A key to understanding the Barrios Unidos theory of change is the realization that this nonprofit organization's programs are designed to model and bring about social change—simultaneously. For BU principals, living the value of their culture and of social justice is even more important than carrying out any one organizational program activity or function. Although successfully developing and replicating effective programs in an essential organizational priority, what is even more central to BU leaders is the task of reclaiming young lives and communities. In effect, BU's work is purposeful and transformative, rather than merely charitable and rote.

Because no one young man or woman, neighborhood, community, or city is completely alike, BU programs are developed with flexible guidelines that respond to and accommodate real-life complexities and variations. The organization's programmatic range is consequently vast. Activities and interventions involving at-risk youth, families, and communities can include teachings about Chicano history in a Kids Club meeting, business practices in a silk-screen enterprise program, or indigenous spiritual ritual in a community gathering to honor an individual's—or a community's—gifts and strengths. For those who seek to understand and replicate this approach it is helpful to know that Barrios Unidos's vision, values, and principles are used collectively as tools to shape all organizational and program activities. The organization's core strategies for change are imbued with equal parts of each.

As a result, it is difficult to provide a static description of any one element of the BU organization. What is more possible to articulate is a clearer understanding of the BU theory of change: the values and beliefs the leaders hold dear, their understanding of the root causes of community violence, the basic changes BU leaders and organizers seek, and the core strategies the organization is employing to realize these changes. A central premise of the Barrios Unidos theory of change is the understanding that the identities of Latino and other socioeconomically disadvantaged youth are shaped by political and class forces that do not always have their best interests at heart. BU leaders believe that much of the disorientation and pain experienced by youth in the barrios and ghettos of this nation is the result of a historical process that has separated these young men and women from their true human identities. For Chicanos, and so many others, identity is inextricably linked to culture. To account for the legacy of cultural separation, all Barrios Unidos program interventions seek to restore in young people, their families and communities a sense of belonging, both to their particular identity groups and to the larger human family.

Since the organization's inception, BU leaders and staff have thus held a steadfast commitment to prioritizing several interrelated objectives:

- Reclaiming and restoring cultural and spiritual integrity as well as dignity within Chicano young people, families, and communities
- Building self-reliance and self-sufficiency across these target constituencies
- Preparing Chicano youth, families, and communities to take a greater leadership role in the building of a more equitable and democratic society

Because these objectives are far-reaching and impossible to achieve in isolation from other progressive community and civic initiatives, resources, and leadership, BU is additionally committed to:

- Mutual learning and intercultural exchange that strengthens pluralism within diverse communities and social, public, and private institutions

- Collaboration and coalition-building that helps to create more peaceful and healthy multicultural communities

These building blocks of the BU approach to youth and community empowerment are actualized through a dynamic array of programmatic strategies. Following is a more in-depth review of these applied interventions, all of which give life to the organization's theory of change. In one way or another, BU's arsenal of interventions—highly interrelated and flexible in application—draws on core investments in education, street organizing, leadership and human development, community economic development, civic participation and community mobilization, coalition-building, and advocacy.

HEALING AND TRANSFORMATION: RECLAIMING AND RESTORING COMMUNITY CULTURE

Then I was standing on the highest mountain of them all, and all around beneath me was the whole hoop of the world. And as I stood there I saw more than I can tell and understood more than I saw; for I was seeing in a sacred manner the shape of all things in the spirit, and the shape of all shapes as they must live together as one being. And I saw that the sacred hoop of my people was one of many hoops that made one circle, wide as daylight and as starlight, and in the center grew one mighty flowering tree to shelter all the children of one mother and one father. And I saw that it was holy.

Black Elk, Lakota Nation Holy Man

CREATING A SACRED PLACE: THE SANTA CRUZ BU CENTER

The Barrios Unidos Center in Santa Cruz is a focal point for cultural preservation and development. It is a hub for intercultural exchange and learning, political education, and organized activism. It is a sacred place to heal and nurture members of the community and to feed their collective spirit. Various BU Center-housed economic development enterprises have amplified and complemented the organization's work in recent years, building on a recent major facility acquisition on Soquel Street. The Soquel Street property supports anchor program components, including BU Productions, Barrios Unidos's core enterprise program. BU Productions generates silk-screen T-shirts, posters, and other arts-related products that generate visibility and revenue for the organization and its work. In addition, the Soquel Street facility houses various small business incubation projects, a childcare facility, and a Cisco Systems-supported technology center. All of these efforts seek to encourage culturally supportive economic empowerment and self-reliance among at-risk Latino youth and their families. Other evolving BU programs respond to related community needs by providing youth- and family-centered counseling and referral services, as well as food and clothing distributions to especially needy community members. The physical existence of the BU Center is not as important as the spiritually and culturally relevant manner in which Barrios Unidos's various programs are administered and conceptualized.

As founding circle and staff member Manuel Martínez observes, "For so many of the young people we serve, there are daily doses of brokenness, neglect, alienation, and condemnation in their homes, schools, and neighborhoods. In so many communities, 'the village' described in the powerful African proverb about what it takes to raise a child is replaced by the subcultures bred of poverty and survival, such as gangs, street life, and escapism through drugs and alcohol. At BU we try to re-create the village by providing an extended family and community, here at our site or in the neighborhoods, schools, housing projects, jails, or detention centers." Indeed, BU leaders have been very intentional over the years in building the organization as a safe haven and spiritual anchor for Latino youth facing often harsh and destabilizing societal challenges. They have encouraged young people and community participants involved in BU programs to see the organization as a sacred place that offers nourishment, security, and an opportunity for collective community advancement.

To dramatize the point, Barrios Unidos leaders have frequently drawn on the story of the sacred tree, which emerged from cultures that are indigenous to North and South America. Traditional belief has it that every tribe, village, community, and nation must have a spiritual center or focal point to both survive and fulfill its highest human potential. The metaphor of the sacred tree has come to symbolize this essential magnet. According to experts at the Canadian-based Four

Worlds International Institute, the Creator planted a sacred tree under which all the people of the Earth could gather to find healing, power, wisdom, and security. The fruits of the tree are the good things the Creator has given to the people: teachings that show the path to love, compassion, generosity, patience, wisdom, justice, courage, respect, humility, and many other life-affirming gifts. These ancient teachings suggest that without the protective shade of the tree, without the nourishment of its fruit, the people would be lost, cease to dream, quarrel among themselves over worthless trifles, and become unable to deal with one another honestly and with humanity.

The Barrios Unidos Community Center has come to represent such a place. The center establishes a focal point or home within the community where young people, adults, and families can regain their cultural bearings. It provides a space for unconditional acceptance, where young people are honored, where their cultural integrity is preserved, and where they can rediscover and celebrate the beauty of their heritage, develop their natural gifts, experience healthy intergenerational relationships, and learn to live responsible and purposeful lives. As spiritual teacher and member of the BU founding circle Liz Ayala has explained it:

> So many of the things we do here are not "funded" programs. The caring and support that youth and families need do not always fit neatly into packaged programs whose outcomes can be quantified and measured as researchers and funders like to do. The first title anyone has who works here is uncle, aunt, brother, sister, or friend. We always intended to be a center *for* the community, not a service center *in* the community. Our main purpose was to be whatever the community and the movement needed. For some of the young people we serve, Barrios is the only real home they have ever known. Where public schools fail and discard our children, we gather them up and do our best to love and educate them. We have been a sanctuary and neutral ground for young people trying to escape gang life and a funeral home for those who never made it out in time. As a spiritual center, we hold sacred ceremonies to heal broken lives and to strengthen community among people from all walks and all colors, in the name of justice and peace.

The center is one of the few places in Santa Cruz or anywhere where Chicano young people and adult residents can find regular, unedited expression outside of their homes. It is a place that supports culturally based communal activities, customs, traditions, and ceremonies. It actively supports a way of life intended to nurture the physical, emotional, intellectual, and spiritual well-being of Latino people. Elder Henry Domínguez is careful to point out that although it was important for BU to acquire land to establish a home base and central gathering place, the binding force of the movement was and remains spiritual:

> The land boundaries that divide our people into *clicas* and gang sets are artificial and should not stand against the unifying bonds of common *cultura*. In the same way, the property lines of the Barrios Unidos Center do not confine the spirit of *familia*, community, and unity that the movement is working to create. The spirit of Barrios Unidos flows from the *corazón* into the homes, streets, schoolyards, jail cells, organized protests and ceremonies in the communities where we serve—anywhere people gather to build unity under the banner.

RITUALS AND PRACTICES TO STRENGTHEN CULTURAL AND SPIRITUAL FOUNDATIONS

The transformative vision at the heart of Barrios Unidos's work is part of the growing movement among Latinos to recognize and recover their spiritual traditions. . . . Transcending many of the boundaries erected in mainstream America, this movement brings together indigenous roots through spiritual practices with Christian beliefs, reflecting a multicultural heritage that draws from Native American, European, and African wells.

Aaron Gallegos, *Sojourner Magazine*

Barrios Unidos's efforts to build from a spiritual "space" have been informed by many sources, partners, and allies. Jerry Tello of the National Latino Fatherhood and Family Institute is a longtime supporter, teacher, and knowledge resource for the founders and staff of

Barrios Unidos. In his rites of passage curriculum, *El Joven Noble* (the Noble Young Man), Tello offers the premise that strength, harmony, and balance in families and communities are rooted in instilling cultural resiliency through spirituality and traditional rites of passage. As Tello points out, "At the base of our culture are direct teachings and traditions to reinforce a sense of identity, respect, *destino* (destiny), interconnectedness, and harmony based on spirituality." The place of spirituality—universal and ecumenical—is central to the Barrios Unidos way.

The leadership of Barrios Unidos describes its community peace and justice work, accordingly, as a spiritual movement. For BU the spiritual dimensions of *Cultura Es Cura* is the lifeblood of the movement, just as water binds the bricks and mortar of the buildings that house the organization. Nane Alejándrez explains the centrality of spirituality to BU's work in this way:

> To us, spirituality and culture are one and the same. Returning ceremony and prayer into its proper place in the life of the community is so critically important to everything we do. We are not about selling religion or proselytizing people, but about embracing the power of spirituality that traditionally has healed and bound our families, communities, and civilizations together as indigenous people. Part of our hope in telling the Barrios Unidos story is to help expand the notions of mainstream society and civic and political leaders on what nondenominational, ecumenical, faith-based work really looks like in the barrios, ghettos, and other ethnic enclaves of America. We are not a denomination or an institutional church, but as much as anyone, faith is central to our movement's efforts to bring wholeness to our people as individuals and well-being to our communities.

On any given day, across all aspects of the organization's life and activities, its spiritual foundation is visible and takes many powerful forms. Upon entering the Barrios Unidos Center one is likely to encounter the aroma of burning sage, *copal*, or cedar that is being used to offer an opening blessing for a meeting, group activity, youth conflict intervention, or community event. Prayer ceremonies, blessings, and sage purification occur before weekly staff meetings and convenings of the board of directors. In the numerous programs BU offers to troubled youth and their families, this aspect of *la cultura cura* is presented to help overcome multigenerational pain that surrounds BU stakeholders and fuels the violence and destruction that is present in their homes, schools, and neighborhoods. These rituals are not imposed, but offered for those who wish to participate. Not all staff, volunteers, youth, parents, or community members who walk through the doors of Barrios Unidos or participate in any of its various programs necessarily embrace the rituals and traditions. However, both are unapologetically and transparently expressed as a central part of the organization's culture, with only one rule: that any ritual or ceremony be conducted with mutual respect, openness, acceptance, and tolerance of other spiritual expressions.

An altar is situated in the common space of the main office where staff, students, parents, and children place sacred items. These include sage in conch shells, religious-themed candles, crucifixes, feathers, rosaries, prayer beads, ceremonial pipes, turtle-shell rattles, medicine wheels, food offerings, photos, and personal effects of loved ones (often deceased)—all to inspire a sense of collective hope and open spiritual expression. As Alejándrez puts it, "Everyone needs to find their own spiritual path. We need these sacred things so we can rediscover the power of love to help us let go of the hatred and forgive."

In this approach, there is a clear influence of the spiritual roots of the Aztec, Maya, Yaqui, and Inca civilizations that inform U.S. Latino heritage. There is also a strong presence of northern Native American ancestral traditions. Broadly speaking, though, the spiritual environment that is nurtured and created at BU is truly open and ecumenical. Throughout the common spaces, personal offices and classrooms of the BU Center, on walls and in other visible places, visitors will typically see images of the Virgin of Guadalupe side-by-side with pieces of artwork depicting Aztec and other indigenous spiritual icons and symbols. They will also likely see drawings or photos of international spiritual and human rights leaders, such as Oscar Romero, Malcolm X, Mahatma Gandhi, Mother Teresa, Rigoberta Menchú, and the Dali Lama.

But the adornments and spiritual references Barrios Unidos leaders feature at the BU Center are not all of traditional and broad public notoriety. In order to ensure that staff and stakeholders do not forget the origins of the organization or the movement, the walls of BU offices and buildings offer permanent memorials to those who have lost their lives to the madness of barrio warfare, violence, and drugs.

The spiritualism practiced by BU elders comes mostly from indigenous traditions of the North and South. As would be expected from a Chicano- or Latino-oriented organization, the syncretism of Catholic and Judeo-Christian influences with indigenous traditions is clearly present, both symbolically and in the practice and daily expressions of faith. At its mountain retreat site, pipe carriers, such as elder Henry Domínguez and Wayne Boyd, pour water during sweat lodge ceremonies for staff, volunteers, students, guests, and community groups. Boyd is a member of the Ojibwa nation and is the resident caretaker and spiritual teacher at the three-acre retreat site BU customarily utilizes. The site contains a sweat lodge, a tepee, fire circles, a natural amphitheatre, an outdoor kitchen, tree houses, and a few small cabins. The retreat site is home to periodic ceremonies, rites of passage rituals, and leadership summits; it also serves as a daily space for spiritual reflection among BU family, constituents, and allied community groups. In the tradition of D-Q University, the BU retreat site is home to spiritual expression and learning about the traditions of diverse indigenous cultures of the Americas. As Boyd observes,

> Creating spaces where the traditions of the tribal nations of the North and those of the South come together is important to the future of indigenous people. It is a prophesy of the eagle and the condor that a great reunification of our people would take place in our time. It is not a coincidence that Barrios Unidos is working to bridge the divisions of Chicano/Latino people in the barrios who see themselves as North or South. The medicine Barrios Unidos offers is part of realizing a greater solidarity and common destiny for all of our people.

Despite the organization's focus on traditional Latino and indigenous spiritual practices, BU staff members, volunteers, speakers, resource people, youth, parents, and community members have always represented faith traditions across the globe. Throughout its past and into the present, the BU family has incorporated individuals devout in various forms of Christianity, Judaism, Islam, Buddhism, Hinduism, and many other religious traditions, working and praying side-by-side. A distinguishing aspect of the organization's culture is that everyone is welcome to bring their gifts and talents to the table at BU. The late Ted Jefferson of the Bahai faith served as a teacher at the César Chávez School. Nghia Tran, who practices Buddhism, has worked periodically as a consultant to executive management. Leslie Sultan, a woman of Jewish heritage, has volunteered to teach *folklórico* dance at the BU Center. Jema Cruz and Dina Torres, who come from devout Catholic backgrounds, run BU-supported Kids Clubs in the Santa Cruz housing projects of Beach Flats and Elizabeth Oaks, respectively. These are all examples of people from diverse backgrounds that have found a common acceptance and home at BU.

Drawing on these various traditions, BU leaders typically begin staff meetings, community events, or larger convenings such as peace conferences or summits with a prayer ceremony designed to create a space of healing and spiritual anchoring for participants. Marylou Alejándrez has explained this impulse to position spirituality at the center of BU's work in terms of maintaining organizational focus on the group's essential and enduring values, more than mere transactional considerations. At the 2001 summit of BU chapters, she expressed this sentiment in these words:

> If we don't start these meetings with our hearts and from a spiritual place, the days will pass with us talking about organizing strategies, raising money, and developing programs without being rooted in common purpose. People will return to their home communities unhealed, disconnected, and with a long list of things to do rather than an understanding of what the work is really about.

The summit at which Marylou Alejándrez shared these words commenced—as so many BU gatherings do—with drumming, participants seated in a circle, and elder Henry Domínguez offering a sage blessing, a prayer, and a sacred song to call the group together. Then came the ritual passing of a "sacred staff." The staff served as a talking stick. Each person held the staff, one by one, taking a moment to share something of particular concern or importance to them individually, organizationally, or as a coalition. On this day, the talking stick ritual offered an opportunity for cathartic release of the stress and pain many were feeling. Some attending BU chapter leaders shared particularly difficult circumstances being faced in their personal lives while others spoke solemnly of recent killings in their home communities that seriously fractured fragile alliances they had worked months or years to establish. Still another participating BU leader shared the loss of a young one, in whom the organization had invested in for several years, to a life sentence in prison. As the talking circle progressed, the inherent pain and complexity of working on the front lines of youth violence prevention rose to the surface. A powerful solidarity filled the meeting venue in the form of tears and heartfelt words of encouragement.

In another powerful moment, Manny Lares, a young leader from one of BU's Southern California chapters in Santa Monica, revealed that in the daily stresses of managing the organization—running from meeting to meeting, fundraising, serving the needs of constituent youth, or putting out fires in the community—he had dangerously set aside his spiritual awareness and grounding. According to Lares, BU's chapter summits (held twice a year) offered one of the few opportunities available to peace warriors like him to regain his spiritual center and sense of healing. That night after holding a sweat lodge healing ceremony for the group, the elder Domínguez reminded participants that the single most important aspect of *La Cultura Cura* and BU is healing, both personal and communal:

> You have chosen work that unfolds the depths of human suffering and the heights of human redemption on a daily basis. If you do nothing else in the course of your organizing, meeting, teaching, mediating, and managing, create the space for healing and spiritual renewal, including your own. Before anything else, remember that a peace warrior is a healer.

Barrios Unidos leaders use traditional community celebrations as a vehicle to strengthen cultural and spiritual foundations that are essential in building cooperation and solidarity in any neighborhood.

For example, mounting *Las Posadas* (the traditional Christmas pageants) during the Christmas season and *Día de los Muertos* celebrations in the fall are staple activities upon which BU builds. These events reinforce appreciation and awareness of the cultural and religious traditions that unite BU family members. Students and parents of the BU César Chávez School for Social Change and participants in BU Kids Clubs, as well as interested community volunteers, usually organize these events with staff support. As with many of the organization's community-building activities, there is always a balance of fellowship, fun, food, celebration, learning, culture, and ceremony.

The *Las Posadas* pageant is traditionally celebrated to mark the beginning of the Christmas season and includes a candlelight procession with singing and music that dramatizes Joseph and Mary's search for lodging in Bethlehem before the birth of Jesus. At BU, the celebration is open to the entire community and may include a dinner, an art show, gifts, crafts, and programs for the children. Food distributions to families in need, music, *danza*, some *teatro,* and a prayer ceremony are also customarily involved. Along with the festivities, it is just as likely that a BU elder or student will offer stories or a play on the mixed Catholic and Aztec origins of *Las Posadas* to impart to young and old alike the importance of understanding, sharing, and preserving traditions.

The commemoration of *Día de los Muertos* is an important and widely celebrated holy day of obligation to pray for deceased family members and relations. As might be expected in an organization that deals with interpersonal and community violence, *Día de los Muertos* is an especially powerful time of the year. It offers BU staff, youth, and their families a special time to remember and honor those who have passed and an opportunity to rededicate their lives to inspiring hope and commitment to change. So many of the young people and families that BU works with have lost loved ones to gang, community, or domestic violence, as well as to alcohol and drug abuse. For that reason, ceremonies, rituals, and teachings during *Día de los Muertos* events are focused on healing, remembering, and honoring those who have been needlessly lost by affirming a collective dedication to stopping the cycle of violence and destruction. BU staff, elders, and spiritual leaders create space at the Center for youth and their families to build sacred altars, offer life-affirming activities, hold prayer ceremonies, assemble talking circles, mount candlelight vigils, organize traditional processions, or conduct sweat lodge ceremonies at their retreat site in the Santa Cruz Mountains.

Invariably, in these activities, the message is clear: reclaiming one's basic dignity and agency as a part of the human family is essential and possible, and reconnecting to one's cultural and spiritual roots is key to healing and self-realization. As Nane Alejándrez puts it,

> During these times, I try to relay to the youth that their innate spirituality is the best way to let go of the pain. I share how the sage, sweat lodge, prayer, and other sacred practices have helped me to heal, let go of the madness, and change my life to help end the cycle of death and needless suffering in our barrios. There is indescribable power in seeing a Sureño and Norteño who were recently mortal enemies praying, healing, reconciling, learning, and growing together as brothers and sisters. Healing of this kind is not just on the individual level, but collective, making us stronger as a people.

LA CULTURA ES CURA: CURRICULUM AND OTHER EDUCATION PROGRAMS

> *I am Joaquín, lost in a world of confusion, caught up in a world of gringo society, confused by the rules, scorned by attitudes, suppressed by manipulation, and destroyed by modern society. . . . I shed tears of sorrow. I sow seeds of hate. I withdraw to the safety of the circle of life. My own people. I am Cuauhtémoc, proud prince and noble leader of men, king of an empire civilized beyond the dreams of gachupín Cortés, who also is the blood, the image of myself. I am the Mayan prince. I am Nezahualcóyotl, great leader of the Chichimecas. I am the sword and flame of Cortés the despot. And I am the eagle serpent of the Aztec nation . . . I am Joaquín.*
> Rodolfo "Corky" Gonzales

The programmatic vision for Barrios Unidos's education work closely mirrors the model of Corky Gonzales's Crusade for Justice Center, which provided a social, cultural, and political base for the

Chicano community in Denver during the 1960s and 1970s. Similar to the Crusade, BU serves as a hub for the community, providing much-needed human services and sponsoring cultural events to foster unity and pride. Many of BU's organizing endeavors mirror the Crusade's *Los Pescadores* (Fishermen's) meetings, which were community forums on contemporary issues to educate, identify, and mobilize local youth leaders. The BU-supported César Chávez School for Social Change parallels the mission of the Crusade's *La Escuela y Colegio Tlatelolco*, which provided a culturally-based educational curriculum focused on preparing future community leaders for the movement.

The community relevance of the César Chávez School is most profound, given the continuing failure of U.S. public educational institutions to serve the needs and interests of Chicano/Latino youth. In the state of California and across the nation, Latino and Latina public school students experience the highest dropout and illiteracy rates of all racial and ethnic groups. Poor school performance and early dropout rates, in turn, resign Latino youth to a life of economic struggle and social marginalization, much of which reinforces their incentives and need to turn to gangs and violence. Like *La Escuela*, its predecessor in Denver, the Chávez School is committed to recovering and enriching the lives of Latino and Latina young people who have been poorly served by America's public education system.

THE CÉSAR CHÁVEZ SCHOOL FOR SOCIAL CHANGE

Established in 1995 and chartered as an alternative high school, the César E. Chávez School for Social Change (CCSSC) draws on the *Cultura Es Cura* curriculum designed by Albino García, Sr. Over the years, Carmen Velásquez, a former teacher, and Liz Ayala, the present coordinator of the school, have refined and expanded many aspects of the *Cultura Es Cura* curriculum. Operated in collaboration with the Santa Cruz County Office of Education, CCSSC enrolls fifteen to twenty-five at-risk students at any given time who are having trouble succeeding in traditional public school settings. CCSSC provides a positive alternative learning environment that combines bilingual instruction in a culturally appropriate academic curriculum. Courses include math, social science, english literacy, creative writing, and history. These courses in turn are complemented by cultural enrichment activities and a five-step Rites of Passage program.

CCSSC faculty and allied staff use a popular education pedagogical model to engage students in subject matter that is culturally, academically, and socially relevant to the at-risk youth the school serves. CCSSC officials, parents, and students are bound by a standard contract outlining the school's academic standards, its code of conduct, and requirements for the Rites of Passage program. The contract also expresses an expectation of meaningful parental and family involvement in the students' and school's work. A council, or *concilio*, comprised of elders (parents or community members), a BU staff member, and two advanced-level students, ensures mutual accountability and guides school decisions regarding activities, petitions and appeals, disciplinary actions, and conflict mediation. The *concilio* is also instrumental in determining the school's core curriculum, which establishes the heart of BU's educational agenda and intended impacts.

DEVELOPING THE CORE CURRICULUM—ALBINO GARCÍA, SR.

To advance CCSSC's important work, BU leaders have pulled together a set of historical and cultural materials, lesson plans, exercises, and other activities that act as a "living" and "evolving" *Cultura Es Cura* curriculum. First introduced in 1995, the curriculum has had many contributors and has drawn from various culturally based rites of passage, youth development, substance abuse rehabilitation, and gang intervention models. Albino García, Sr., who came to BU in the early 1990s around the time the nonprofit organization was getting off the ground, has been the principal architect of the CCSSC curriculum throughout its evolution and development.

When García came to BU, the organization was growing by leaps and bounds, using organizing approaches rooted in culture and spirituality to add chapters in California and other states. But, in large part, the BU founders were working in ad hoc fashion. They had never comprehensively documented the history, cultural traditions, rituals, and ceremonies that were essential elements of the personal and community change process they were seeking to model and promote. Nor did they even know how best to assemble all of the lessons they had gleaned over the years into a coherent, comprehensive model. García quickly focused on the need to create a "living" curriculum others could be taught to use. In effect, BU's founders needed to undertake a collective discovery process to consolidate and formalize the core base of learning that would ultimately institutionalize the organization's practices and teachings. By definition, this took time and involved numerous iterations of knowledge- and resource-mapping. As Albino recalls it all:

> When I arrived [in 1994], the organization already had a solid framework of strategies rooted in *cultura*, spirituality, organizing, economic development, the arts, and popular education. What Nane [Alejándrez] invited me to do was to help take this to the next level and work with staff to develop a curriculum that melded the various aspects of cultural/historical education, behavioral change, personal development, gang intervention, substance abuse prevention, violence prevention, principles of nonviolence, family preservation, leadership development, community consciousness, and social activism. The population and barrios we serve have intersecting needs and challenges across all of these areas. It was not about simply developing a gang prevention curriculum but creating something that dealt more fully with the roots of dysfunctional subcultures that were created by poverty, discrimination, alienation, and injustice. We wanted to design a curriculum that built on the movement principles of the organization and that could be used as a guideline across all of Barrios Unidos's programs and community activities. I like to refer to this as a "multiple worlds" model that prepares young people to behave in healthy, disciplined, and constructive ways in personal conduct, peer relationships, at home, and in the streets, [as well as] within institutional settings, [so they can become] positive forces in society.

To develop the BU curriculum, Albino drew logically from several other culturally based frameworks he had helped to develop and test in his previous work experiences in gang prevention, substance abuse recovery, juvenile offender intervention, youth leadership development, and such alternative education programs as Sunrise House, the

New School, Gang Alternatives North and South (GANAS), and
Rivals in the Redwoods. At the same time, Albino and his BU colleagues wanted to break ground and create something powerfully new
and unprecedented. Their collective experience had told them that,
while established models could be helpful, real progress in violence
intervention and prevention specifically targeted to at-risk Latino
youth required something that did not yet exist. "We were trying to do
something that to our knowledge was groundbreaking and new," says
García. "Our goal was not just gang diffusion or drug aversion but
realizing behavioral change, cultural healing, and reeducation to
replace the dysfunctional and profoundly instilled subcultures of
gangs, the streets, and drugs. We were trying to help young people
forge positive identities with a new code of conduct rooted in the values of a common *cultura*."

The purpose of the curriculum is simple enough. Its goal is to create a powerful learning framework built on life-affirming values and
the conventions of a shared *cultura* that can literally replace the
destructive ways of the streets that have destroyed or threatened most
of the young people that BU works with. As García further explains it,

> In the curriculum, we take the [most] powerful influences
> in at-risk youths' lives, such as the search for identity and
> belonging, rites of passage to manhood/womanhood, desire
> for status and respect, devout loyalty and *palabra* [word of
> honor], along with distorted notions of *carnalismo* [brother-
> hood], *machismo, comunidad, familia, confianza* [trust], and
> *cultura*, and replace these corrupted adaptations with uncon-
> ditional love, exposure to history and heritage, cultural educa-
> tion, affirmative rites and rituals of adulthood, ceremonies,
> and traditional modes of communal support. Transformative
> learning of this nature requires tough love and compassion,
> creating a trusting environment of acceptance while at the
> same time working with [youth] to honestly confront the
> destructive consequences of negative subcultural values and
> norms that they have been living by. We acknowledge that we
> are asking them to give up the only truth or belonging they
> have known to make positive changes in their lives. For the
> majority of these young people, giving up the negative expres-

sion of their colors and street life in the name of common culture is the most difficult decision they have ever made.

Because the BU curriculum seeks to replace the negative aspects of gang subculture with positive forms of cultural education, self-identity, belonging, and affirmative rules of initiation and status, the *Cultura Es Cura* approach is by definition "alternative." The curriculum was designed to transcend classroom instruction. BU teachers, therefore, must be prepared to engage students by focusing their experiences on learning inside and outside of the classroom. Moreover, while traditional school settings might view experiential learning as a set of incidental extracurricular activities to enhance in-class learning, the *Cultura Es Cura* curriculum calls for an explicit integration of community-based activities into each individual student's development. As a result, learning experiences at the Chávez School may engage students as much in extended community volunteer work or projects in a given neighborhood as in short-term internships or field trips designed to expose them to life alternatives, opportunities, and social responsibilities. In each case, classroom learning and external exposures are matched by a heavy dose of authentic experiences in community engagement and the reality of positive lifestyles; this is what finally distinguishes BU's educational approach.

At CCSSC, the intellectual and practical realities of students, based on informed reflection, choice, and action, collectively comprise their learning experience. Individual and community advancement are seen as the dual outcomes of this conscientiously integrated approach to learning. Invariably, the Chávez School achieves levels of success with its students that more conventional schools have not. Since its inception in 2002, the school has operated as a moderate-sized alternative school serving grades 9 through 12. Since 1995, the school has effectively served hundreds of at-risk Latino students referred by the county office of education or the juvenile court system—over 50 percent of the CCSSC student population is referred by the juvenile courts.

An internal survey tracking a sample pool of 300 CCSSC students demonstrated an outstanding level of success. When one considers some of the debilitating contextual factors that define the educational experience of the CCSSC student body, its achievements and impacts are even more remarkable. For instance, prior to coming to the Chávez School, most BU students were expelled or on the brink of permanent expulsion from public schools due to failing academic performance and behavioral issues. Many possessed unacceptable school attendance records, including chronic truancy. Most of these students, moreover, have been the subject of serious interventions due to behavioral problems, including multiple incidents of violence, and gang-related and/or substance abuse problems. Finally, more than half of these students have had one or more contacts with the juvenile justice system.

The specific markers of impact the school has on at-risk Chicano youth are noteworthy. Fifty percent of the students included in the above-referenced survey were able to lift their academic performance substantially and return to a public school setting after spending at least two semesters at CCSSC. The school boasts the highest attendance rate of any alternative school program in Santa Cruz County and has achieved an 80 percent reduction in student suspensions and expulsions compared to area public schools that predominantly serve Latino students. Fully 80 percent of the BU student body survey sample went on to receive a high school diploma from CCSSC or another accredited high school, or passed and received a General Education Diploma (GED). Perhaps most strikingly, 60 percent of the students captured in the survey have gone on to continue their education in vocational or professional training programs beyond the high school level.

Beyond these impressive academic indicators, students at the Chávez School are eligible to benefit from important corollary investments that complement the positive effects of their formal educational experience. This added benefit traces to the deliberate integration of the Barrios Unidos Rites of Passage Program into the Chávez School's overall schematic. The program, which considers the individual's and the community's healing, growth, and well-being, establishes the crowning moment of young BU students' transition from adolescence into adulthood.

THE RITES OF PASSAGE PROGRAM

The five steps of the BU Rites of Passage Program are based on Aztec cultural symbols. These inform various levels of growth and responsibility, as well as tasks that form Chávez School student graduation requirements. Mastering these rites or milestones of growth is intended to advance each young person to the next level of personal development and leadership. Within the César Chávez School for Social Change, each of the five required developmental levels takes approximately four weeks to achieve. The various levels of attainment are linked to attendance, academic performance, adherence to school traditions and rules, relations with staff and peers, completion of five designated tasks within each required stage of personal growth, and monthly *juntas* (meetings) with family members. Known as the "Level System" by BU leaders and students, the five developmental levels that BU family members strive to achieve are as follows:

> *Tochli* (Rabbit)—This first step or stage represents a new beginning and an opportunity for self-development. It builds on a comprehensive inventory of problem areas or risks that BU youth face coming into the organization, such as gang involvement, substance abuse, and criminal activity. Assessment of the impact of these risk factors on the youngsters establishes, in turn, the basis for strategic interventions and prevention activities that will inform each youth participant's subsequent experience at BU.

> *Akatl* (Reed)—This second step focuses on building a foundation for family. It helps participating youth and their families to better understand and trace their history, to identify opportunities for improving relations, and to develop plans and strategies to resolve family conflicts.

> *Tekpatl* (Flint)—The third step commits BU youth to lifelong study, comprehension, and analysis. It focuses especially on encouraging students to actively engage in issues facing people they know in their families and communities, including physical disability, neglect of the elderly, homelessness, child abuse, and health issues such as HIV-AIDS. During this stage, BU youth are required to volunteer in a chosen area and to prepare a detailed report on their experiences.

Kalli (Home Refuge)—A fourth step of the BU Rites of Passage Program concentrates on leadership. Here, BU youth are encouraged to establish their own sense of what leadership is and to embrace the need for, and the responsibility of, exercising leadership in their own lives. They study other leaders in their peer group, in community settings, and in world history to sharpen their understanding of how to become responsible and effective leaders; they also engage in applied and peer-based leadership learning activities.

Naui Ollin (Constant Movement)—This final step represents the student's culmination of learning, growth, and responsibility across the Rites of Passage Program spectrum. It concentrates on each student's personal conduct, place in the community, and leadership style. A crossing-over ritual for the student into *Naui Ollin* marks his becoming an advanced student leader and includes going before the César Chávez School *Concilio* to review lessons learned along the way and to receive the elders' blessings to move forward. At this stage, each student is offered support and sponsorship by an elder to engage in a traditional fasting, vision quest, or sweat lodge sitting as part of their crossing over to the *Naui Ollin* level. The passage concludes with a traditional ceremony in which each student chooses an Aztec name and publicly embraces adulthood and the responsibilities of community leadership.

Throughout this twenty-week journey, students are engaged in a rigorous supporting combination of academic instruction, skills-building activities, life counseling, parental exchanges, and cultural enrichment programs. Since its inception, the BU Rites of Passage Program at CCSSC has witnessed innumerable transformations of at-risk youth into responsible young adults and leaders. Linked to the more tangible indicators of success, such as high rates of school attendance and graduation—and a near universal drop in juvenile criminal recidivism among CCSSC students who have completed this Rites of Passage Program—are profound behavioral changes that have typically occurred in the individual lives of these young people.

The survey of BU students referenced above showed significant positive changes in attitudes and behaviors among participants regarding violence, individual and social responsibility, and their quality of home and peer relationships. These improvements included transformative aspects of personal development, such as constructive problem-solving, goal setting, and economic self-reliance. Perhaps the most salient indicators of success related to the BU Rites of Passage Program model concern leadership, violence prevention, and gang involvement. The BU data on Chávez School student performance shows that over 80 percent of its graduates have ended their gang affiliations. Ninety percent no longer consider violence as a constructive means of resolving conflicts. An even greater number, 95 percent, now consider volunteerism that contributes to community well-being and social change as a core priority in their lives. BU recognizes that the outcomes reflected in these data, while gratifying and encouraging, should in no way be interpreted to suggest that solutions to the risks facing the Chicano youth and families it serves have been achieved. But they do acknowledge the potential efficacy and replicability of their impressive intervention model.

Barrios Unidos's remarkable success in positively redirecting the lives of at-risk Chicano youth and their families did not occur, however, without struggle. Despite having met with impressive success in recent years, initial efforts to build an effective learning curriculum into BU's budding charter school (and other program areas) created large challenges that warrant examination.

THE CHALLENGES OF IMPLEMENTING BU'S CORE CURRICULUM

Several challenges emerged at the outset of BU's efforts to develop CCSSC and its innovative curriculum. Some of these involved the reality that despite BU's deep commitment to the cause of violence prevention and its creative approaches to keep at-risk youth out of harm's way, the competing risk factors facing even BU's most promising young leaders were powerful and ever-present in their lives. This meant that, often, steps forward with the young people would be matched with disturbing steps backward. In the worst cases, some teenagers in the BU family fell back into a life on the streets, many of them ending up incarcerated, some of them severely wounded in gang- or crime-related conflicts. In the worst cases, a few of these young people were killed in violent exchanges with rivals or the police.

These realities made success an almost insurmountable proposition for BU leaders, particularly during the mid-1990s when California gang- and gun-related violence was reaching epidemic proportions.

BU's early challenges in gaining traction with its school-based and program interventions were further complicated in this context by public referral agencies, especially the public schools. These institutions tended merely to pass along the most troubled youths in the system for remediation in BU's fledgling programs. According to Albino García, Sr., "Those earlier days gave the strong impression that some of the referral officers at the Office of Education were deliberately trying to sabotage and discredit the César Chávez School by sending the most hard-core youths from other alternative high schools in Santa Cruz and Monterey County to a degree that would prevent us from being able to succeed. They sent us many young people who were deeply rooted in the gang scene with multiple criminal offenses. Some had serious drug addictions, non-gang-related behavioral problems, or learning disabilities that we were ill-equipped to handle."

Being trapped between the pathologies of the streets and the questionable motivations of some public officials put BU in a position not unfamiliar to many Latino organizations and individuals seeking to advance social change. In this no-win situation, the organization redoubled its efforts to show positive impact on the lives of the youths in its charge, including those most hardened by past exposure to the streets and the penal system. It did this both out of a deep spiritual commitment to and concern for these young people, as well as a reluctance to provide public authorities with any hint of credible evidence that BU was not institutionally capable of making a difference. As BU's García would later explain, "We took the challenge, not wanting to give potential critics a foothold to discredit us."

But the real-life circumstances and contradictions facing BU leaders in this early work were often clearly larger than their ability to contain them. Occasionally, things blew up, and the pressures and dangers of life on the streets beyond BU's control would subsume BU youth otherwise committed to a path of peace. BU leaders facing these realities struggled in their initial years to find a simultaneously practical and intellectually honest way to respond. According to García,

We never wanted to create the illusion of a fairy-tale ending for everyone we have tried to reach over the past twenty-five years. Tragically, Barrios loses young ones to the streets, violence, incarceration, and drug addiction every year. We have testified as character witnesses at trials determining life sentences, caught promising kids shooting heroin in our bathrooms, and buried some of the best and the brightest we have encountered.

These real-life challenges would test Barrios Unidos teachers and push them to reach agreements on what saving and changing troubled young lives looked like through BU's early years as an emerging institution. BU leaders had early intense discussions therefore about whether and, if so, how to introduce certain codes of conduct within the CCSSC curriculum or control counterproductive behaviors on the BU campus. Some wanted to make the school a no-gang-colors zone. Most (though not all) agreed that CCSSC have a zero-tolerance policy for students caught carrying weapons or using drugs or alcohol on campus grounds—indeed, early on, offenses in this category were made grounds for immediate dismissal.

Some, like Albino García, felt that "in order to succeed with integrity and credibility, BU needed to be as disciplined and demanding as it was loving and compassionate." Although carrying out strict codes of conduct was difficult at times, BU leaders in this camp felt strongly that the organization had to impose nonnegotiable standards of compliance to conditions of probation, drug treatment requirements, and sobriety for all students as well as staff. Others in the BU leadership set, including Nane Alejándrez, believed in using an approach that created a more tolerant, nonjudgmental, and safe space for change. Alejándrez believed that, over time, establishing anywhere BU worked as neutral ground—a place of love, acceptance, and learning—would naturally lead the youth to leave their gang allegiances behind. By being too formulaic and inflexible, he felt BU would risk losing kids who might otherwise be spared the worst of the streets through a high-accountability but more tolerant and realistic disciplinary regime.

Internal differences of opinion along these lines were not solved overnight. Rather, considerable conversation, negotiation, and accommodation was required to find a durable consensus. Some issues proved more complicated than others to resolve. "We struggled over the mandate of no colors," Albino García would later recall. "At issue for me was striking a balance between accepting gang-committed youth for who they were versus challenging them to be renewed from jump-street as peace warriors." García and other BU leaders wanted these young people to strive for more in their lives, to see the self-defeat inherent in killing one another over territory rather than collaborating to build up their neighborhoods and their collective powers. The youths' distinctive gang colors came to reflect a focus on their darker instincts rather than the more positive values of *la cultura cura*. García and others wanted to challenge BU youth to find the strength to choose *la cultura cura* and to consciously relinquish their colors. As Albino has commented,

> The codes of the gang and streets are crystal clear. I believed we needed to set our own clear standards by getting the young people's *palabra* (word or oath) that they were going to do what it took to change destructive behaviors and to learn a new way. We wanted their *palabra* of loyalty to the values of *cultura*, a commitment to try new things and work hard, to have respect for school traditions and sacred rituals, showing *ganas* (desire), personal responsibility, and an obligation that transcended colors. The youth had to understand that they had to give up something (allegiance to a counterfeit culture and destructive behaviors) to get something in return: the beautiful birthrights of their heritage and an opportunity for new life.

Nane Alejándrez and others had the same aspirations for the youths, to be sure, but they saw the situation differently as a practical matter. They felt that it was okay for the young people to retain identification to their barrios, neighborhoods, or regions, even including open association to their neighborhood's gang colors, as long as this identification was no longer used for destructive or divisive purposes. As Nane explained it, "Homeboys and homegirls can be proud of where they came from and still be brothers and sisters, north and south, under the banner of *La Raza*." Similar divides revealed themselves over issues both practical and philosophical as BU leaders struggled to define an institutional culture for BU. Ultimately, agreement over core values and the basic framework BU would employ at the César Chávez School would be forthcoming. Honest, unfettered debate and exchange would produce a working consensus at each turn. Rather than bury their disagreements, BU leaders took the time needed to passionately and transparently examine their diverse positions. They surfaced and acknowledged their differences and worked through them by building on what they fundamentally all agreed on. Everyone at BU fundamentally agreed that the essential goal of the organization and CCSSC was to replace the street subculture without condemning young people for having sought respect, belonging, loyalty, community, status, and identity through gangs in the first place.

In the end, BU leaders retained as aspirations the highest standards and principles of expected youth behavior at the school and throughout the various BU programs. At the same time, as a practical matter, they agreed to err on the side of flexibility and case-by-case intervention strategies in order to accommodate the inherently complex realities of BU youths' lives. By balancing aspirations with real-life contingencies, BU leaders have found a way to maintain a developed sense of community accountability while also achieving impressive results with the deeply challenged youth they serve.

In seeking to strike this keen balance BU has at times soared, while on other occasions it has struggled. A large part of the equation where it has struggled has had to do with integrating new leaders and staff as BU has grown over the years. Complementing the work of more seasoned movement veterans and youth organizers, such as Alejándrez, García, Marciano "Chango" Cruz, Manuel Aparicio, Manuel Martínez, Liz Ayala, and Marylou Alcjándrez, in recent years have been younger BU leaders such as Steve Vigil, Kathy Domínguez, Frank Gonzales, and Maribel Gallardo. While all of these individuals have come out of some form of barrio experience, they have all had to be carefully mentored, trained, and integrated in order to enhance their experience-based "street sensibilities" to better serve the BU mission, philosophy, and core constituency. Perfecting their evolution as BU leaders has been time-consuming and painstaking. Considering BU's particularities, this is understandable. As Albino García has observed,

> It was one thing to design a curriculum; it was another to train everyone and get them on the same page. I felt staff had to know the curriculum cold and certainly had to model what they were trying to teach. We had some folks working or volunteering at Barrios who were still walking in both worlds (the world of the streets from which they came and the world we were trying to create at BU). We wanted our staff and volunteers to not only teach our methods of change, but also to model our values and principles in their own behavior—in essence, to walk the talk.

Achieving this consonance proved to be difficult in the early stages of BU's formalization and start-up of the César Chávez School for Social Change. But this was not the only educational program area that created early problems for the organization. BU leaders also faced challenges after seeking to institutionalize when they sought to standardize educational programs and pedagogy across the entire set of BU pursuits. Over the years, in fact, the application of the BU curriculum and tenets in affiliated Kids Clubs, off-site high school and middle school programs at various public schools (administered through Barrios Unidos Clubs) and juvenile halls has been uneven—taking root strongly in some areas and less effectively in others. The problem is largely one of transferring knowledge and practice to the organization's growing number of chapters extending beyond Santa Cruz.

The fact that BU staff and volunteers increasingly come from varying experiences personally, professionally, and geographically is inherently challenging. Because BU has a strong commitment to developing leaders straight from the communities it serves, the organization's range of staff and volunteer skill sets can vary greatly. Inexperience, or experience with competing organizing models, is frequently a large factor in relation to BU's challenge to standardize approaches and impacts. "Some younger staff and volunteers are freshly off the street," Albino García points out. "They are only recently removed from being on the receiving end of the work. Others are former teachers or counselors or have similarly worked in more traditional service organizations." García stresses that the elasticity of BU's approach is a strength because "it possesses the flexibility to be adapted to the various environments and foci of BU programs whether in schools or juvenile halls, in varying leadership program models, or in gang intervention curricula." At the same time, he admits, "you want to achieve a level of consistency."

Beyond the aforementioned internal challenges, where program consistency is concerned, BU has faced some resistance and unevenness in implementing its culturally centered curriculum in several external settings. Despite a long-standing relationship with public schools and juvenile justice centers providing more mainstream services such as tutoring, counseling, mentoring, and basic education, for example, BU has encountered institutional problems at such locations owing to its Chicano-centric approach. Many school and justice system officials with whom BU has partnered in this work have either misunderstood, misinterpreted, or purposely misrepresented the BU curriculum as an attempt to preach racial nationalism and cultural separatism, owing to its heavy emphasis on Latino cultural and political subjugation in U.S. political history and the resulting need for Latino community empowerment.

BU leaders strongly reject the contention of some mainstream critics that the organization's programs are designed to espouse nationalism or racial separatism. Elder Henry Domínguez likens the self-awareness elements of BU's curriculum to the cultural building blocks of true democracy and sovereignty for the Chicano, Latino, and *Indio* communities of the United States. "In a truly free society," Domínguez asserts,

. . . people enjoy the inalienable human right to know their true history and express their culture across all areas of their life. If the nation we live in is built on the concept of a federation of states operating as a union, then our democracy is a collective of different cultures living together on principle. The ideal of *E Pluribus Unum* (i.e., out of many, one) has not always been lived up to, but it remains our highest aspiration in American democracy. For Chicanos and indigenous people, our culture is the source of our strength. It is what bonds us to family and community, engenders respect for others and the earth, and what leads us to acknowledge and give allegiance to a higher responsibility and purpose in life.

BU's need to defend its philosophical and educational approach at CCSSC and in its other programs intended to discourage Latino gang warfare is part of a now decades-long debate over multiculturalism in America. The roots of that debate are political and ideological by definition; but politics and ideology aside, it is simply undeniable from a practical standpoint that BU's novel way of educating and engaging at-risk Latino youth has produced real benefits to individuals, families, and communities. Indeed, notwithstanding various challenges over the years to standardize and administer its culturally based curriculum and programs, BU leaders have found a way to positively impact the lives of thousands of at-risk Chicano youth in ways that others have not. Their work has helped to change and save lives, even despite considerable environmental, material, and institutional obstacles.

THE POWER OF RESULTS

For close to a decade, BU has applied a core curriculum across its signature programs and various ad hoc community activities in now hundreds of community and institutional settings. Many experts have come to consider BU's work a model of best practice in violence prevention, youth development, and community-building. Young people have typically come through the doors of BU on a path to self-destruction, relegated to lives of marginality, lingering desperation, and struggle. They have emerged from BU's influence as markedly more self-reliant people who possess newfound tools to find their greatest potential and a heightened expression of their humanity. They have learned that freedom and empowerment at the individual, family, and community levels flow from the deeper understanding and prolongation of their cultural heritage and traditions. They have learned, moreover, that true *cultura* is expressed through one's heart, intellect, enterprise, ingenuity, spirituality, and service to society.

Because of this work's practical success, increasing numbers of private funders and other champions have emerged in recent years to help BU expand its work more broadly across communities nation-wide. The segment that follows examines BU's efforts to establish a chapter base to that end.

Growing Leaders through Chapter Building

There are many hundreds of elders, activists, and leaders in com-munities across the country who identify themselves as part of the Barrios Unidos family or who simply embrace BU's principles through their efforts to end violence. These leaders have established the base for a nonviolence movement in Chicano barrios that BU has led over the past two decades. The development of this movement was the result of conscientious organizing on the part of BU founders. From the beginning, these leaders understood that the task of extend-ing BU's vision and values would require committed organizing efforts across the nation to expand the organization's constituency. Such constituency development in turn would necessitate a program-matic strategy to build a formal network of BU affiliate organizations or chapters. BU leaders had become aware of other organizational efforts that had achieved success and broad public impact through multicity network building, including leading nationwide organizing or constituency-building groups such as the National Council of La Raza and the Pacific Institute for Community Organization (PICO). They developed the early belief that a multisite organizing base would maximize BU's opportunities to encourage a national peace move-ment in America's barrios. Chapter development thus emerged early on as a core organizational strategy to expand the BU model across the state and the nation.

BARRIOS UNIDOS CHAPTERS

The twenty-seven cities that have operated recognized Barrios Unidos chapter affiliates include the following locales:

California—San Francisco, San Mateo, Modesto, Chico, Gilroy, Hollister, Fresno, San Jose, Salinas, Brentwood, Santa Rosa, Mor-gan Hill, Watsonville, Bakersfield, Venice, Santa Monica, San Diego, and (headquarters) Santa Cruz.

Other Cities and States—Washington D.C.; Fairfax/Prince William, Virginia; San Antonio/El Paso, Texas; Yakima/Tri-City, Washington; Phoenix, Arizona; Omaha, Nebraska; and Chicago, Illinois.

BU chapters have taken a wide range of formations over the years, from independent organizations with paid staff to less formalized, grassroots volunteer efforts adapting the BU model in varying ways to their local context. There have been as many as twenty-seven chapters active in localities across California and other states of the United States. Fourteen chapters were active as of the writing of this book. BU chapters have played an important role in building local Latino community and youth leadership on violence prevention issues across the nation. Through education and advocacy programs, community organizing efforts, and peace initiatives, BU affiliates have produced an effective cadre of peace warriors and a broad range of conflict intervention and prevention strategies.

BU has advanced this work out of its own headquarters in Santa Cruz, California, under the formal banner of the National Coalition of Barrios Unidos. Coalition members in turn have pursued diverse, locally driven activities with technical support of the Santa Cruz chapter in areas including multiethnic coalition-building, public policy analysis, civic education, and organizational and fund development. Some BU-affiliated groups have elected to develop their own nonprofits, borrowing the techniques of such programs as the Barrios Unidos Kids Clubs, BU high school chapters, and the Barrios Unidos Juvenile Hall Transition Program. Others have chosen instead to organize on an ad hoc grassroots level using the cultural values, principles, and practices of the BU movement.

It has been an ongoing challenge for the BU headquarters to provide the necessary technical, organizational, and financial resources to respond to the many communities that have requested chapter-building support. Even from the organization's earliest days, as the founding leadership and professional staff of Santa Cruz BU was codifying its programs—structuring a formal nonprofit entity, building core institutional and capital assets, and learning to operate and sustain BU as a functioning enterprise—they were being called upon to teach allies elsewhere to do similar work in various communities across the country. While some aspects of BU's technical assistance and support process were straightforward, others were not. As Otilio Quintero has put it,

> Providing organizing support to numerous communities seemed easier when we were in the same boat as the communities asking for help, that is, operating primarily as a grass-roots movement. The *cultura*-based programs and services of Barrios Unidos are simple social math: healing individuals plus strengthening families equals a stronger community and a stronger society. The curriculum developed by Albino García and others on staff gave us a tool to teach this stuff. The challenge was that people wanted the recipe for the Santa Cruz organizational model. Folks wanted the formula for the cultural and spiritual dimensions, yeah, but they also wanted the practical road map to the property acquisition process, establishing the charter school, BU Productions, the violence prevention framework, and accessing essential public and private funding. Our challenge was to package the various aspects of Barrios Unidos's work into a framework that could be passed on. The dilemma was that the language and the methods, as well as our ability to teach, were only being discovered as we went along.

Partly on account of these factors, BU affiliates have experienced mixed success over the years in trying to emulate the Santa Cruz organization's core programs, innovations, and substantial resource-building accomplishments. Variations in local leadership capacity, funding and institutional support, and basic serendipity, have largely determined the kind of success local BU chapters have achieved over the years. BU's own limitations in being able to provide in-depth, ongoing technical assistance to the field has also played a role in this connection. Over the years, all told, less than half of the communities that have supported a BU chapter have developed a viable nonprofit organization or moved beyond operating as fledgling service programs working under the fiscal sponsorship of another nonprofit group. Failing to develop a stronger local institutional base has limited BU's ability to become a more dynamic mobilizing force for spreading the principles of the movement nationwide. But this is not to say that BU has lacked national significance or impact. Indeed, many BU affiliates—even those that have remained essentially grassroots volunteer-organized efforts (some operating only with small grants or contracts, educating and developing local leaders while working in partnership with other groups)—have helped to promote substantial community-building and change.

In Washington, D.C., for instance, former gang member and college graduate Luis Cardona asked for support to establish a BU chapter after meeting Nane Alejándrez at a violence prevention conference in 1994. Already at the time an effective organizer of gang-affiliated youth and a mediator of disputes in the district's largely Latino Mount Pleasant and Adams-Morgan neighborhoods, Cardona was drawn by the cultural and spiritual elements of the BU movement. Being that Cardona and many of the Latino youth he was working with were Central American (or Latin American) rather than Chicano, he adapted much of BU's cultural education content to accommodate Mayan and other heritage traditions more appropriate to his street organizing and school-based education/program constituents. Cardona is presently one of the most recognized advocates and organizers of young people from street gangs in the nation's capital.

Other BU grassroots leaders and affiliates have found strength and impact by collaborating with highly credible local institutions. For example, Alex Santillanes of Yakima, Washington, adopted BU's philosophy and formed a successful chapter in cooperation with the local Catholic diocese. The church supplies him with a youth center to organize his own local versions of BU's Kids Clubs, juvenile hall interventions, school-based learning programs, leadership development efforts, and violence prevention models. Under the BU banner, Santillanes now organizes the largest annual violence prevention conference in the state of Washington, convening young leaders and diverse professional advocates, including educators, clergy, local law enforcement and government officials, small business representatives, and service providers to seek common solutions to community violence problems.

The most active of the Barrios Unidos chapter affiliates, not surprisingly, are located in California. The California Coalition of Barrios Unidos (CCBU) is comprised of a diverse set of grassroots organizations working in both rural and urban settings. At its peak, the California Coalition included seventeen active community affiliates. Significant changes have altered the level of activity within the coalition at various times, but CCBU has consistently established a base for important organizational gains in leadership and influence.

The San Mateo chapter, for example, has gone through several structural iterations since it was established as a cooperative venture of local college students and community organizers, including Alejandro Vilches and George Galvis. The present director, Maribel Andrade, emerged from a youth leadership circle to stabilize the chapter under the fiscal sponsorship of El Concilio, a local social services agency. The San Mateo organization builds on an increasingly formalized array of violence prevention programs, including a *Calles* Project (street outreach), a GANAS program in local middle schools and high schools, two Kids Clubs and a tattoo removal project.

Much like San Mateo, several other California chapters have expressed the desire to move toward greater institutionalization and development. The cities of Salinas, Fresno, San Diego, Santa Monica, and Los Angeles (Venice) have established chapters that offer effective boilerplate programs, such as Kids Clubs, Teen Lounges, youth and parent groups, juvenile hall transition projects, GANAS, and HIV/AIDS education programs. These affiliates also support cultural activities such as *danza, folklórico*, and arts and crafts. Along the way, many of these chapters have faced challenges to growth and stability that are common among grassroots nonprofit groups—frequent transitions in staff and volunteer leadership, limited organizational capacity and infrastructure, and resource development and management deficits. Over the years, however, leaders of these chapters have shared the common characteristics of sheer will, commitment, and perseverance. Such fortitude has served to keep these groups alive in the most dire of circumstances. The ability to overcome the many challenges they face perennially and still achieve success has been their hallmark. Oftentimes, this has required uncommon resilience and substantial rejuvenating efforts. For example, following the departure of the Fresno organization's founding director, Maggie Navarro, other local leaders emerged from the ranks to build on ten years of organizing by Homer Leija to establish the site as one of the strongest BU chapters in the state.

A large part of the story thus has to do with the spirit and dedication of local BU supporters and the organization's uncanny capacity to produce unusually dedicated and resourceful leaders. In Salinas, long-time activist Antonio Avalos and his fellow organizers have struggled for years, providing essential services on a shoestring budget in the city's crime- and violence-riddled eastside, with little support from local institutions. Similarly, BU chapters in Santa Monica, Venice, and San Diego have effectively organized and provided services for years, despite lacking considerable institutional and financial assistance. Such groups have established a strong community presence even while struggling to build the necessary resource base to be more effective players in their local public policy contexts.

None of this work has been easy under the circumstances, but it has been done with what can only be described as unquestionable resolve and belief on the part of BU leaders regarding the importance and righteousness of their cause. This compelling collective spirit has sparked the attention of mainstream leaders and institutions that have shown growing interest in providing support for the CCBU in recent years. In 1998, recognizing the potential of the BU model (and spirit) to expand knowledge that can advance the fields of violence prevention, community-building, and youth development in California, the David and Lucile Packard Foundation and the William Randolph Hearst Foundation both provided significant grants to Santa Cruz Barrios Unidos. The support of these leading funders helped BU to pilot an organizational capacity-building initiative involving five members of the CCBU. Local chapters in San Mateo, Fresno, Salinas, Santa Monica, and San Diego were chosen to participate in this work. These five chapters were selected on the basis of their readiness to benefit from intensive technical assistance and long-term organizational planning support.

The Packard- and Hearst-funded initiative enabled Santa Cruz
Barrios Unidos to develop a comprehensive training module focused
on local asset mapping. It also positioned BU to develop important
program, organizational, and fund development goals designed to
build the capacity and long-term sustainability of BU chapters. This
work has since produced varying degrees of success relative to BU's
efforts to support chapter activities within and outside of California.
However, important lessons learned in the process of pursuing this
work have pointed up three not-easily-achieved requirements that BU
leaders must effectively address in order to secure successful chapter
development beyond Santa Cruz. These include:

Capacity-Building—Effective grassroots nonprofit networks
rarely occur in a vacuum; typically they require considerable
outside investment and coordinating assistance from a strong
intermediary organization. The ability of the national organization in Santa Cruz to provide both substantive and sustained
support to multiple communities wishing to replicate its
model and develop local BU chapters requires that it further
develop its own capacity and staying power as an intermediary. The provision of ad hoc or substantially time-limited
technical assistance supports to nascent or developing chapters seeking to establish a viable program based on the BU
model has not yielded lasting results.

Leadership Development—Despite the presence of committed, vibrant, visionary, and capable peace advocates in local
communities, building the level of management skills and
competencies necessary to sustain a viable nonprofit enterprise like Santa Cruz Barrios Unidos requires strategic investment in grassroots leaders. Developing such leaders in support of BU chapter-building goals thus calls on BU to support
more intensive local-level learning and skills-building strategies. It also requires BU investment in longer-term technical
assistance efforts focused on community-based leadership
development.

Sustainability and New Approaches—Sustainability is perhaps the greatest challenge facing local organizations and
leaders involved in community-building work that helps to
prevent violence. But in recent years, as rates of juvenile

crime and violence have dropped (in part owing to ill-advised, draconian policies) and violence prevention has declined as a funding priority, it has become increasingly difficult for violence prevention groups—especially those operating at the neighborhood level in communities of color—to compete for sustaining resources. In this context, groups like BU must learn to advocate for public and private support in new and different ways, promoting projects in allied fields that have historically been, or recently become, more accessible to funding sources. Such fields principally include child, youth, and family welfare; community economic development; education; public health; and poverty reduction.

These lessons have helped to crystallize the vision of BU leaders in creating a Barrios Unidos Institute. The envisioned institute would centrally focus on efforts to support violence prevention in local communities, broadly expand field capacity and knowledge, and facilitate movement-building in community peace work across the United States and in other nations. Given recent realities and trends, the need for such work cannot be overstated. Even now, nearly a decade after the organization's first funded investments in developing a stronger BU organizational network, many BU affiliate organizations—like many nonprofit organizations in general—continue to face fundamental sustainability challenges. They are typically underfunded and overwhelmed by the ever-growing demands they are increasingly called upon to meet.

Yet, as they always have, BU's local leaders and champions continue to forge ahead. In defiance of all odds, BU chapters consistently find new ways to sustain themselves and to thrive, even while struggling to survive. In practical terms, the Packard and Hearst Foundation investments in the nascent chapter-building work of BU have helped to water the young roots of these fledgling local peace efforts. As importantly, these investments have helped to move BU national leaders to new levels of insight and determination in their efforts to develop more effective strategies in the years ahead. They have helped BU leaders to imagine Barrios Unidos less as a regional leader in the field and more as an anchor intermediary institution dedicated to advancing community peace efforts on the national and global stage during the years to come.

Peace Summits: Connecting and Organizing Multicultural Leaders

Since the early days of its involvement with the Coalition to End Barrio Warfare and through organizing efforts involving its affiliate chapters, Barrios Unidos has sponsored peace summits and conferences to promote the violence prevention field, organize communities, and advance the goals of the broader movement. In allied efforts dating back to 1993, in partnership with organizations including The California Wellness Foundation and the Simba Circle (Rescue, Release and Restore, Inc.), BU has advanced the use of summits and conferences in ways that have increased the violence prevention field and intercultural exchange and partnership. Taken together, conferences and summits supported and/or significantly shaped by BU have involved some of the foremost U.S. multidisciplinary practitioners, researchers, and community leaders committed to preventing gang, youth, family, and community violence. Unlike many gatherings convened by mainstream institutions, the gatherings in which BU has most heavily invested its vision and resources have drawn extensively on the leadership and experiences of young adults, parents, and grassroots leaders directly affected by violence, in order to examine issues and solutions in the most authentic way possible. It is from this practice of direct engagement and accountability to its constituency that BU has developed its ongoing work on the ground and fashioned its organizing mandate for the community peace movement. The César Chávez Peace Plan, discussed in the segment that follows, is a direct result of these dynamic historical gatherings.

THE CÉSAR CHÁVEZ PEACE PLAN

During 1995 and 1996, BU organized a series of four peace and unity summits in Santa Cruz, El Paso, San Antonio, and Washington, DC that led to the conceptualization and adoption of the five-point César Chávez Peace Plan (CCPP). The focus of the summits was to fashion a national violence prevention agenda that drew from the best thinking emerging in the country at that time in fields ranging from public health and juvenile justice to youth development and community-building. These gatherings brought together thousands of Barrios Unidos affiliate members and allied advocates of the community peace movement to develop an organizing framework designed to bring coherence to the movement nationally. According to a BU summit document,

> The César Chávez Peace Plan will be used as a strategic organizing platform to promote and implement a peace process throughout California and other parts of the country. In order for the plan to work, we must include all segments of society, government, business, churches, and other community institutions that share our vision for a new tomorrow. To address the issue of violence in our communities, the plan offers a broad national and community-level framework of strategies to mobilize the full breadth of human, institutional, public, and private resources to realize healthy and peaceful communities.

BU affiliate chapters have adopted the César Chávez Peace Plan as a template and local organizing platform. They have used it accordingly as a means to advocate for increased resources to directly mediate violence, support barrio youth and families, and advance more humane and comprehensive social policies. According to OT Quintero, "Barrios Unidos felt that the symbolic adoption of the César Chávez Peace Plan was important to building greater focus and momentum in the community peace movement nationally. It was the first step in mobilizing around a greater vision and promoting collective responsibility for realizing healthier and stronger communities. We believed that the values and vision that César Chávez had for the farmworker movement was at the heart of the plan."

In April 1996, the five-part César Chávez Peace Plan was adopted by the National Coalition of Barrios Unidos at a Peace Summit in Washington, DC and presented to the staffs of the White House and members of the U.S. Congress. The plan called for:

- Federal and state support of community peace agreements and truces
- Broad national implementation of viable violence prevention models

- Creation of "barrio enterprise zones" for youth-centered, community economic development
- National initiatives to create alternatives to incarceration, address the root causes of youth violence, and prevent police brutality
- Development of a youth-centered network to build and distribute resources for violence prevention and social investment

The César Chávez Peace Plan has become the blueprint that guides the advocacy and movement-building work of BU locally, regionally, nationally, and internationally. While broad and universal application of the Peace Plan's framework outside of Santa Cruz is still in development—sustained progress in key areas such as successful policy advocacy and brokering local peace agreements is only beginning to show organization-wide results—the BU framework for change is compelling and increasingly far-reaching. The aspiration to establish Barrios enterprise zones has been particularly elusive given the complexities of advancing community economic development investment in low-income Latino communities and the organization's only very recent entry into this field. Yet, BU's increasing focus on economic opportunity as an essential aspect of justice for youth in America's barrios reflects a very significant intellectual trajectory in organizational consciousness based on a clear recognition that economic deprivation is a fundamental root cause of youth and community violence in Chicano/Latino neighborhoods.* BU leaders see the Chávez Plan's provisions on community asset building as a central strategy for change. According to OT Quintero,

> The approach of the César Chávez Plan is holistic. It focuses not just on bringing to an end the symptoms of violence but on changing its root causes. The plan begins from the premise that peace is only possible where communities nurture healthy people and families. In the plan individual and community development goes hand in hand. Developing leader-

---

*BU Productions has grown from a limited micro-enterprise concept, i.e., the design, production, and sale of a culturally based signature apparel line that could generate resources while providing skills training and employment opportunity for at-risk barrio youth, to a far more comprehensive economic development strategy consistent with the provisions of the César Chávez Peace Plan.

ship and human capacity comes first. Developing assets, generating capital, creating jobs and adequate housing, promoting community-centered economic networks, and re-investing in social infrastructure creates a full circle of development. Community peace is only possible when the civic and economic life of the community is conducted in ways that are equitable, inclusive, and life-affirming to all.

NATIONAL MOVEMENT-BUILDING: INTERETHNIC PARTNERSHIPS AND INTERCULTURAL EXCHANGE

Gleaning the lessons of the civil rights movement, the farmworkers struggle, and the contemporary quests for criminal justice reform and immigrant and refugee rights, BU leaders have come to recognize the power of working in solidarity, partnership, and coalition with other culturally diverse communities, organizations, and movements dedicated to achieving social and economic justice. Over the years, BU has placed great value on engaging in intercultural exchange and learning to promote greater cultural fluency among its leadership, constituents, and others involved in the community peace movement. Multicultural partnerships promoting peace and community empowerment in low-income communities of color has enabled BU to extend the social value of its work beyond Latino population centers and constituencies. Two important engagements have shaped the BU leadership's commitment to this work as an organic part of the peace and justice movement: the Kansas City Peace Summit of 1993 and the organization's ensuing collaboration with Simba Circle (Rescue, Release, and Restore, Inc).

THE KANSAS CITY PEACE SUMMIT

The Urban Peace and Justice Summit held in Kansas City, Missouri, in 1993 (the Kansas City Peace Summit) has been called the first constitutional convention of the community peace movement in the United States. The brainchild of the late Carl Upchurch, the summit was initially envisioned as a way to bring together the country's leading gang networks: the Bloods, the Crips, the Conservative Vice Lords, the Gangster Disciples, the Black Gangster Disciples, the Latin Kings, the El Rukhyns, the Cobras, and the Stones, as well as

Norteños and Sureños and other gangs flourishing on the streets of major American cities. The idea of gathering these leading gangs was to establish a national agenda for addressing violence and its causes. Numerous developments across the country had spurred Upchurch to organize the summit. First, in the aftermath of the 1992 civil unrest in Los Angeles, Southern California community organizers and gang leaders associated with the Bloods and the Crips, respectively, had brokered an unprecedented local truce. The truce garnered significant regional attention and inspired similar efforts to suspend gang violence in African American communities elsewhere in the country. Parallel violence moratorium efforts involving the Coalition to End Barrio Warfare and BU in California and across the Southwest created a unique opportunity for cross-racial solidarity on the issue. Mainstream church organizations, such as the World Council of Churches, as well as major public and private institutions, including the Centers for Disease Control and The California Wellness Foundation, were simultaneously beginning to support efforts to position youth violence prevention as a national research, funding, and policy priority. Such leading institutions ultimately helped to finance and legitimate the justice summit's organization. These converging factors served to create the opportunity to bring together a gathering of unprecedented magnitude.

Carl Upchurch, a community organizer with a deep, long-standing commitment to youth advocacy, seized the opportunity to propel the urban peace movement into the national spotlight. His goal was to simultaneously help broker a national moratorium on gang violence while also working to fashion a public policy agenda to address the root causes of social and economic violence in America's cities. Dr. Ben Chavis, a United Church of Christ executive who would later head the NAACP, provided early financial support for the summit. An initial announcement for the event outlined various topical concerns to be covered. The topics fell under key title headings, such as Challenges of Gaining Empowerment, New Visions for Urban America, Economic Justice, and Police-Community Relations. The summit trumpeted in a new vision for the urban community peace movement, one that looked beyond myopic gang prevention and intervention suppression strategies to promote instead a comprehensive social-change agenda intended to increase public and private investment in the nation's minority youth.

As Upchurch writes in his book, *Convicted in the Womb* (NY: Bantam, 1996), "My vision for the summit was that a working group of people would talk about solutions to urban problems and about sustainable gang peace." For the summit's lead organizer, the historic gathering was "about more than just gang violence and truces." As Upchurch saw it, the summit was about economics. "If there are no jobs," he commented, "then there is nothing to look to in the inner city; if there's no hope, then violence becomes an outgrowth of frustration."

Convened on the one-year anniversary of the 1992 Los Angeles civil unrest, April 29, 1993, the Kansas City Peace Summit established an unprecedented platform for a new generation and brand of grassroots leaders of color to gain national voice. In a courageous and brilliant move, lead summit organizers, looking to signal the need for cross-cultural coalition-building, decided early on that the historic meeting's success required a biracial convening structure. Fred Williams of Common Ground in Los Angeles and BU's Nane Alejándrez were accordingly appointed to cochair the summit, making it the first major jointly convened gathering of African American and Latino community peace activists on a national level in U.S. history. There had been some early trepidation among summit organizers that people on both sides of this unprecedented collaboration might not be ready to support a formal black-brown alliance. This fear was quickly dissipated, however, when Wallace "Gator" Bradley, a spokesman for the Gangster's Disciples of Chicago, announced a truce for all Gangster's Disciples across the country—African American and Latino—during the summit's opening ceremonies.

The accord was significant in that it signaled a coming together of historically antagonistic Latino and African American factions while providing a powerful nod of approval for the solidarity and leadership of summit cochairs Williams and Alejándrez. The Chicago leadership's gesture established a harmonious tone for the summit, leading to other important participant agreements and decisions that set the stage for a constructive exchange overall. None of these favorable out-comes were preordained. As Alejándrez recalls,

> Kansas City was one of the first forays by Barrios Unidos into the national scene in community peace work across black and brown lines. There was a very strong African American presence, and one group could easily have dominated the agenda of the summit. However, with the announcement of the Gangster Disciples accord, my nomination as cochair with Fred Williams, and the approval of African American summit participants to dedicate the convening to the memory of César Chávez, we knew the solidarity was genuine. Philosophically, the leadership of Barrios Unidos was already committed to interethnic solidarity but the summit put our principles to the test, as many leaders on the *Raza* side of the equation were lukewarm to the idea at best. Some believed we needed to get our own house in order before such coalition work and, to be honest, there was some backwards, narrow, nationalist atti-tudes as well. We overcame resistance in our own ranks because we knew participating at the summit was the right thing to do. That is why I accepted the role of cochair with Fred.

Ultimately, a common wisdom prevailed among the African American and Latino summit participants, despite what certainly must have been, at times at least, a divided set of viewpoints on the merits of building the gathering around a multiracial agenda. At bot-tom, all of the convening's constituents seemed to share a deep hope in the possibility that old divides and turf battles, even racial ones, could be meaningfully addressed at the summit. The formal remarks of Ben Chavis at the historic conference underscored the real and potential power of black and brown solidarity to achieve profoundly significant things. As Chavis expressed it,

> What brings us together is blood and lives. This is a sacred event. A spiritual bond has come between us. This is not a secret meeting. We don't have a hidden agenda. We come forth to say to the world and to say to the people in our communities that brothers and sisters can come together across lines of culture and ethnicity, and we can make a dif-ference. . . . We're not only going to come together, we're

going to stay together, because the adhesion that brings us together is blood itself. We are going to come together in a way this nation has never seen. This is why the establishment is so afraid of this summit. They know that if we stop killing each other, this summit has the potential to change the course of American history.

In addition to creating a space for unprecedented interracial dialogue on the issues, the Kansas City Peace Summit enabled a new generation of grassroots youth leaders to set forth a national vision for the community peace movement. The gathering coincided with what communities and others in the then-emerging field of violence prevention were saying about the issues: comprehensive initiatives were needed to tackle the root causes of violence, such as poverty, injustice, and the ongoing manifestations of institutionalized racism. The summit's major conclusions and proposals for responsive initiatives reflected this collective wisdom and are still relevant to the community peace movement today. In effect, summit participants made a strong case for:

- Public and private investment in community-based education and youth development initiatives that promote self-determination, character development, cultural understanding, leadership, academic achievement, skills-building, and responsible social involvement
- Restoration of public funding for parks and recreation, as well as after-school and cultural programs serving children and youth in poor communities
- Economic development efforts that include employment, small business financing, affordable housing, and more accessible health and human services
- Organizing to oppose federal and state "three strikes" legislation mandating minimum prison sentences for multiple offenders and the sentencing treatment of multiple misdemeanor offenders as felons
- Public policy advocacy to rescind anti-gang programs, such as the federally supported Weed and Seed Initiative

- Adoption of a major national initiative to comprehensively address the root causes of violence in its various forms across the nation, including gang violence, domestic violence, sexual assault, and child abuse
- Public education campaigns to shift the trend of national sentiment and policies leading to the criminalization and demonization of poor youth and young men of color

The hope of establishing a lasting national truce and implementing the summit's comprehensive agenda for an urban peace initiative was short-lived due primarily to a lack of public and private will to create the necessary supportive resources. Many of the participants, however, did take the gathering to heart and effectively pursued implementation and related advocacy of the summit's core ideas and strategies in their home communities. As Otilio Quintero has commented,

A lasting legacy of Kansas City will be the leaders it lifted up and gave legitimacy to in both the Latino and African American communities. Barrios Unidos and other participating organizations took along many of their own young leaders, knowing the event would make a deep impression, and a good number remain active community peace organizers to this day. In terms of creating traction for an urban peace initiative in communities across the country, the lack of outside support doomed the effort from taking root. In many respects, Barrios Unidos was in a better position than many other groups present in Kansas City to begin to implement the initiatives discussed because we were already building an organizational infrastructure and were part of the [Wellness Foundation] Violence Prevention Initiative. Not only did the summit validate our direction as an organization and movement, but it also introduced us to some important partners in the African American community that helped us get to where we are today. The flag of interethnic solidarity was firmly planted, and many lasting relationships were created. Good people, like Gaylord Thomas, Khalid Samad, Jitu Sadiki, Fred Williams, Twilight Bea, and Daude Sherrills of the Los Angeles truce movement, have remained in our circle of friends and allies.

The Kansas City Peace Summit undoubtedly helped to inform, inspire, and advance the broader community peace movement in America. The solidarity work that has emerged over the past twelve years since the summit has informed best practices in the field of violence prevention and urban peace work, while creating and helping to sustain a broad agenda for social change that still guides the movement today. As sociologist and longtime BU supporter Dr. John Brown Childs observed in the aftermath of the Kansas City summit, "The Kansas City summit remains a great example of trans-communal action to achieve social change. It reflected multiculturalism at its best, where grassroots alliances work respectfully and constructively to achieve peace and justice in poor communities."

In fact, many groups, organizations, and individuals formed meaningful partnerships as a result of the Kansas City summit. To this day, they continue to work together on common interests, sharing expertise and jointly advancing advocacy efforts to promote progressive violence prevention policies and reforms in criminal and juvenile justice, prison administration, and law enforcement.

For BU, the single most influential ally produced by the summit was Gaylord Thomas, an official in the Evangelical Lutheran Church of America (ELCA) and founder of the Simba Circle (Rescue, Release and Restore, Inc.). Indeed, in time, Thomas and his innovations at Simba Circle would have a profoundly weighty impact on BU leaders. It is accordingly important to examine in some detail how and why this came to be the case and to what ends where BU's work is concerned.

THE SIMBA CIRCLE (RESCUE, RELEASE AND RESTORE, INC.)

The connection between Gaylord Thomas and Nane Alejándrez was instantaneous and powerful. Both men shared leadership experiences in the civil rights arena and as Vietnam veterans and postwar antiviolence activists. They also shared uncanny similarities in organizational mission and approach. What Alejándrez was trying to do at BU to restore the self-esteem and prospects of Chicano gang youth, in terms of placing Latino heritage and culture at the heart of the organization's philosophy and programs, Thomas was seeking to do within African American youth by pioneering an Afrocentric rites of passage program. Also, Alejándrez and Thomas shared strong interests relative to their mutual appreciations of spirituality and community economic development. In taking up the work of social ministries within the Lutheran faith, Gaylord Thomas was naturally involved in spiritually driven work; his support of poor people and families in the community development programming of the ELCA's Division of Church and Society was widely recognized.

It wasn't long before Thomas developed an immediate appreciation of BU's mission and a keen interest in supporting BU in realizing its community economic development vision. In fact, the ELCA made one of the initial investments in BU Productions, Barrios Unidos's T-shirt silk-screen business, to help the organization purchase production equipment and draft a business plan. The collaboration resulted in an important intensification of BU's business focus and intercultural learning. Based largely on the ECLA support provided by Gaylord Thomas, BU Productions was able to grow into a significant revenue-generating vehicle for BU, ultimately producing annual profitability in the $200,000 range. The collaboration with Thomas also helped to establish a fruitful platform for advancing opportunities to engage black and brown youth program practitioners in strategic leadership exchanges.

Indeed, Gaylord Thomas's connection to BU turned out to be particularly important for exposing BU leaders to a powerful youth-supporting program model related to multicultural leadership development. About the time Thomas and BU leaders met, the African American church official was just beginning his Afrocentric youth empowerment group, the Simba Circle (Rescue, Release and Restore, Inc.). In due course, Thomas's youth program would become a model for refining BU's leadership development curriculum.

The Simba Circle is a Lutheran-based network of organizations in the Midwest United States that serves young at-risk African American males. Its educational program model is rooted in both ancient and contemporary schools of thought that ground participating youth in African heritage, history, culture, and spiritual traditions. The curriculum draws on the Seven Principles of Kwanza known also as the

*Nguzo Saba** and the ancient Egyptian moral code of MA'AT.[†] Although an Evangelical Lutheran Church-supported program firmly rooted in Christian principles, the Simba Circle readily incorporates the spiritual traditions of many faith communities. At the same time, its approach to youth and community empowerment builds on a unifying philosophy and policy analysis of American history that explains and ultimately challenges institutionalized racism. The program seeks to celebrate traditional African culture in ways that help to prepare young African Americans to build healthy gender roles, marriages, families, communities, and social relations. The Simba Circle has served hundreds of young African American men over the years through its annual summer camp at Strawberry Point, Iowa, and year-round programs operating in several Midwestern cities, including Chicago, Milwaukee, and Columbus.

The Simba Circle's many distinguishing complements to BU's values and organizational aspirations in the Latino community context formed a logical basis for cross-fertilization. The close parallels in outlook and objectives between BU and the Simba Circle naturally led the leadership of both groups to consider formal partnership opportunities in the aftermath of the 1993 Kansas City Peace Summit and Gaylord Thomas's subsequent supportive engagement with BU Productions. By the mid-1990s, the organizations formally commenced an annual leadership exchange that has continued to the present. In the regular exchange of staff and volunteer specialists, Barrios Unidos and the Simba Circle have established one of the nation's most dynamic intercultural and interfaith partnerships in the youth and community development fields.

---

*The *Nguzo Saba*, or the Seven Principles of Kwanza, is an Afrocentric value system developed by Dr. Maulana Karenga. The seven principles are *Umoja* or unity, *Kujichangulia* or self-determination, *Ujima* or collective work and responsibility, *Ujamma* or cooperative economics, *Nia* or purpose, *Kuumba* or creativity, and *Imani* or faith.

[†]MA'AT (Virtues, Principles, and Declarations) derives from the ancient Egyptian divine law of truth, justice, and righteousness. Written 2,000 years before the Ten Commandments, the Seven Virtues, Ten Principles, and 42 Declarations of Innocence are among the world's oldest sources of moral and spiritual instruction. Many see them as the foundation of modern social order.

Each year the two organizations exchange delegations of elders, movement leaders, staff, and volunteer specialists to teach, celebrate culture, and share spiritual ceremony at the Simba Circle summer camp and the BU warrior circle spring camp, respectively. The BU delegation typically consists of some partnering combination of elders Henry Domínguez or Albino García, Sr. and/or his son Albino García, Jr. The BU leaders conduct sweat lodges, drumming circles, and indigenous dance ceremonies for youth and adult participants of the Simba camp. Other representatives have included Nane Alejándrez, Otilio Quintero, Yvonne de la Rosa, and youth activist George Galvis. These BU leaders have organized cross-racial teaching exchanges with Simba Circle principals in history, the cultural arts, and social justice studies. Simba Circle delegations to BU's spring camps have included key founding leaders of the organization: Gaylord Thomas, Louis "Baba" Dodley, Shedrick Sanders, Jerome Dabney, Pastor Venice Williams, Pastor Sean McMillan, and Mae and Jcohn Jackson. Simba Circle delegations have also included poets, spiritual leaders, mediators, community development specialists, and experts in team-building and intercultural leadership development. These African American leaders have not only benefited from BU spiritual and program support, but have also assisted Barrios Unidos leaders and have substantively advanced BU programs through strategic technical assistance related to the organization's interethnic peace work in California juvenile halls and prisons.

The partnership between BU and the Simba Circle has been invaluable for both groups as they have sought to pioneer nonconventional, culturally centered faith-based work in the budding field of community violence prevention. Their alliance across racial and geographic lines has modeled inspirational possibilities for American society in community-building. Some, however, have not readily encouraged their important work and partnership. Simba Circle, like BU, has encountered challenges from conservative mainstream leaders and institutions because of its focus on identity-based education and progressive social activism. Often, the organization has been labeled as separatist, ultranationalist, or militant. Simba Circle nation builder, Pastor Sean McMillan, has summed up and responded to such views in the following terms:

The blanket indictment that the only response oppressed people can conjure up is hatred, violence, and separation is offensive. We don't teach hate; we teach young people to love themselves. Loving one's self doesn't equate to the hating of others. Self-love is not, and should not be, a threat to anyone. Americans of European descent and assimilationists need to understand that the world does not revolve around their notions of what is good, what is appropriate, right, beautiful, or spiritual. They need to accept that there are other world cultural perspectives, values, and traditions that are just as valid when considering what constitutes the "American Way." Everyone has the inalienable right to tap into what makes them distinct, because it is in that distinction that the common humanity with others becomes more apparent.

The criticism that the work of Simba Circle and BU is divisive or outside the spectrum of accepted American civic engagement is curious considering the history and core aims of both organizations over the years. In so many ways, the work and partnership of these organizational networks models the kind of community self-help and inter-ethnic solidarity that have served as hallmarks of the American experience since colonial times. In the design and implementation of their violence prevention program initiatives, individual organizational practices, and public education and advocacy endeavors, both groups have modeled the highest principles of American democracy, pluralism, and tolerance. As one Simba Circle elder, Louis "Baba" Dodley, Sr., recently expressed it, "Imagine a society where people enjoy the freedom and beauty of self-awareness, tolerance, and understanding of others and a safe environment where people are encouraged to express and exchange worldviews with dignity and mutual respect under the unifying principles of democracy and the higher universal tenets of ecumenical spirituality—that is the vision we share with Barrios Unidos."

Indeed, the cross-racial bonds and community-building that BU and Simba Circle leaders have advanced over the years stand as exemplars of America's best possibilities moving into the twenty-first century. The organizations' partnership is one of only a small number of enduring intergroup alliances that have brought together inner-city gang leaders and youth networks to forge community peace across the nation. In this connection, Simba Circle's influence on BU's organizational development has been profound.

BU's engagement with Gaylord Thomas and his colleagues at Simba Circle (Rescue, Release and Restore, Inc.) have fundamentally advanced the organization's leadership and work. It has helped the organization to tap essential technical and financial support. It has exposed BU to important new program approaches that complement and further its institutional mission. It also helped to expand still further BU's cultural reach and access to informed national leaders in the violence prevention field. All of these benefits have combined to make BU and the Simba Circle stronger and more effective organizations, notwithstanding doubts and cynicism in some circles concerning the two organizations' outlook and methodologies.

Promoting Community Self-Reliance and Self-Sufficiency

BARRIOS UNIDOS AS A CATALYST FOR SOCIAL ENTERPRISE

From BU's earliest days, the dream of its elders has been to establish a culturally centered space for Chicano/Latino leaders and youths to help advance the values and achieve the aims of a community peace movement in America. Given the nature of BU's agenda and its progressive political implications during a period of growing conservativism across the United States, the organization's leadership has been compelled increasingly to rely on a long-range plan for financial self-reliance and self-sufficiency. Enterprise efforts have been a central element of this evolving strategy. Building on what was most natural to the organization's core youth constituencies, BU Wear, the brand name for a BU Productions' clothing line of culturally themed silk-screening art and casual wear, became the logical early focal point for organizational revenue generation.

Initial efforts to raise funds from youth creations in these domains operated at a small scale and largely in the context of home production. But eventually BU found an important and growing market for these products. It also recognized that expanding organizational production capacity in silk-screen and T-shirt design and product distribution could help to address the perennial socioeconomic challenges facing BU's core constituency of at-risk youth. Organizational engagement in such activities, it turned out, enabled BU to create meaningful employment and income-generating opportunities for many of its youth adherents. In time, these considerations combined to turn the attention of BU's leaders more centrally to community economic development and the need for a more significant organizational profile in the field.

BU's resulting endeavors ultimately engaged the organization in an array of business and expansion activities. These involved real estate, various small business ventures, and efforts to establish a Barrio Enterprise Zone (BEZ) on Soquel Avenue in BU's Santa Cruz headquarters community.

FORMATIVE STEPS IN COMMUNITY ECONOMIC DEVELOPMENT

During the formative stages of Barrios Unidos's organizing work, small revenues made through silks-creen production and the sale of culturally themed T-shirts enabled organizational elders to pay small organizer stipends to help cover their BU-related work expenses for gasoline, supplies, meetings, and educational materials. Over the years, BU T-shirts became a trademark tool for organizational outreach and recruitment. Start-up BU chapters were given shirts at cost so they could in turn be sold at a profit to support local organizing efforts, pay for Kids Clubs, and support other network-building activities. The elders' underlying vision for BU Productions quickly evolved. Based both on the need for increased organizational revenue and the community value-added of new employment opportunity for at-risk youth, BU leaders soon began to work toward developing a full-service silk-screen operation as a small business that could produce and market a signature line of T-shirts and clothing while creating jobs for BU's young members. BU principals believed that the enterprise could be developed and expanded over time to become both self-sustaining and profitable. Today, the production, marketing, and sale of BU clothing helps to generate approximately $200,000 in annual revenue.

The initial thinking of BU founders was that revenue in this range (a large sum by grassroots community standards) would more than suffice to help them achieve institutional stability and would contribute significantly to BU's long-term sustainability. The realities of what it takes to effectively run and sustain a nonprofit organization quickly forced a reevaluation of these assumptions. In fact, as BU activities and plans grew on other fronts, so did its revenue needs. Over time they substantially exceeded proceeds generated by the organization's successful T-shirt line.

"We saw ourselves becoming the McDonalds of the T-shirt business: two billion sold, you know," recalls Otilio Quintero. "Until one day we sat down and started to do the math about how many T-shirts it would take for the enterprise to be self-sustaining and feed profits back into the organization to subsidize other work. We still see the potential for developing a signature product line through BU Productions and BU Wear, but to generate additional revenues in the shorter term we had to consider what economic development meant more broadly for our movement and what other approaches might be available to us."

In the ensuing organizational dialogue and strategizing that took place, BU leaders turned once again to Chicano history and culture. In their discussions these leaders surfaced two stark insights gleaned from Mexican American experiences in the civil rights and community peace movements. The first was that Chicanos are a land-based people who must reclaim their connection and rights to ancestral lands. A tragic irony in this connection was that contemporary Chicano/Latino youth were killing each other in neighborhood turf wars for land that they did not even own. The second insight was that poverty and its attendant dysfunctions are at the root of violence and demanded that economic development become an even more integral aspect of BU's mission and organizational design.

An important realization among BU leaders involved in this exchange was that, indeed, ownership and asset deficits continued to be defining challenges for BU's core group of youth members and their families. Even in the progressive Santa Cruz community that housed the organizational headquarters, there existed no concentration of Latino-owned businesses, properties, or social enterprises of which to speak. Consequently, BU leaders began to ponder the need and possibility of creating a targeted zone of Chicano/Latino capital formation. As Nane Alejándrez recalls,

> The teachings of César Chávez, Reies López Tijerina, and Corky Gonzales regarding the connection of economic justice, land ownership, self-reliance, and community-centered economics were never more influential to us than right before we purchased our Soquel Avenue property. The epiphany was that we needed to acquire land and develop assets to create the kind of employment and change we were seeking in communities. The whole idea of the Barrio Enterprise Zone (BEZ) was to declare the imperative to stimulate economic development as part of an overarching set of community-building strategies. The BEZ complemented the human development functions of the program-based Barrios Unidos Institute we were seeking to develop.

THE BARRIO ENTERPRISE ZONE (BEZ)

The first step BU's leaders took in creating a Barrio Enterprise Zone was availing themselves of the knowledge and resources required to realize such a vision. These leaders—products of the streets who were scarcely educated in matters of high finance, business, and real estate matters—knew well that they would need considerable technical support and funding to succeed in this endeavor. They also realized the effort would require early support from important political leaders. To initiate their campaign to establish a BEZ, BU principals turned logically to a longtime ally and supporter with considerable civic influence: Santa Cruz mayor Scott Kennedy. Mayor Kennedy instructed the BU leaders to develop a concept paper and a statement of need for the BEZ that he could present to the city council and other essential institutions whose support would be needed to make the venture a reality. In making the case for the BEZ, BU leaders had to identify and map a geographic area of Santa Cruz that met the Community Redevelopment Agency's definition of an economically depressed area. This included a demonstrated dearth of public and private investment in business and affordable housing and poverty indices showing low-income levels, high rates of unemployment, and poor educational achievement. After examining pockets of poverty in various Santa Cruz communities, BU leaders ultimately focused on documenting the case for developing the economically depressed area of Santa Cruz known as the Soquel Corridor.

BU leaders next turned their focus to the challenge of identifying an appropriate and affordable property in the proposed zone that could be purchased and then developed as an enterprise center. After considerable searching, they discovered an old hardware store complex located on the Soquel Corridor that was encumbered in foreclosure litigation. It was being offered for sale at a price of $1.6 million. BU decided to take a chance and made a purchase bid on the property despite not having a bank-approved financial package in place. At this point, a combination of welcomed serendipity and good old-fashioned political patronage from important institutional leaders helped BU to close the property deal. Notwithstanding the uncertainty of BU's financial capacity, the judge presiding over the property's legal disposition decided to clear the way for the organization to purchase the land. Then, as good fortune would have it, BU was quickly able to secure a community development block grant to finance the purchase down payment, a loan guarantee from the U.S. Department of Agriculture, and a full mortgage loan from the Santa Cruz Community Credit Union. The Credit Union loan was the largest it had ever underwritten in Santa Cruz up to that time.

The necessary political support to make the deal possible was of a mixed order. While some local leaders, including Mayor Kennedy, were facilitative, other local officials and members of the Santa Cruz government bureaucracy presented challenges and roadblocks to BU's leadership. In some cases, BU's progress in attaining the Soquel Avenue property was not achieved because of establishment authorities, but rather in spite of them. Reflecting in retrospect on the process required to purchase and develop the first BEZ in Santa Cruz, Otilio Quintero has commented,

> Like we did when we established the nonprofit, we just jumped in headfirst. We knew very little about real estate acquisition, financing requirements, government loan

processes and programs, or the politics of community development. However, despite having important allies, this time no one was giving us anything. The whole process of acquiring the land was not without its lessons, struggles, and disappointments. For one, Barrios Unidos found it very disheartening to have to jump through so many hoops to find support for the land acquisition in a city that had so few public resources dedicated to helping poor Latino families. Moreover, the city and local institutions only begrudgingly acknowledged the presence of, or responsibility to invest in, poor barrios in Santa Cruz.

As a land acquisition requirement, BU produced a long-term plan to develop the BEZ. Its phase one plan proposed the purchase of a parcel of property large enough to house a Barrios Unidos Community and Cultural Center (i.e., BU's long-envisioned Institute). The Center would comprise roughly 2.5 acres with three residential units, office space to house all of the existing BU programs and administrative operations (including the César Chávez School for Social Change), and storefront space presently being rented to four small community businesses. The larger scope of the BEZ as projected by Barrios Unidos leaders in a second development phase (now in progress) included plans to increase BU's programmatic capacities in job creation, preparation, and training. It also called for stimulating small business through the ongoing acquisition and management of local property assets and technical support for micro-enterprises and other community development ventures. Moving into these areas of work represented an entirely new realm of engagement and leadership for the organization.

Since committing itself to this agenda, BU has moved deliberately to integrate its economic development activities with its human development work. In order to help maximize prospects for consonance and reinforcement in the relationship between these two anchor elements of BU's mission, the organization's leadership has established priorities for proceeding in the area of economic development. Four basic priorities thus guide all BU economic development decisions and activities. These include the following:

- Developing the potential and capabilities of community residents to be economically self-reliant
- Promoting community-centered economic development practices and structures
- Creating new assets that generate capital, employment, affordable housing, small business enterprise, and economic growth in low-income neighborhoods and communities
- Promoting sustainability by recirculating resources, as appropriate, into promising new community and human development enterprises

Although Barrios Unidos has not officially designated itself as a community development corporation (CDC), it has increasingly taken on the properties of a CDC in its Santa Cruz headquarters community. BU's distinctive model of integrating Latino community and youth culture, as well as asset- and institution-building in its core work, establishes an increasingly promising model for other locations and multicultural populations all across the United States.

Moving into the Future: The Barrios Unidos Institute

As BU has ventured into new fields, such as economic development, it has redoubled its efforts to ensure the long-term visibility and impact of its informing program work with at-risk youth and families. Today, in order to achieve this aim, BU elders are working to develop a sustainable program entity: The Barrios Unidos Institute. BU's evolution from organization to institution is far from complete; indeed, this work is barely getting started. But this new direction in organizational focus constitutes one of the most important decisions the organization's leadership has undertaken in BU's nearly thirty years of activity.

As now conceived, the multipart mission of the Barrios Unidos Institute (an elaboration of BU's current work) will be to educate through the preservation of cultural heritage; to promote social and economic innovations, and model public policies, that build community and expand opportunity; and to prepare intergenerational leaders for a life of learning and service. In these ways, the broad scope of the Institute's work will support human and community development, civic engagement, and the advancement of pluralism, justice, and democracy.

After twenty-seven years of work, BU leaders have amassed the credibility and resources to achieve this next level of institutional development. The necessary knowledge, values, and strategies are in place, and, for the most part, the BU movement is healthy and strong. The *Cultura Es Cura* curriculum is embedded in the César Chávez School for Social Change and many of the organization's other programmatic efforts. Chapter-building work has surfaced the need to develop a stronger intermediary capacity within BU to provide support for affiliates. Community economic development programs are succeeding and have led to the development of an exciting long-range organizational sustainability strategy.

The California Wellness Foundation, The California Endowment, the David and Lucile Packard Foundation, and other important philanthropies have made major financial commitments to support BU as it negotiates a successful transition into the future. The steadfast support of cornerstone benefactors like these has been an essential factor accounting for the organization's many successes over the years, especially over the past decade. Continuing support from such leading funders will facilitate BU leaders in their quest to realize the envisioned BU Institute—an achievement that will consolidate BU as an anchor organization in the Latino rights community and the broader social justice field.

Summing Up and Looking Ahead

To sum up where the events and developments covered thus far have brought BU strategically and programmatically, the information provided below summarizes the essential means and projects that BU has cumulatively developed over the years to establish its present institutional profile. These summaries in turn speak to BU's theory of change and its core strategies as an organization. They reflect the fundamental belief of Barrios Unidos principals that multicultural respect, partnership, and community-building are the basic engines that drive social change. They also demonstrate BU's unbending commitment to integrated strategies that promote social, political, and economic justice.

SANTA CRUZ BARRIOS UNIDOS PROGRAM STRATEGIES

Since their very first forays into organizing for peace in the barrios of California, BU's founders drew from an array of culturally-based strategies to bring about change. The following is a brief overview of the organization's strategic priorities as of this writing. Each area that is highlighted includes a corresponding description of objectives. It is important to note that as BU has evolved in its organizational journey, it has increasingly integrated these strategic priorities to a point where there presently exists a high degree of seamlessness and interplay between and among them.

Education: BU educational program strategies focus on a multiplicity of inter-related aims, including:

- restoring cultural and spiritual traditions through dynamic formal and informal educational program methods
- promoting multidisciplinary academic instruction
- imparting an understanding and appreciation of history
- engendering positive identity and self-esteem
- developing critical reasoning skills
- encouraging creativity and ingenuity
- building character
- promoting values that support the centrality of family, appreciation of others, and respect for nature
- informing a sense of responsibility relative to civic and communal life

Street Organizing: BU's street organizing work is informed by the following strategic priorities:

- conducting outreach in community, school, and institutional settings
- identifying and supporting youth in at-risk circumstances
- building trusting, caring relationships through individual and group counseling

- sponsoring mentorship, supplemental education, and tutorial programs
- organizing positive group activities in the community
- providing conflict mediation support
- encouraging truces that suspend gang and interpersonal disputes
- administering community advocacy training
- championing cultural awareness
- advocating healthy behaviors relative to substance abuse, sexual relations, nutrition, and physical fitness

Leadership and Human Development: BU seeks to develop visionary people and social capital through strategic activities, including:
- providing leadership-learning and character-building opportunities to needy, at-risk youths and community members
- supporting culturally-based education, skills development, and volunteer service projects
- training youth to become responsible leaders who contribute to the well-being of their families and to the social, economic, and civic life of the community
- enlisting a continuum of intergenerational leaders (including children, youth, adults, and elders) in collective efforts to build community and advance society
- recruiting, training, and employing community workers in responsible positions that expand their leadership insights and capacities

Community Economic Development: BU supports strategic efforts to increase community economic capital and benefits by focusing on the following priorities:
- promoting community economic advancement and self-sufficiency
- pursuing socially responsible community-based land development
- managing property and business assets in ways that expand community wealth and well-being

- supporting education, job-preparedness, and skills-building programs that bolster individual and community capital
- fostering entrepreneurial ventures and micro-business enterprises

Civic Participation and Community Mobilization: BU champions public engagement and democratic vitality through strategies, including:
- mobilizing youth and adult community residents to effect improvements in the policies and practices of public and private institutions
- encouraging an informed citizenry and public
- building the human and institutional assets of traditionally disadvantaged youths and families in ways that facilitate their engagement in democratic processes
- developing the skills and resources of barrio youths and residents to advocate effectively for the common good
- advancing partnerships, multi-sector engagements, and working collaborations that support increased participation in civic and community decision-making

Cultural Arts and Community-Building: BU regards the cultural arts and community-building as essential anchors of social awareness and community peace. It encourages advancements in these areas by:
- providing a central communal space for practicing spiritual ceremony
- celebrating the arts through the sponsorship of regular exhibits and programs in music, dance, poetry, literature, crafts, and storytelling
- promoting alternative forms of cultural expression
- lifting up important religious and multicultural traditions
- supporting rites-of-passage ceremonies, commemorations, and other cultural celebrations that encourage social cohesion and community-building

Coalition-Building and Advocacy: Finally, BU pursues social change through intentional efforts to work in coalition with other groups and with an eye to progressive advocacy. It advances these priorities by:

- providing grassroots-organizing support to neighborhood and community leaders across California and the United States
- encouraging the development of BU chapters and other social-change efforts guided by similar values, principles, and core strategies
- mobilizing regional and national peace movements in collaboration with multiracial coalitions and alliances
- advocating on cross-cutting nonviolence and justice issues that affect multicultural constituencies
- participating in selective policy advocacy and reform campaigns on issues ranging from criminal and economic justice to humane immigration policy and education

Santa Cruz Barrios Unidos Core Program Summaries

César E. Chávez School for Social Change (CCSSC): CCSSC was established in 1995 as a chartered alternative high school. CCSSC offers students—most of whom have experienced major problems in conventional school settings—a positive educational environment. It develops leadership and self-esteem through culturally appropriate academic courses and developmental learning, using a five-step rites-of-passage curriculum. Classes currently offered at CCSSC include instruction in history, the arts, computer literacy, cultural dance, English, Spanish, math, creative writing, and job preparation.

The Barrios Unidos Multimedia Center: The BU multimedia center is a fully equipped computer and video production center that was established to provide basic computer and video production instruction to students of CCSSC, as well as BU Kids Club participants, local K-12 public school students, parents, and members of the community at large.

Community Education and Outreach Projects: BU supports a broad range of community education and outreach projects, including:
- The Fresh Lifelines for Youth Project (FLY): FLY provides outreach, instruction, training, and counseling to young people on probation concerning their rights and responsibilities under the law

- Barrios Unidos Clubs: BU Clubs sponsor weekly support activities for local high school and middle school students, such as topical workshops, culture- and skills-building programs, mentoring, and one-on-one counseling
- Gang Alternatives North and South (GANAS): GANAS offers street outreach, mediation, counseling, educational and peer support, and cultural enrichment activities targeted to gang members and gang-affiliated youths, with an eye to encouraging their broader engagement in non-gang-related pursuits
- Kids Clubs: BU Kids Clubs provide daily outreach, after-school care, tutoring, mentoring, and cultural, educational, and recreational support to children and their families residing in low-income housing units and surrounding neighborhoods
- Juvenile Hall Project: The BU Juvenile Hall Project sponsors weekly meetings and counseling, mentoring, skills-building, and other support for incarcerated youths, with the aim of preparing them for constructive reentry into their communities and society upon their release
- Barrios Unidos Parent Groups: BU Parent Groups offer counseling, family-service referrals, and peer support to local adults whose children are involved in (or at-risk in relation to) gang and/or related criminal activity
- Young Fathers Project: The Young Fathers Project offers counseling and other support to young fathers in such areas as responsible manhood and parenting; it also assists project participants with referrals to available health and human services and job-training opportunities

Warrior and Adelitas Circles : In order to complete annual rites-of-passage requirements for CCSSC students and to nurture other young people involved in BU's work, BU organizes a week-long retreat where elders, peer leaders, mentors, and select instructors lead group dialogues, or circles, to impart the cultural and spiritual heritage of Latino people. The circles seek to prepare participating youth for healthy development and transition into responsible adulthood. Accordingly, these gatherings support activities that instill cultural understanding, positive self-esteem, and respect for others. Boys and young men involved in these activities participate in warrior circles, while girls and young women participate in "Adelitas" circles— Adelitas were the female soldiers in the Mexican Revolution.

The California Prison Project: The California Prison Project provides community, spiritual, educational, and cultural support to incarcerated individuals of Latino and African American heritage residing at state correctional facilities. Current project activities are supported at California's Tracy (DVI), Solano, and Soledad prisons. Through this work, BU encourages multicultural inmates to embrace peace and constructive life paths, both within and outside of the prison walls.

The Barrios Unidos Cultural Center: The BU Cultural Center offers a communal gathering place at no cost to a wide range of community groups. Center activities include historical celebrations, community events, and topical educational and civic awareness programs. The Center also supports classes in *Tai Chi*, Mexican folkloric and Aztec dance, traditional Native American drumming, art, and music.

Community Economic Development: BU community economic development projects support short- and long-term strategies designed to encourage organizational and community self-sufficiency. Major activities in this program area include:

- *Barrio Enterprise Zones*: Through Barrio Enterprise Zone development, BU pursues the purchase, development, and management of property assets for community benefit. A two-acre multipurpose complex currently under development on Soquel Avenue in Santa Cruz establishes the first Barrio Enterprise Zone. The property is being developed into a multiuse facility serving as a hub for community development programs, cultural and civic activities, education and training, the César E. Chávez School, a technology learning center, an incubation site for small business and micro-enterprise development, and affordable housing.
- *BU Productions*: BU Productions supports on-site professional silk-screening workshops that generate trademark clothing (i.e.,

the BU Wear brand). This work in turn produces considerable organizational and community income, as well as job-training and employment opportunities for at-risk youth involved with BU Productions.

- *New Business Enterprises*: Through internal seed funding, BU will soon selectively capitalize new BU enterprise projects that advance its economic justice and development agendas. Projects under consideration include developing a Barrios Unidos Cultural Café and Bookstore and an on-site, accredited childcare program.

The story recounted thus far has sought to capture the origins of the Barrios Unidos movement, the hard work and journeys of some its key leaders, the birth of BU as an organization, the evolution of its work and mission, and the organization's challenges and opportunities looking to the future. Because the BU story is so inextricably linked with the work of many longtime progressive leaders—many of whom are contemporary pioneers of the struggle to achieve justice, equality, nonviolence, and true democracy in America—it is important at this point to assess BU's historical and evolving work in the view of a select number of these individuals. The chapter that follows, therefore, seeks to capture the collective wisdom of several particularly respected and accomplished friends of BU and the community peace movement: Dolores Huerta, Harry Belafonte, Tom Hayden, Constance "Connie" Rice, and Manuel Pastor. These essential voices on civil rights and community peace bring a special insight to the meaning of BU's important contributions to the movement. To be sure, each of these distinguished individuals holds a special place in the pantheon of BU family members and associates.

Nane Alejándrez in Nairobi, supporting the Fair Trade movement of local coffee growers.

Nane meets with elders in Tanzania. Supporting the Fair Trade movement in Africa is one area of cooperative advocacy with Gaylord Thomas of The Simba Circle.

Warrior Circle—Nane Alejándrez and Simba Circle founder, Gaylord Thomas. BU and the Simba Circle organize an annual exchange in cultural education, social history, the arts, and spiritual ceremony for Latino and African-American youth.

Warrior Circle—Elder Henry Domínguez, Morning Prayer Circle —the camp is held every spring in the Santa Cruz retreat site purchased by Barrios Unidos.

Walter Guzmán, Henry Domínguez, Nane Alejándrez, Nghia Tran dedicating a mural at the BU Barrio Enterprise Zone in Santa Cruz, California.

Nane Alejándrez and Angela Davis—UC Santa Cruz Conference on Prison and Justice System Reform. Education and advocacy across a broad spectrum of social justice issues is central to BU's mission.

Barrios Unidos Productions—the silk-screening business is part of the first Barrio Enterprise Zone being developed by BU on its two-acre property in Santa Cruz.

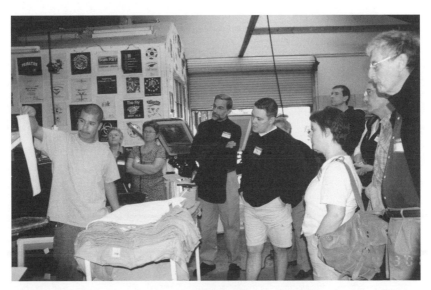

BU Productions—Joaquin Alejándrez demonstrates the silk screening process to a delegation from Ireland. BU Wear can be found throughout the United States and many countries around the world.

Instruction at Barrios Unidos César Chávez School for Social Change, where students receive multi-disciplinary instruction and tasks related to their rites of passage to adulthood.

Liz Ayala (far left) with students from the César Chávez School for Social Change at Barrios Unidos.

Youth Skit—Día de los Muertos teatro. César Chávez School students follow the movement tradition of educating and healing through the arts.

Intercultural Holidays—Las Posadas and Drum Circle Ceremony. The BU family celebrates with an inter-tribal delegation of supporters during the Christmas season.

Solano Prison drum ceremony—BU supports cultural celebrations, educational exchanges, and solidarity work with a cadre of intercultural leaders among inmates in three California prisons.

Big Mountain, Arizona. BU sends an annual delegation of supporters to the Sundance ceremony. Nane Alejándrez, Otilio Quintero, and Liz Ayala are regular supporters.

Barrios Unidos Youth Warrior Circle Camp—BU elders, teachers, and nation-builders pose with rites-of-passage youth graduates.

2004, First Annual Barrios Unidos Adelitas Circle Camp—The young girls and women of the BU Kids Club and César Chávez School celebrate their first rights-of-passage class.

Part IV
Essential Voices on Civil Rights and
Community Peace

Introduction

We cannot seek achievement for ourselves and forget about the progress and prosperity of our community. . . . Our ambitions must be broad enough to include the aspirations and needs of others, for their sakes and our own. . . . When we are really honest with ourselves, we must admit that our lives are all that really belong to us. So, it is how we use our lives that determines what kind of [person] we are. It is my belief that only by giving our lives do we find life.

César E. Chávez

The history of Barrios Unidos and of the contemporary community peace movement in America is intricately connected to the long legacy and lessons of the civil rights movement. The tenets that define human rights and democracy inevitably flow from the enlightened convictions and actions of real people. Such people, through experience, sacrifice, and the exercise of principle, compel us to fulfill our highest humanity. In telling the BU story, it is vital to document how its work has been informed and perceived by important leaders and allies in the quest for social justice. Over the years, BU has been fortunate to garner the support of countless multicultural leaders of consequence. This segment of the BU story highlights the reflections of five particularly important observers and champions of its work to put in relief their informed sense of BU's significance and continuing promise as an agent of social change.

Dolores Huerta

Dolores Huerta is cofounder of the United Farm Workers of America, AFL-CIO (UFW), and president of the Dolores Huerta Foundation. She is the mother of eleven children and has twenty grandchildren and five great-grandchildren. Huerta was born in the mining town of Dawson, New Mexico. Her father, Juan F. Fernández, was a veteran, miner, field worker, union activist, and state assemblyman. Her mother, Alicia St. John Chávez, was a businesswoman, community leader, and activist. After her parents divorced, she moved with her mother and four siblings to Stockton, California. Huerta was influenced by the activism of her mother. Early in her career, she became a grammar school educator. Believing she could do more by organizing farmworkers, however, she left teaching. Huerta's early civil rights work included serving as a founding member of the Stockton chapter of the Community Services Organization (CSO). She later founded the California Agricultural Workers Association in 1960. In 1962, after the CSO turned down a proposal by César Chávez to organize farmworkers, Huerta joined Chávez and his family in Delano, California. There they formed the National Farm Workers Association (NFWA), the predecessor of the UFW. In 1965, the NFWA joined Filipino members of the Agricultural Workers Organizing Committee to strike against Delano grape growers. The two organizations merged in 1966 to form the United Farm Workers Organizing Committee. In 1966, Huerta negotiated a watershed contract with the Schenley Wine Company, the first direct collective bargaining agreement involving U.S. farmworkers. She directed the monumental national grape boycott of the late 1960s and early 1970s and spearheaded many hard-fought union victories yielding the ultimate enactment of the California Agricultural Labor Relations Act. The act empowered workers to organize and collectively negotiate fair contracts. It strengthened labor rights by establishing farmworker health and unemployment benefits, grievance procedures, and protections against poor working conditions, pesticide exposure, and other workplace abuses. Working with Chávez over more than thirty years, Huerta helped to found the Robert Kennedy Medical Plan, the Juan De La Cruz Farm Workers Pension Fund, and the Farm Workers Credit Union. A board member of the Fund for the Feminist Majority, Huerta is considered one of the nation's leading feminists and has been inducted into the National Woman's Hall of Fame. She founded the Dolores Huerta Foundation for community organizing to support Communities in Action, a grassroots leadership development initiative in low-income underrepresented communities.

The central role that spirituality and nonviolence has played in the civil rights movement is something that needs to be passed on and understood by students of history and the leaders of today. The farmworker movement could never have been built without its spiritual base. The hardships and sacrifice of the people from the very beginning of the movement took a lot of faith, both in God and in the cause itself. César Chávez and the early organizers of the union took a lot of ridicule and scorn, not only from those that opposed the union's goals, but from our own families and people we grew up with in the community. People thought César was crazy for doing what he was doing, questioning his motives, calling him a *flojo* (lazy) who didn't want to work, even questioning his fidelity and character to discredit his integrity.

My own family questioned me and thought I was off my own rocker for becoming an organizer and leaving a good stable job as a teacher. Here I was a mother with young children, in the process of divorce, and leaving my job to go organize with César in the movement. Many of the early core organizers drew from their spiritual belief systems or faith for resolve and strength both personally and as leaders. A lot of people believed the other way, that we didn't have a chance to organize an effective union such as the United Farm Workers (UFW) to serve *campesinos* and other poor farmworkers. Other union models that we were learning from were successful because they were able to gather some financial resources from their membership and allies of the labor movement. It was first and foremost an act of faith to believe we could succeed in organizing some of the poorest and most disenfranchised of the poor.

As the real organizing began, the strike drew a lot of anger, intimidation, and violent tactics from the opposition to break our resolve both to build the union and to use nonviolent principles and tactics to achieve its goals. The resolve to stick to nonviolence was seriously tested in the early days, as people were getting brutally beaten and attacked by strikebreakers and opposition forces. César and I believed that the only way to create a mass movement for farmworker justice and equality was through the moral power of non-violence. We also understood that nonviolence does not work without faith; without a spiritual base we knew that the sustained individual and collective determination needed to endure the hardships and win the difficult battles ahead would crumble.

NONVIOLENCE AND SOCIAL CHANGE

Ours was truly a spiritually based vow to nonviolence values and nonviolent social change. However, for us to be truly successful it would be critical to communicate and teach the values and principles of nonviolence across the rank and file, the workers and organizers of the union. César and I drew heavily not just from Mahatma Gandhi's teachings on nonviolence, but on the brilliant tactics and strategies that he used as an organizer. There was a moral authority and power that flowed from Gandhi's liberation movement in India that greatly influenced the civil rights struggle here in America. César read all he could get his hands on regarding Gandhi's work, philosophy, strategies, and tactics. I also studied his works and was greatly influenced by his revolutionary organizing tactics and how others like Dr. Martin Luther King were applying them.

César also drew from his personal experience and background having grown up exposed to community violence. His mother, Juana Estrada, tried to protect him and teach him the value of life, to survive with integrity against the adversities of poverty, and to dedicate whatever he did to honor and preserve humanity. César's political and social philosophies were built from the personal value system developed in his mother's home but also those that flowed from his understanding of *cultura* and history. Both César and I understood that choosing nonviolence went against the traditions of the proud revolutionary history of our people to achieve liberation. Our embrace of nonviolence also went against the grain at a time when so many in the Chicano movement and other sectors of the civil rights struggle saw the use of violence to overcome injustice and oppression as legitimate.

In the mid-1960s, there were very influential groups and leaders within the Chicano movement who were condoning, if not advocating, violence as a tactic both to protect ourselves and to achieve social change. Certain leaders in the Brown Berets and powerful voices of the time, such as Corky Gonzales and Reies López Tijerina, did not discount violence as a legitimate response to injustice and oppression. César and I realized that we were going against the grain of a more historical revolutionary mind-set and the customary reliance on violence that was really dominant among the leadership of the time. People within the Chicano and the broader civil rights movements made fun of Dr. King, the SCLC, NAACP, and César for promoting nonviolence, calling them a bunch of wimps and *vendidos* (sellouts). Critics charged that we were being ineffectual through nonviolence and would end up selling out the movement. Although the criticism was hard to take at times and placed a lot of pressure on us to show success, we believed that history would prove nonviolence to be the right way to achieve victory.

César and I always felt responsible for teaching and leading by example, especially in the realm of living and working by nonviolent principles. We knew that it took a great deal of sacrifice and discipline to practice nonviolence, but we also trusted that nonviolence had the greatest potential for transforming people and society. At the same time, we had the tremendous challenge of communicating these values and organizing principles to workers who knew very little if anything of Gandhi and his victories or of the organizing philosophies of Dr. King. César and our lead organizers regularly taught and talked about nonviolence principles and tactics in the course of organizing and recruiting workers to the UFW movement. We also tried to infuse these values into the culture of the union. It didn't take very long before our success in infusing nonviolence principles into the union would be put to the test.

An early test came in 1969 when the Teamsters invaded a UFW organizing site. After a peaceful demonstration and march on Sacramento by the union, the Teamsters had moved into the fields in our absence and were waiting for our return. Dozens of farmworker organizers were beaten, assaulted, and intimidated, requiring a mass response meeting by the union. At the meeting, many organizers and workers were frustrated and angry about the violence they were being subjected to by the Teamsters, and they wanted to respond in kind. It was one thing to be nonviolent to the growers and labor contractors, but what about these Teamsters who were directly brutalizing and victimizing UFW members? This meeting marked an important crossroads for the union as César called on the organization to stick to nonviolence in the face of the unwarranted violence against us. He asked every member to make a standing vow to nonviolence. This prompted a lot of discussion and *pleito* (argument). Opinion was split and agreement on nonviolence was not automatic. It was not until César stood up and issued an ultimatum: if the union resorted to violence, even in response to it, he would leave and start another effort based on nonviolence. César made it clear that he wanted nothing to do with a group that used or promoted violence to achieve its ends. He said that if we turned to violence against our enemies, then we would ultimately use it against each other.

From that moment on, nonviolence took root across the rank and file of the union. There was clear acknowledgment that nonviolence was to be our guiding principle. It would be misleading to say that this proclamation was not without some significant disagreement, internal conflict, and the need for collective accountability. For instance, I remember one time on a picket line where I was serving as captain, a Teamster began verbally abusing, instigating, and physically harassing some union members. All of a sudden, one rather large UWF supporter from another union that was on the picket line in solidarity with us snapped at the relentless abuse. This large man stormed to his car, pulled a large chain from the trunk, and proceeded to head toward the Teamsters with serious bad intent. He was so angry, and there I was at

103 pounds at the time, trying to stop him from giving in to violence. Finally, I just grabbed onto the chain and wrapped my body around it knowing he would have to swing me as well to be able to use it as a weapon. This must have been some sight to those watching! Ultimately, I just told him to get off the picket line if he couldn't stand with us in nonviolence. He left and complained, but my decision was upheld.

In Delano, forty strikers and union organizers, men and women, were waiting for strikebreakers to get off work so we could tell them about the strike. Suddenly, a large group of Teamsters, conveniently accompanied by a couple of police paddy wagons arrived. Without warning, the Teamsters marched toward us swinging 2 x 4 wooden boards. They knew they had the upper hand, because the conservative district attorney would not issue arrest warrants or aggravated assault complaints against them. I ordered all of our women to the front with their arms held up. The Teamsters banged the women's arms with the boards but the women stood their ground. Despite these aggressive provocations, the Teamsters could not get the men—who demonstrated great discipline—to jump in as the women were assaulted. This demonstration of nonviolence forced the Teamsters to back off, kept people from injury and jail, and prevented a bloody riot.

SPIRITUAL AND CULTURAL CENTER OF THE MOVEMENT

Cultural and spiritual symbolism was at the very core of the UFW movement and provided a powerful imagery to all who participated in and supported the movement. Most of us really drew on spirituality for strength and to help keep us focused. It became a part of the UFW culture that before every march or large organizing activity we held a mass or prayer service. There were nonbelievers within the ranks of the union who did not agree with the "religious" orientation of the movement. But the reality was that spirituality was a fundamental part of life for much of the leadership and the vast majority of the members. On the march to Sacramento, for example, the image and statue of *La Virgen de Guadalupe* served as a focal point of cultural unity and strength. The issue was discussed at a planning retreat of the UFW leadership where it was decided that she was part of the spiritual dimension of the movement and an important cultural symbol from which many poor Latinos took inspiration and found common purpose.

During this period there was a fatigue factor setting in among organizers, and outside support was waning. The march on Sacramento was intended to refocus our attention and to gain newfound support for the strike. The march route purposefully went through farming towns with large Latino *campesino* populations where we could educate, recruit, and garner new supporters. César wanted the theme of the march to be *penitencia* (penance) and forgiveness. His focus was to bring healing within the union and to reaffirm our higher purpose. The *Virgen* was a guardian of the poor and a powerful symbol of this calling. Another important intent of the march was to achieve a spiritual cleansing of the movement and to lift our organizers and leaders to a higher moral plane.

César and I both believed that the righteousness of the movement required that the marchers and strikers walk by the highest possible principles in relation to the cause. There were a lot of internal tensions, ego trips, and petty disputes emerging over things like resources and titles that were poisoning morale, damaging relationships, and hurting the union's working environment. These problems were surfaced in a healthy way by creating a spiritual setting where, in a mass open confessional and reconciliation between members, people cried, prayed, and forgave. César's hope for cleansing, refocusing, and reinvigorating through this important spiritual process came to be as members vowed to move forward and walk together guided by a higher authority and purpose. Manuel Vásquez, who understood the important symbolism of the *Virgen* and the spiritual dimensions of the movement, became the captain who helped to lead the Sacramento march.

An important aspect of the UFW experience was building community solidarity by providing creative outlets and avenues for cultural and human expression. In this regard, the contributions of Luis Valdez and El Teatro Campesino, providing the steady presence of theatre, music, and song, were immeasurable. Songs and *corridos* are an important tradition that helped our people to express what they were feeling. They captured the pain, the hope, and the vision of what we were trying to achieve and create. The *actos* (skits or plays) developed and performed by Teatro were critical to organizer morale. They inspired purpose and the ongoing dynamic of education within the ranks of the movement among both new and old members alike.

The *actos* educated and motivated, reinforced the focus of the union and humanized the cause. Their themes articulated our common values, principles, and purpose while rejuvenating our spirit—all of which was needed in the daily toil of the struggle. It is important for aspiring leaders and the young ones coming up to appreciate the sacrifice required of them to bring about social change. For those of us in the UFW, organizing work was arduous as days went from four in the morning to eleven at night, seven days a week, with campaigns lasting months and even years. We greeted workers in the morning and were there when they got off work; we visited the strike breakers in their encampments at night to educate and organize. The demands of organizing a social movement are continual, extreme, and intensive. This is the price of success. I say this not to put our sacrifices over the sacrifices of others, but to reinforce the fact that change requires deep commitment; hence, the great need for the constant presence of spirituality and expressions of *cultura* to encourage healing, release, the sense of our humanity, and the inspiration to face each new day.

IMPORTANT LESSONS, ACCOMPLISHMENTS, AND UNFINISHED BUSINESS

There are many important lessons, milestones, and accomplishments that occurred as the result of organizing and protest by the largely poor Mexican American and immigrant communities of California that are buried in mainstream accounts of history. An important example is the case of *Méndez v. Westminster*, which foreshadowed the landmark case of *Brown v. Board of Education*. This case arose from the fruit groves and urban communities of Orange County where, in 1944, Gonzalo and Felicitas Méndez fought against the racial segregation of their daughter in a local public school. On February 18, 1946, a federal district court in California ruled that "the general and continuous segregation in separate schools of children of

Mexican ancestry is unlawful." The historical contributions of farm-worker and other Latino organizers in building foundations and creating footholds across the various stages of the movement are too often overlooked when recording the advancement and progress of civil rights.

The stories of the thousands of women who contributed to both the UFW and the broader civil rights struggle need to be captured and told as well. The reality is that there were many women playing important leadership roles across the rank and file of the movement that just aren't told and recognized, even in our own peoples' telling of history. The women were there! All anyone needs to do is look at photos of the Chicano Moratorium organizing actions or UFW picket lines, marches, and organizing meetings: women were usually front and center. Within the UFW and among its supporters, various women played key roles, including Helen Chávez, María Magaña, Antonia Saludado, Josephine Soto, Sister Huranal, Zacarina García, Jan Peterson, Alegría de la Cruz, Vivian Levine, and Barbara Macry—I could go on and on. There are so many women who contributed, all of whom deserve being mentioned, acknowledged, and remembered. Young men and women today should know these names so they can learn from their lives and follow their example.

The civil rights accomplishments of the 1960s and 1970s laid the foundation for much social, economic, and political advancement among Latinos, Blacks, Asian Pacific Americans, and others. It gave birth or new momentum to various fronts of the civil and human rights struggle, such as the environmental justice movement and the women's movement. But despite the end of legal segregation and exclusion, gains in voting rights, and some economic advancement for poor people of color, none of the major goals of civil rights have yet been achieved. The struggle is a work in progress with too many poor people still being left behind. For instance, education for our people is surely better now than it was in times past, at least in important respects due to the Méndez and Brown decisions; yet our schools continue to fail the vast majority of poor Latinos and African Americans today.

There have been inroads into higher education, and we have more educated Latinos than ever before, but claiming anything resembling equity would be false. The dismal failure of contemporary schools in preparing young Latinos to pursue or succeed in higher education says we are failing as a country to live up to the intent of the Méndez and Brown court decisions. Beyond the legal responsibility is the moral responsibility to educate all people. Education is the great equalizer. It is virtually impossible for the majority of people to step out of poverty without this stepping-stone. The achievement of educational equity and reform is perhaps the most critical area of unfinished social business for the movement today. But the next real battlefront of civil rights in America will revolve around economic rights. In the years to come, the broad agenda of economic rights, and especially ending poverty, will be a catalyst to bring all of the nation's progressive splinter movements together again.

TODAY'S PRIORITIES FOR REVIVING THE MOVEMENT

None of the unfinished business of the struggle, especially the structural eradication of poverty in America, will go anywhere unless people organize. The path to ending poverty and achieving the broader unfulfilled aims of civil rights cuts across the many fronts of economics, education, health, housing, environment, criminal and juvenile justice, political representation, civil liberties, and race relations. This broad swath of persistent concerns renders it important to prepare for a long-term nonviolent campaign. On top of this aspect of organizing for social change is the importance of continuing to do the work related to rebuilding and strengthening the fabric of our communities that have suffered so much harm from generations of oppression, discrimination, and injustice.

This is why the work of Barrios Unidos is so important and why I have established the Dolores Huerta Foundation (DHF). The DHF continues the legacy of Fred Ross, Sr. and César E. Chávez in grassroots community organizing by training organizers and assisting communities to take social action with their own indigenous leadership. On the one hand, Barrios Unidos seeks to educate, train, and prepare young leaders and families to get involved, to organize, and to see their responsibility in achieving change in their communities and society. Barrios Unidos programs and initiatives prepare young Latinos to be part of, and to exercise leadership in, the movement by reconnecting them to their history and *cultura*. This in turn provides healing and reconciliation to these young people, their families, and their communities. Just as the right-wing and conservative elements in this country have established a strong infrastructure of schools, institutes, think tanks, and grassroots groups to develop leaders and fuel advocacy of their agenda, so must we. The work of groups like Barrios Unidos to develop greater human potential, economic resources, and social infrastructure in communities is important to the long-term empowerment of our youth and the poor.

The direct and future impact of Barrios Unidos in working with youth and families that have been neglected and cast aside by society—gang members, at-risk youth, violence survivors, incarcerated children, adults, and their families—is the opportunity to give each of these groups a unique and crucial role in the movement. Restoring the cultural and spiritual fabric of our communities so we can better care for and rear our children may be the most important thing Barrios Unidos leaders do. In doing so, they serve as the voice and conscience that reminds America to go back to making kids and youth a national priority. Investing in tomorrow's leaders starts at birth.

I hope that this story helps to generate greater support for culturally based preventive programs in the community. Such programs help parents to develop healthy children and youth by involving them in positive educational, cultural, recreational, and service opportunities that prepare them to be responsible, caring, and compassionate human beings. I want to thank Barrios Unidos for not selling out and staying true to its vision, especially with regard to promoting leadership with youth and women.

Barrios Unidos needs to get its message of peace out to the world. The organization approaches education, leadership development, and social change with rare integrity and honesty. Its spiritual message is one of reconciliation, something the world and the contemporary civil rights movement need desperately. Barrios Unidos works with the untouchables in American society. The UFW worked with the poorest of the poor. It was always an honor to work with people who held their dignity and humanity when they were exploited and cast aside by mainstream society. Movements must be led and comprised of the people they serve in order to succeed. Self-determination is what Barrios Unidos represents in the community. Its leaders' values mirror those of the people they serve, and their actions model what the people wish to achieve. The dignity and humanity of our people will always win out over oppression and inhumanity. ¡Sí, Se Puede!

Harry Belafonte

Harry Belafonte is a world-renowned singer, actor, humanitarian, and activist. He is widely recognized in the United States as the king of calypso music. His career as a performer spans over fifty years. Early in his performance career, Belafonte broke racial barriers on screen, on stage, and across the musical genres of jazz, folk, American standard, and contemporary pop. Born in Harlem, New York, Belafonte was the son of Caribbean-born immigrants. He learned early in life the importance of activism and human rights through his mother's support of the labor movement. Belafonte has always considered himself an activist and humanitarian first and a performing artist second, using his celebrity as a platform for promoting racial equality, peace, and justice. In the 1960s, he became intimately involved in the civil rights movement, providing direct support to Dr. Martin Luther King, Jr. Working with Dr. King and other movement leaders, Belafonte engaged in direct activism and organized support for the Southern Christian Leadership Conference and the NAACP Legal Defense and Education Fund. As head of a fund-development committee, Belafonte raised essential resources for various civil rights campaigns and legal defense trials, facilitating the involvement of other sympathetic celebrities, civic leaders, and supporters. Belafonte is recognized as an ardent voice of nonviolent social change and an advocate of civil and human rights in America and abroad. At great personal and professional cost, he has walked side-by-side with national, international, indigenous, and grassroots leaders, such as Nelson Mandela, César Chávez, Dolores Huerta, Maya Angelou, Sidney Poitier, Stokely Carmichael, Jim Brown, and Arthur Ashe, as well as Nane Alejándrez, Bo Taylor, and countless other grassroots movement figures. Over the years, Belafonte has been an increasingly active and vibrant international voice challenging human rights violations, injustice, and inequality. In the United States, he has also played a significant role in opposing U.S. military and interventionist foreign policy, the criminalization and mass incarceration of individuals of color, and the perpetuation of violence in communities and the media.

I'm excited and honored to be included as a voice on this important, yet largely unknown, story of the work of Barrios Unidos. I hope this book inspires a new dialogue in America about civil rights, the community peace movement, and the need to better understand the experience of poor Latino and African American youth. I'm often fascinated by the fact that young people of color are hunting for answers to questions as to the present state of things, yet they seem either unaware of, or to have dismissed almost entirely, any in-depth references to the history from which they come. There is a tragic loss of history taking place that threatens to stifle progress in civil rights and the progressive movement for social change.

I am also taken aback by the lack of knowledgeable references to those who have laid down the guidelines for the movement or who have pioneered methods on how to conduct social processes to change the way people experience life. I'm speaking about reaching the poor and disenfranchised, those who are in the midst of the severe economic oppression and distress that continues to devastate so many lives in America today. It seems to me that it has never been more important to learn from the work of César Chávez, Dr. King, Minister Malcolm X, Dolores Huerta, and other amazing men and women who have led in the struggle for justice. There are so many leaders and great social thinkers who framed social movements of the past. Everyone must build on and learn from those that came before. These people helped us to envision the magnificent higher ideals upon which we hoped the post-civil rights society would be shaped.

It is an old adage but a true one: know history and apply its lessons or be condemned to relive its failures and tragedies. It worries me that too many young leaders are either not being educated on the rich legacy of the civil rights movement or have just turned their backs on the history of struggle, dismissing that history as old-fashioned and irrelevant. This selective amnesia is central to what young people face today. It is understandable that they look for new methodologies and ways to deal with current issues, but it is exceedingly dangerous not to be grounded in the history of where they came from or to lack a sense of the value and validity of the knowledge at their disposal. In one sense, every generation must be responsible for itself, a notion that is fundamentally empowering. But it is also wise to know with some clarity where we came from, what the struggle was like for those that preceded us, what was accomplished in the face of overwhelming odds, and how seemingly impossible victories were achieved.

The Barrios Unidos César Chávez School for Social Change is a model for this kind of education and empowerment. It is fundamental to the mission of the school to reconnect young ones to their history and heritage—to the legacy of struggle from which they came—and to provide them with a clear understanding of the examples set by leaders such as César, Dolores, Rigoberta Menchú, Corky Gonzales, Dr. King, and Malcolm. The school helps its students know not just who these people were, but also the magnitude of what they did and how they did it. The critical importance of the school's approach is that it goes beyond solely academic instruction to the teaching of applied principles and methods of social change. All students, fledgling activists, and agents of change need historical context for continuing the struggle for civil rights, but they also need the skills, tools and practical instruction. Nonviolence 101: Theory and Application should be a graduation requirement of the César Chávez School.

NONVIOLENCE AND SOCIAL CHANGE

It seems to me that the community peace movement—and particularly groups dealing with the gang culture, such as Barrios Unidos and Unity One in Los Angeles—could draw much wisdom from even more deliberate study of what went on before them. Most obvious is the powerful set of principles and strategies to emerge from civil rights and nonviolent social change. I believe that nonviolence is the answer. Learning how to apply the principles of nonviolence in a strategic, meaningful, and critical way can create the human space to collectively solve the social dilemmas of today. I would implore all young leaders and activists to verse themselves in the Gandhian principles of social change and the more modern applications of Dr. King and César Chávez. Nonviolence is the greatest gift to humanity by these great leaders.

By unleashing the power of nonviolence as an instrument to recreate society, today's community peace leaders can breathe new life into the various fronts of the broader social justice movement. As a matter of fact, if one was to take a quick survey of history, they would discover that nonviolence not only gave us voting rights, which for too long were denied to us as people of color, but also nonviolence brought an end to institutionalized apartheid, legal segregation, and systematic exclusion. It was the moral underpinnings and humanity of nonviolence that created the mass political will to achieve the change associated with *Brown v. Board of Education.* Even advances in women's rights, such as *Roe v. Wade,* can trace their achievement to the effects of nonviolent struggle. Until today's generation studies these historical examples and gains greater understanding of the power of nonviolent action, it will lack perhaps the greatest tool passed down from the past to create the world we all desire and deserve.

IMPORTANT LESSONS AND UNFINISHED BUSINESS

The successes of the civil rights movement centered on ending legal apartheid, segregation, exclusion, and sanctioned white privilege. It certainly created opportunities over time for the social, economic, and political advancement of many blacks, Latinos, and other poor people of color and women that had previously been denied. Many people including myself benefited from these hard-fought changes in America. But we must not forget that some forty-five years into the civil rights struggle, the prevalence of suffocating poverty and its attendant oppressions still defines daily existence for the majority of blacks, Latinos, Native Americans, and other forgotten inhabitants of this nation. The malady of poverty knows no boundaries when it comes to race, but we must be honest and acknowledge that it is concentrated more in some communities than in others. Clearly stated, the greatest war of the civil rights movement—ending poverty—still remains to be waged and won.

Dr. King, at the time of his assassination, had just begun to devise a clear agenda for the civil rights movement to end poverty in America. He recognized that the demands of economic change would require a radical reordering of economic structures and priorities in this country. It was his intent to bring attention to those living in the lowest experience in the human chain in America. He hoped to establish that it was morally wrong and counter to the principles of democracy to allow people to suffer the indignity and inhumanity of abject poverty. It was his aim to organize a critical mass of people across lines of race, class, and creed who believed there was no reason for, or reward in, sustaining and profiting from the poverty of others.

The "Poor People's Campaign" that King envisioned along with Phillip Randolph, the leadership of the SCLC, and a multiracial coalition of other national leaders, was to unveil a detailed social change agenda after a mass nonviolent demonstration modeled after the historic march on Washington, DC It had the potential to be the largest demonstration in the history of the protest movement. Sadly, when Dr. King went to Memphis, Tennessee, to support organizing efforts of local garbage workers—people hovering on the lower rungs of the economic ladder—he was senselessly killed. By this time there were specific plans, coalitions, and a leadership infrastructure that had been created to initiate the Poor People's Campaign. The second phase (the first phase being the end of legal apartheid and discrimination) of the civil rights movement fell into some disarray after Dr. King's death due to the absence of a voice with his moral authority on poverty or any other issue. Instead, we were left with a power vacuum, turf battles, infighting, and outright obstructionism. To make matters worse, the proximal assassinations of Malcolm X and Bobby Kennedy only amplified the movement's disarray and diffusion. In many ways the most pressing next phase priority of the movement—the poverty question—was abandoned.

The astute student of history will trace the resurgent bold agenda of the right-wing elements in the country to this time. Taking advantage of the loss of focused leadership and direction on the left, they began to organize extensively at the grassroots level within fundamentalist churches and took control of local institutions like the PTAs, school boards, and city councils, while setting up the regional and national political machinery to wage campaigns and elect policy makers to push back civil rights gains. Although there have been some progressive advances in legislation, public policy, and the courts to further civil rights, the groundswell of conservative backlash has mainly eaten away at these gains over the past thirty years. The steady erosion of social, economic, and political advances in civil rights has brought us to the point of crisis we find ourselves in today under the second coming of President George Bush and the prevailing conservative agenda.

GETTING THE MOVEMENT BACK ON TRACK

For the civil rights and progressive movement to get back on track, there will have to be renewed commitment to the kind of far-reaching vision, goals, and change agenda that will be necessary to end poverty. Leaders will have to show the kind of decisiveness and willingness to sacrifice that was demonstrated in the first phase of the movement. From the big picture to the simplest details, we need to do what conservatives have done and return to the community and put organizing back into the movement. There is no substitute for creating a groundswell of consciousness and commitment to the values and principles of civil rights. Sadly, for the movement to regain its fervor and dynamic force, we need to remove obstructionist leaders. Somewhere along the way, communities relinquished their voice of self-determination to social brokers and politicians. Too many leaders, elected or otherwise, come out of an exceedingly corrupt process that renders them mediocre and/or accommodationist. If poor communities want dramatic change, they need to stop looking to these types of leaders as strong, principled voices with their best interests at heart.

The community needs to retain leadership within itself, working collectively to nurture a dynamic, organic vision that sustains the broad participation of people in the decision-making process: the political and moral voice being a collective voice. It is this organic kind of leadership within a community that holds elected officials, government, and private institutions most accountable and responsive. Lifting up new leaders and promoting a collective brand of leadership within and across communities is thus critical to building momentum and restoring vibrancy to the movement. Until we lift up leaders who are informed, educated, and prepared to be rooted in the values, principles, methods, and vision of the movement, we will be mis-served and misrepresented. The movement needs leaders that have the guts, strength, and power of moral conviction to lead in the way the most effective leaders of the past have led.

The greatest opportunity to galvanize the movement still today is among the young; this has always been the case. The role of youth and students in the antiwar and civil rights movements is one of the greatest legacies of that bygone era. Were it not for young organizers in the antiwar efforts focused on Vietnam, there would have been far less accountability and attention to the issue. Today, it is up to the young to assume leadership and rise up against the war in Iraq, to rebel in a systematic way against the inadequacies and inaccessibility of education, to protest against mass incarceration and suppression, and to prepare themselves for a protracted and sophisticated nonviolent campaign to end poverty. Groups like Barrios Unidos need to prepare and organize a critical mass of organizers in the poorest communities of urban and rural America—anyplace where young ones and families live in misery. A new Poor People's Campaign, led by the young and the poor, may be the tonic to revive the movement. Poverty touches every walk of human life, creating the dysfunction and social upheaval that destabilizes the world for all. Poverty is everybody's business.

OTHER CIVIL RIGHTS PRIORITIES

It is an absolute imperative to reform the administration of justice in America. There is no greater priority than reforming the justice system from top to bottom, including the various departments of justice, attorney general offices, and youth and adult correctional systems at every level across the nation. In the aftermath of September 11, 2001, there is a dangerous and almost unbridled power vested in the federal Department of Justice (DOJ) through the Patriot Act and other executive branch edicts that have seriously diminished civil liberties and accountability to the public. The apparatus of checks and balances for protecting and preserving civil rights and civil liberties of the poor have all but been gutted.

The criminal and civil courts are failing to serve a higher good and the public interest, as intended in their creation. For instance, the criminal and juvenile justice systems have achieved levels of incarceration unprecedented in modern global civilization. The net effect of this mass incarceration has decimated poor black and Latino communities through what amounts in some communities to social, political, and economic genocide through the physical removal and disfranchisement of adults, young men, children, and women from family and civic life. Due to the draconian focus on punishment versus rehabilitation, individuals leave prisons or juvenile detention centers unredeemed, uneducated, unskilled, and often retrenched in the antisocial subculture mentality that led to their detrimental behaviors in the first place. The outcome is that these human beings are taken further from a future of meaningful connection to and participation in their families, communities, and society than when they started. Certainly a civilized nation rooted in the highest spiritual and democratic ideals can fashion a more humane, restorative, redemptive, and conciliatory approach to the administration of justice.

It is without doubt a tragedy of the times to see a critical intent and purpose of one of our greatest moral victories in civil rights, the court decision of *Brown v. Board of Education*, to go unfulfilled after fifty years of struggle. At a threshold level, every taxpayer in this country deserves the right to access a free and quality education. It is the right of every child to know how to read, write, and creatively ponder the highest quality curricula and instruction possible in this day and age. Instead, we are witness to the dismal failure of public education in serving the needs of poor African American and Latino children—a fact that is irrefutable given the data on academic performance, dropout, retention, and graduation rates, and enrollment in higher education programs. Education remains the most important determinant of social, economic, and political access and achievement. Educating our children is among our highest and most unequivocal responsibilities as a nation. It is not an unreasonable proposition to assert that the quality of education for the poorest among us is the key indicator as to the state of our democracy and civilization.

THE BARRIOS UNIDOS MOVEMENT

The most powerful statement that Barrios Unidos makes about itself is that it is a spiritual movement. This is important because we can look upon history and see that the most significant movements—for better or worse—have been motivated, at least in theory, by spirituality or religion. In effect, Barrios Unidos follows in the positive spiritual traditions of Gandhi, Dr. King, César, and Malcolm following his pilgrimage to Mecca. Its tenets also mirror the deep spiritual inclinations of each of these leaders' indigenous ancestors and relations. Barrios Unidos offers a way to remake oneself, to reconcile, and to create and re-create community. The only way for a community to talk to itself is to come together with a sense of higher purpose and human healing; this is where people find a deeper appreciation of their human mind, heart, and soul—where commonality and shared humanity is found. Standing together in such a space, people can focus on the kind of humanity they desire to experience, a place where they can begin to imagine and in fact create the kind of world they desire.

This kind of spirituality engenders the creation and positive exchange of a universal framework of principles upon which respectful relationships and community are forged. The cornerstone tenet is to treat others as you would like to be treated. Spirituality is also there to incite positive and constructive action against the objective realities of injustice and poverty. When people understand and practice the higher tenets of most spiritual traditions, there is invariably a connection or relationship between spirituality and activism. True spirituality is neither a debilitating opiate nor a license to impose one's will on others. It does, however, provide each person with a moral base upon which to act toward the change of unjust, inhumane social circumstances that diminish life, such as poverty, exploitation, racism, discrimination, violence, and all forms of human oppression.

When I look at Barrios Unidos I am glad that the organization saves young people by giving them back their culture, providing essential knowledge, discovery of identity, a sense of purpose, and the wherewithal to resist the deadly lure of gangs and destructive violence. The question for Barrios Unidos as an organization and movement is whether it has reached the threshold where it is building off decades of changing lives to take this work to the next level. The next level I'm talking about requires that Barrios Unidos leaders set social objectives for the movement and community to help create more tangible change. These objectives need to be focused on achieving some identifiable benchmarks that Barrios Unidos constituents can organize around and work to bring about. For example, within their immediate realm of influence, Barrios Unidos leaders can set social objectives related to reforms in juvenile and criminal justice, or make change in ineffectual public schools in the communities they serve, or advance some of their economic development initiatives to create job or entrepreneurial opportunities that foster self-reliance.

Similarly, these leaders must be a steadfast voice of conscience against injustice, such as police abuse, discriminatory law enforcement practices like racial profiling, and gang injunctions that brand and criminalize youth and entire communities. They must exercise their leadership in promoting comprehensive solutions to gangs beyond suppression, mass incarceration, and unchecked demonization by public institutions and media pundits. Our young have been transformed from human beings who can be reclaimed and restored to subhuman social pariahs that are readily discarded as refuse. In our day, we picked our battles, such as the bus boycott in Montgomery. It certainly wasn't the most pressing issue on our plate, but we picked one objective, focused, and won to demonstrate the power of nonviolence. A simple act of nonviolent civil disobedience made a profound statement on the power of our movement and provided a building block for future resolve. Achieving social objectives on our overall platform for change brought a validity and resolve that grew with each victory. This is what Barrios Unidos needs to do: establish clear social objectives around which its various areas of work can be more concretely organized, thereby establishing itself as an even more catalytic force for change.

CLOSING THOUGHTS

There is a T-shirt that Barrios Unidos produces that is one of the best I have ever seen. It is the classic beautiful picture of Che Guevarra wearing his beret and underneath is written the caption, *"We Are Not A Minority!"* This is exactly what Barrios Unidos teaches and needs to continue to impress on its constituency: namely, that they are in fact not a minority. Getting rid of that minority mentality is critical to people of color in America. If you are poor, you are not a minority! If you are Latino, you are not a minority! If you are a woman, you are not a minority! If you are in prison, you are not a minority! We need to stop calling ourselves what our oppressor calls us. We need to understand as people of color that we are whole human beings and that collectively we have power and that we must begin to exercise and apply that power. We need to harness the power of cultural identity, purpose, spirituality, new belonging, connectedness, and collective activism to create change. Barrios Unidos has shown a commitment to working in this way.

The story and example of Barrios Unidos is an inspiration to everyone in the movement, but the organization is just hitting its stride. I implore Barrios Unidos to reach even farther and do all in its power to make its promising plans and initiatives a reality, including the development of my proposed platform of social objectives that can contribute to the entire movement. Everyone is watching, especially the naysayers out there, to see if Barrios Unidos can continue to live up to its ideals. In this book, BU leaders are putting forward a set of bold and exciting initiatives to advance economic justice and self-reliance through the principles of the César Chávez Peace Plan and the first Barrio Enterprise Zone. The institute model aspired to by the organization hopes to educate, prepare, and mobilize an army of peace warriors as principled leaders in the community peace movement. It will be up to its leaders to connect the vision of Barrios Unidos to what is taking place elsewhere in the nation and internationally, to advance self-determination and human rights. I believe they will.

When I think of Nane Alejándrez, Otilio Quintero, and all the others at Barrios Unidos, I know we come from the same kind of hope; we come from the same kind of love and the same kind of desire for a better world and nation. We need now to support one another and hold each other accountable, to be in step with the heart and aspirations of our communities. We need to uphold the values of the movement, walking together to fulfill the dream.

Tom Hayden

Tom Hayden is a social and political activist and writer. He is widely recognized as one of the most steadfast voices of the progressive movement in America today. Hayden came into the national spotlight as a student activist opposing the war in Vietnam and supporting the cause of civil rights in the 1960s. Of Irish American descent, Hayden was born in Detroit, Michigan. He later attended the University of Michigan, where he cofounded the activist group Students for a Democratic Society (popularly known as SDS). Between 1964 and 1968, he lived in Newark, New Jersey, where he worked with impoverished inner-city residents as part of the Newark Community Union Project. After witnessing the city's race riot in 1967, Hayden wrote the book entitled, *Rebellion in Newark: Official Violence and Ghetto Response.* He also played a lead organizing role in the demonstrations at the 1968 Democratic National Convention in Chicago, Illinois, where he was arrested and tried as one of the "Chicago Seven." During the early 1970s, Hayden made several high-profile and controversial visits as a peace activist to Cambodia and North Vietnam. Over the course of more than forty years of activism, Hayden has remained a compassionate and provocative voice for peace, justice, and equality in America and abroad. He was elected to the California Assembly in 1982 and the California Senate in 1992, serving seven consecutive terms in office. During his tenure, Hayden was recognized as an unwavering liberal leader on policy issues concerning women, African Americans, Latinos, Holocaust survivors, immigrants, refugees, the poor, and youth. He is a prolific writer, having authored nine books including his two most recent: *Rebel: A Personal History of the 1960s* and *Street Wars: Gangs and the Future of Violence.* Hayden remains an active friend and partner to hundreds of youth and grassroots leaders and community organizations involved in community-centered initiatives to prevent violence, mass incarceration, and the criminalization of minority youth.

In the early turmoil of the 1960s, I think I was just a young man looking for or trying to live up to a set of American values that I thought were being betrayed. Over that decade, the identity of being an Irish American, of being white, of being male—all these identities were being challenged very effectively, which left me searching. I believe this process of people seeking identity both of self and in relation to everyone else in multiracial, multicultural America remains very important. The civil rights movement was a powerful catalyst for getting people to grapple with democracy in terms of power and oppression in relation to race and injustice. For people of color, searching was a process of revolt, reconciliation, rediscovery, reaffirmation, and reclaiming.

Sadly, what could have been an era of radical reform of everything that was wrong with this country turned out in some ways to be a failure. By the mid-1970s, the Chicano and black nationalist movements were blocked, their character morphed into the issues of crime and "law and order" by forces of conservative backlash. This spin was the foundation of Richard Nixon's War on Crime. I think everybody fell for this notion except for those with no choice but to survive—those people that came out of the war zones of poverty in the barrios and ghettos. For people like Nane Alejándrez, it was not a case of criminality but of survival and redemption: these were individuals who found victory over oppression and injustice in ways that others did not.

In some respects Barrios Unidos grew out of what the civil rights movement left behind and those needs were too deep to address. I can remember important leaders like Magdaleno Rose Avila, later of Homies Unidos, who remains an important voice in the community peace movement to end gang violence today, cutting her political teeth as a hard-core Chicano nationalist under the tutelage of the late Corky Gonzales. On the African American side, you had the product of the Nation of Islam, Malcolm X, who took on the symbol of X as an expression of self-determination. The taking of his name was a powerful metaphor for reclaiming his identity and rejecting that he had to become separated from his African heritage.

The issue of coming to terms with identity is important for white people in this country as well. I think it is essential for white people to abandon the idea of whiteness, but not for them to think that out of some sense of guilt or loss of self they can become pseudo-black or pseudo-Latino, which you see a lot in hip-hop culture. If you break the search down to national origin, culture, ethnicity, and even the class of one's descendents for the dominant white groups—English, Irish, Italian, Jewish, and German—there are some significant traditions of heritage, settlement, and organizing that should not be lost. I think an honest recollection of groups like the Molly Maguires, who were immigrant Irish workers in the coalfields, is important in America. For ethnic whites, assimilation came to mean accepting the white Anglo-Saxon Protestant package. This sometimes means being ashamed and reprogrammed to the point of absolutely forgetting that your ancestors got here on a boat, had their rebel sensibilities swallowed in racism and expansionism, or may have committed gangland crimes to stake their place on the social and economic ladder.

The bridge to the respectability, legitimacy, and privilege of middle- and upper-class status too often taken by white Americans is selective amnesia or innocence by disassociation. They don't want to embrace their gangster past except while watching the movies. But the responsibility to own the history of one's people is something we all inherit. Looking back on the anxieties of my parents in gaining this class status, I understand this now to have been their shame of our poor Irish past. Assimilation of this kind is damaging. It's a way of cleansing and absolving conscience, of wiping the slate of history clean.

The reclaiming of identity that Barrios Unidos is based on, to me, is a healthy application of culture. The cultural cure that Barrios Unidos speaks of could be extended to non-Chicanos. This reclaiming of culture by non-Chicano, nonindigenous people would be good medicine for everyone, white people and others. The focus on healing and reconciliation with regard to history, the present, and the future would be good for the nation as a whole. It is amazing to me how threatened people are by multiculturalism, because demographically we are a multicultural nation. In principle, we are a pluralistic democracy (*E Pluribus Unum*). It was never realistic to force everyone to adopt one cultural standard and perspective. Commentators sited in this book and elsewhere have likened the requirement of conquest as being the destruction of indigenous and Mexican identity, resulting in the creation of *cholos*. These *cholos* or "lost boys" were being educated by a colonizing force to adopt a new identity that they really could not. This in turn partially explains the formation of alternative life ways or subcultures, such as gangs, along with their structural economic exclusion.

LESSONS OF THE CIVIL RIGHTS MOVEMENT

The student movement of the 1960s helped to end the legal segregation that controlled the destiny of over 25 million people in the South. Had Vietnam not come along, the combination of civil rights and the War on Poverty might have become a broader revolution. The antiwar effort split the focus of student activists. In this regard, I often question whether it was an accident that the country went to war. Some say war is the health of the state, the way it manages its domestic conflicts. I've heard it said that there's nothing like a war to clean out those barrios and ghettos and get those folks into the Army. In wartime periods the powers that be can then claim they have no money for social programs to create jobs, affordable housing, education programs, and healthcare. War creates a pretext to take the energy and focus away from domestic problems and conflicts.

It is moving to me that Nane Alejándrez was drafted in 1968, the year of my own crisis—a very bad time to be sent to war. I deeply admire Nane's own path to overcome the struggles of the barrio, compounded by the trauma of war, addiction, and resettlement in a domestic war zone upon his return. There were thousands of poor young men from the barrios and ghettos of America who survived the ravages of war only to return home and be swallowed up in the dire circumstances of their chronically neglected communities. This is a microcosm for what happened to the movement because of the war. The movement was stalled because Vietnam sapped all the energy, idealism, and public resources that would otherwise have gone to waging a domestic war on poverty. The stalling of the movement and the unchanged circumstances in America's impoverished barrios and ghettos set the stage for gangs to flourish. Whatever glimmer of hope that was created in these communities for long-term advancement by the civil rights movement was dashed.

Civil rights did have tangible benefits for a fortunate few—a finite strand of African Americans, Latinos, Asian Pacific Islanders, Native Americans, and women. There was some growth of the middle class. It was like the movement created a few slots for those that fit the traditional mold of American advancement. For the most part, though, young brothers and sisters of color in the poorest communities were left only with aspirations that were ultimately frustrated by the lack of structural change socially, economically, and politically in this country.

I remember talking to a Black Panther by the name of Kumatsi who was reflecting on the advancement of Julian Bond, someone he greatly respected and admired. Kumatsi thought that in some ways the advancement of the Bonds of the world was in a way more frustrating because it shut the gate for people like him. Bond was educated at a top university, fair skinned, and an articulate orator. He comfortably fit the mold acceptable for advancement. Kumatsi did not blame people like Julian Bond for this, but he knew that these were the prototype individuals who would be the success stories for civil rights, leaving nothing for the more representative prototype of the ghetto. This similar phenomenon played itself out in barrios and ghettos across America and was almost a perverse consequence of the civil rights movement.

The civil rights movement created consciousness and aspiration for the underclass in these communities but provided no real bridge to cross into the working class or middle class. Certainly, civil rights did not solve the class issues in this country. Some will say this is due to the ongoing presence of racism and discrimination. The equation of race cannot be ignored. Many ethnic whites were lifted up into the middle class during the expansionist periods between 1890 and the 1930s, thus providing working-class alternatives for a generation of white ethnic gang members. Many more whites ascended between the 1930s and the economic boom following the Second World War. The question is whether a similar set of circumstances will occur to lift up poor blacks and Latinos.

ADVANCEMENTS IN RIGHTS, RACE, AND PRIVILEGE IN MULTICULTURAL AMERICA

The elimination of legalized racism in America is the greatest accomplishment of the civil rights movement, without question. The victory has many outgrowths essential to the extension of civil liberties to nonwhites. The right to organize, including the right to organize unions, at least in theory, came with legal protections that did not previously exist for people of color. There was also the creation of a foothold for the advancement of women through affirmative action, along with attendant new protections against discrimination.

The legal mechanisms that were achieved established some important platforms for advancement. Although Republicans have effectively whittled down the once broad and promising spectrum of affirmative action, legal protections against discrimination as well as equal opportunity provisions in employment and business have all had a positive impact. All of the legal protections that allowed people to go to court, to achieve a handle in the system to protect the rights of poor people, were significant achievements. These protections and legal remedies did not exist prior to the civil rights movement. Important historians, like my friend Howard Zinn, may go too far in minimizing the impact of these reforms and saying the overall system of privilege was preserved. These criticisms have some validity because many reforms fell short of what was envisioned while others have been repealed. Regardless, I believe that the legal reforms, empowerment reforms, and enfranchisement reforms of the twentieth century were significant accomplishments that came at great expense and sacrifice.

I would also add as a critically important advancement the expanded opportunity and content of high school and university curricula. It is absolutely valid to remain dissatisfied with the existing inaccessibility and unaffordability of higher education. At the same time, the hundreds of thousands of students that have attended American colleges and universities in recent decades have been more even-

handedly educated than my generation was. Access to books by progressive scholars and social commentators, such as Howard Zinn,
Luis Rodríguez, and Malcolm X, were once only available on the
streets. Access to books like this in the classroom has offered access
to fresh knowledge and perspectives that could fuel political awakening, activism, and reform. For instance, when I was going through my
own process of discovery and meltdown at the end of the 1960s, I read
Dee Brown's *Bury My Heart at Wounded Knee*, a simple and straightforward account of the Indian massacres. The book reminded me of
what I witnessed in Vietnam. Being faced with such an honest account
of history was a transformative process for me. Books like these were
typically not written and published prior to the sixties. In the last quarter century, the door has been opened for the writing of books that
have torn the lid off of hidden, distorted, and unspoken realities in
American history.

There is now a backlash by conservative elements in this country
to rid the public dialog of "political correctness." This term to me is
simply making the conscious effort to get history straight. A country
that doesn't get its history straight doesn't have a future. For instance,
the idea that has been spoon-fed to us that this country is God's gift to
the earth or that the pilgrims were on a religious journey to regener-
ate the world anew—these ideas are now so dead on arrival in our
schools that it threatens the very foundations of white privilege. To
date, there has been no truly honest accounting of history in America
that adequately explains slavery, racial segregation and exclusion, the
near annihilation of native populations, annexation of ancestral lands,
neo-colonialism of foreign lands and populations, and the intractable
disparity of poverty and privilege along lines of race. The moral dismantling of the fairy-tale version of American history upon which the
institutions and structures of privilege are based is a vital outcome of
the civil rights era. What remains as a national imperative is unfold-
ing a process of public dialog and learning that provides an honest
treatment and accounting of history so we can reconcile as a people
and move forward.

PRIORITIES FOR CONTEMPORARY CIVIL RIGHTS

There are three continuing fronts for the civil rights movement that deserve much more expansive discussion than we have space for here. These deal generally with addressing seismic shifts in the U.S. population base, sweeping workforce transformations, and dangerous educational trends. The first matter requires a fundamental commitment to deepening multiculturalism, especially in classrooms and the media. Taking this country and its institutions toward a true multicultural identity is a growing national imperative. More than ever in our modern history, pluralism is an essential requirement for American society and democracy. Large shifts in the U.S. economic base implicating more and more foreign-born workers (many of them undocumented) and the outsourcing of many jobs overseas pose another key concern for the movement. Labor reform must be part of a larger agenda of structural economic change if America is to achieve greater equity in the years ahead. Such change is important so that working-class African Americans, Latinos, and immigrants in particular, as well as poor whites, can be elevated to a living wage or middle-class wage. Finally, in order to bolster the educational opportunities of increasingly disadvantaged youth in our public schools, movement leaders need to secure state-of-the-art resources, facilities, curricula, and instruction from preschool to twelfth grade. In addition, we need to link these educational investments to affordable higher education opportunities for any young person that wants to attend a college or university.

Beyond these clear priority concerns, a major new civil rights imperative that has emerged in recent years is the need to initiate a comprehensive reform of U.S. law enforcement, adult and youth correctional, and justice systems. Rather than focusing on rehabilitation and reconciliation, the punitive approach now in vogue just makes the crime and violence problem worse by hardening the hardcore and devastating entire black and brown communities. Through disenfranchisement and mass incarceration, a large cross section of these communities is disempowered to play any meaningful role in the social, economic, and political life of the nation.

ADVANCING THE COMMUNITY PEACE MOVEMENT

The evolution of the community peace movement (and related fields such as violence prevention) provides a great strategic breakthrough for countering the devastation of law and order policies. Rather than responding to the root causes of violence and crime, the shortsighted responses popular in America today offer mostly suppression, social controls, and mass incarceration as solutions. The field of violence prevention has provided a more holistic way to balance the immediate concerns of public safety with the longer-term requirements of creating healthy people and healthy communities through social change. This is important because liberals tend to link crime to poverty and economics. Conservatives counter that ending poverty is a long-term proposition at best and safety is an immediate concern, thereby justifying policies of mass incarceration and suppression. The spectrum of prevention (e.g., early prevention, prevention, intervention, rehabilitation and reentry) has offered a bridge by providing both a science-based and a more humane approach to treating violence as a condition that can be healed. The public health community framework for violence prevention provides civil rights advocates an alternative language that can be utilized and promoted across political spectrums.

Barrios Unidos stands at the intersection of the peace and justice movement in America. It represents an essential voice among social justice leaders within the United States, addressing the war occurring on our streets while working directly with the people who have been left behind, notwithstanding the lingering historical gains of the civil rights era. As an organization and a movement, Barrios Unidos is saying two things that people in marginalized American communities want and need to hear: first, that the civil rights movement needs to account for those left behind, particularly poor families, imperiled youth, and incarcerated brothers and sisters; and, second, that it is imperative to end the unacceptable levels of violence and death among youth in communities, schools, and homes across our nation. America needs to be awakened to the reality that violence is not just manifest in Iraq, Columbia, South Africa, and Afghanistan—the distant shores of other lands. The devastation of violence is deeply present in the communities of our nation. It is not inconceivable to project that as many American lives will be lost in the inner cities of California during the coming year as in the war in Iraq.

The voices of leaders like Nane Alejándrez, Alex Sánchez, and Luis J. Rodríguez bring a new face of humanity and possibilities for transformation that most of America never see or hear. These are the voices of former gang members, addicts, juvenile offenders, prisoners, homeboys, and homegirls. Introducing America to the voices of poor, former gang members and ex-prisoners who have changed their lives with the right resources and support systems is important. Accepting these voices, the voices of the lost boys and the forgotten, as legitimate guides to community transformation is so vital to advancing the movement. What seems to trip up even the most compassionate liberals, moderates, and conservatives seeking honest solutions to crime or violence is the issue of individual responsibility and accountability. Barrios Unidos has stepped up and said that there are pathologies that lead to antisocial and destructive behaviors, but let's then also address the roots of these pathologies in the vestiges of poverty, broken community cohesion, cultural alienation and dislocation, and the trauma of extended exposure to violence with no economic on-ramps to the middle class.

CONCLUSIONS

Barrios Unidos is a leader in the community peace movement and an important constituency-based participant and catalyst to further civil rights. There is power in the fact that Barrios works across generations and is able to mobilize youth (12 to 24 years old), young adults (25 to 30 years old), adults (31 to 65 years old), and "elders" (those over 65). The participation of an intergenerational constituency is important for the revitalization of the struggle. Once young people "graduate" and move on to the workaday demands of professional life and parenting, their involvement in progressive youth groups or activism is too often discontinued. Reaching back to reenergize and mobilize this group will be important to mounting a protracted campaign against poverty.

I hope that this book incites discussion and sheds new light on the history that has affected the lives of so many in the barrios of this country, that homeboys and homegirls can see themselves in the hope and transformation of the community peace movement. On the practical side, owing to the richness of Barrios Unidos's organizational model, change theories, and work in multiple communities, I hope the book offers some critical self-analysis that people and communities can learn from and model. For example, I know from firsthand experience that there have been some real challenges in establishing and sustaining affiliate chapters in different communities. Why is this so and what are the lessons? What can the Barrios Unidos experience offer to efforts seeking to develop movement organizations in multiple communities? The story is so compelling and powerful, but should not be taken in or portrayed as a fairy tale. There is often more to be learned from our challenges and missteps than our successes in the movement.

Barrios Unidos has shown the capacity to spread its vision to other leaders who embrace their message. It has nurtured, educated, and prepared many peacemakers. Barrios Unidos offers a creative spark, new insights into community-building, and a contagious energy that can awaken and prepare a new mass of activists for the movement. The organization has a vision in its name and a concept that can be helpful to communities across the country. Its story offers instruction in the lessons and methods of advancing peace and justice. In many ways the real story is not contained in the pages of this book but in the thousands of lives Barrios Unidos has touched. Although the organization has been around for twenty-seven years, its story and legacy as an agent of social change is still in the making.

Constance "Connie" Rice

Connie Rice is an attorney and cofounder of the Advancement Project. She is one of the most widely recognized contemporary civil rights lawyers and progressive voices in the country. Born into a then-all-too-rare, middle-class African American household, Rice was driven to excel in her education and professional pursuits by her family as a way of contributing to her community and society. She fondly remembers her grandmother checking her report cards and telling her, "I may not know how to read and write, but I know what an A grade looks like." Formerly the West Coast Regional Legal Director of the NAACP Legal Defense and Education Fund, Rice has litigated major cases involving the preservation and advancement of civil rights protections. Through litigation, policy advocacy, and principled leadership in multiracial coalitions, she has helped to advance progressive and community-centered campaigns designed to improve police accountability, public transportation access, and juvenile justice. The Advancement Project works with communities to build a just multiracial democracy through the strategic use of law, policy advocacy, and strategic communications. Through its Community Justice Resource Center, the Project provides resources to activists, attorneys, and community organizers involved in racial and social justice initiatives. Since 1992, Rice has been a supporter and advocate of the cross-color gang truce and urban peace movement in Los Angeles and across the nation, working with Barrios Unidos, Unity One, Amer-I-Can, and several other violence prevention initiatives. In 2002, she collaborated with Harry Belafonte, Catholic Cardinal Rodger Mahoney, Los Angeles County Sheriff Lee Baca, and others to establish the Urban Peace Prize, a prestigious award presented to distinguished individuals and groups whose efforts are dedicated to ending violence, reclaiming personal responsibility, and restoring community.

I am honored to be a part of the support base for the work of Barrios Unidos. The work that Barrios Unidos does on the ground and the leadership it provides in the community peace movement is critically important. My role in advancing the movement has been that of a classically trained civil rights lawyer. I was born and raised into what I call the middle-class "B.U.P.P.Y.," or black urban professional, experience. By the time I entered the civil rights arena, all the dragons of segregation, such as Jim Crow and the *Brown v. Board of Education* decision, had been slain. The first phase of civil rights ended legal apartheid and the second phase was to have been dedicated to ending poverty. Yet, by the time I entered the struggle, everything in the movement became a shade of gray as most of my contemporaries and I worked mostly on preserving affirmative action, antidiscrimination, and equal protection through the big stick of litigation.

In my own awakening as an activist, I had an epiphany of sorts. Despite all of the important work those in the legal arm of the movement where doing to protect the gains of civil rights, there remained an entire third world residing in many cities and rural areas across the country. Some forty years after the Civil Rights Act, there is still a whole sector of the American scene that dwells in poverty, as destitute and endangered as people in many underdeveloped nations. It dawned on me that focusing on affirmative action, preserving contracting quotas and college admission numbers, was like concerning ourselves with the bug in the sink when there was a velociraptor in the shower, the raptor being the impoverishment that places people in real peril. The ghettos and barrios of today resemble third-world war zones that Thurgood Marshall wouldn't recognize.

Looking at things from a historical perspective, the assassinations of Dr. Martin Luther King, Jr. and Malcolm X robbed the civil rights movement of two sources of great inspiration, vision, and moral leadership. In their absence, competing agendas and jockeying for influence diffused the civil rights movement all over the map, missing what should have been the biggest issue of the day: namely, what was happening to the underclass. At the time of his death, Dr. King had turned his attention to fashioning an aggressive war on poverty: the Poor People's Campaign. Unlike the campaign to end apartheid in America that had enlisted the leadership of the middle class as advocates for change, the focus of this new campaign was to mobilize the lower ranks of the economic ladder. Dr. King envisioned a massive grass-roots effort that would give voice to those at the bottom of the economic well, such as the working poor that today continue to hang on by a thread.

I liken the effect of civil rights to a donut phenomenon. By this I mean that many of the gains of civil rights helped to lift some poor African Americans, Latinos, and women into the middle class—the body of the donut representing these substantive advances by some. However, the vast majority of poor people of color were left in the donut hole where there is nothing. In this void there is no village, only the miseries and social dysfunctions of daily poverty for families and children. Instead of focusing on the movement requirements of creating the kind of social change necessary to end poverty, we have centered on litigation to protect our gains. Having won the battle of legal apartheid in America, litigation seemed to lose its attachment to the movement. When you concentrate on litigation instead of the movement equation of realizing larger-scale social change, you are bound to lose energy and power.

In waking out of my own middle-class slumber, I realized that the most vibrant third rail for civil rights was picking up where Dr. King had left off. We are missing the boat by not placing our focused efforts on ending poverty, the effects of which are literally wiping out people in these forgotten communities. For instance, the alternative underground economy of cocaine and other illegal drugs is devastating many barrios and ghettos. There is close to 75 percent incarceration among African Americans in some Los Angeles public housing projects. That is annihilation! Numbers are 50 to 60 percent for Latinos in housing projects like Ramona Gardens. Families are losing an entire generation and community of men to incarceration related to drugs, gang association, and street violence. Even a ferocious feminist like me knows that if you take the men out of the community, the community dies. Going back to my epiphany, I came to realize that I could worry about middle-class discrimination and sex discrimination later.

There was annihilation taking place in the poorest communities I cared about; annihilation is more deadly than discrimination.

The sector of people with which Barrios Unidos and Unity One work come from the economic underclass. These are children, youth, and adults who face the most devastating manifestations of poverty. Unfortunately, the pitfalls of poverty are magnified when you introduce the drug economy. This economy is thriving in both poor urban and rural settings. Too many poor African Americans, Latinos, and whites who are unable to earn a living wage turn to the drug economy for survival, despite facing the prospect of serious consequences. For people who live outside the vice grip of poverty, it is difficult to fathom the daily sufferings of living at or below subsistence levels, where the only prospects of changing your station are downwardly linked to a life in prison. Most people in this situation choose to live honestly and with dignity, scratching out a living as best they can. Others, who surrender to desperation, frustration, hopelessness, and perhaps even rebellion, grab the poison golden egg. It is tragic that in the poorest communities of America the options are so few and the circumstances so dire that good people are left to see selling drugs—despite the inevitable prospect of prison—as their only way to attain a better life.

Sometimes it seems that America has given up on ending poverty. Most poor people still do not have a legitimate way of getting to the American table. It is this forgotten sector that needs to be the primary target of contemporary civil rights. Groups like Barrios Unidos that do work in this sector—addressing the hard-core manifestations of poverty such as gangs, community violence, broken homes, drug economy and addiction, unemployment, and offender reentry—are essential to revitalizing the movement. By providing programs that promote education and skills development, civic leadership, economic self-reliance, family preservation, restorative justice, and community-building, these kinds of organizations represent the front line in the battle. Such groups are in the best position to prepare and mobilize those most affected by poverty and pick up where the Poor People's Campaign left us.

It is important to understand that those who promote community peace, gang alternatives, and violence prevention do not usually or automatically contextualize their work as part of the ongoing struggle for civil rights. Many have come to embrace the values of the struggle, such as nonviolence, but didn't go to a Gandhian course or study the work of César Chávez to get there. The various fronts traditionally associated with civil rights are not always the immediate driving force for community peace workers. They come to this intersection organically from their experience on the streets and the conditions in their communities. Typically, this occurs over time as they expand their work to address the root causes of violence. The commitment and identification of such leaders relative to civil rights comes directly from working at ground zero of the struggle.

NONVIOLENCE AND THE COMMUNITY PEACE MOVEMENT

In examining the legacy of civil rights, we can start with the abolitionist movement, which at its core was about human rights. We have to deduce that the abolitionist movement didn't work, because we needed a civil war to end slavery. Post-slavery efforts to end segregation and second-class citizenship moved toward a nonviolent transformational model. The beauty of the civil rights movement was that it was a "velvet revolution." We must never forget that there were people who died in the struggle, but it wasn't a conventional war where thousands died in armed conflict. The application of nonviolence by Gandhi, Dr. King, and César Chávez is the greatest gift to humanity in the twentieth century. We have since witnessed the power of nonviolence used by Nelson Mandela in South Africa and liberation movements around the world. The philosophy of nonviolent revolution prevented a second civil war in America to end segregation. In a contemporary context, leaders and organizers in the community peace movement, such as Barrios Unidos, have come to embrace this tool more and more.

What amazed me about the gang truce that took root in the community of Watts in Los Angeles after the civil unrest in 1992 was that organizers came to nonviolence organically. These gang leaders and organizers weren't versed in the philosophies and tactics of Dr. King, but knew that violence had to be taken out of the equation to change the circumstances in their lives and in their communities. Prior to the civil unrest, the mayhem of gang and community violence that defined daily experience on the streets left no space for organizers of the truce to gain traction. The street wars in Los Angeles during this time had begun to claim lives at unprecedented levels. The violence-riddled Jordan Downs housing complex and other public housing projects resembled war zones. There were ten to fourteen deaths on an average weekend in these communities with children sleeping in bath-tubs, closets, and on the floors to avoid stray bullets. These wartime survival practices had become accepted realities of daily life.

Some skeptics of the truce movement claimed that its real moti-vation was to end the anarchy of escalating violence that was hurting the drug trade. Honest reflection might verify this motivation for some who came to the table, but the bottom line for most participants was that too many fathers, children, and innocents were dying. Fathers, sons, brothers, uncles, and entire families were being swal-lowed up by deadly violence. Regardless of the motivation, bringing a stop to the violence required the embrace of nonviolent organizing to achieve the desired truce. The truce leaders were looking for peace treaty models when they approached me for assistance. They asked for a copy of the peace treaty between Arabs and Jews in the Middle East (i.e., the Sinai Egyptian Israeli Peace Accords), claiming that "if they can do it, so can we." At this point they weren't so much interested in civil rights issues as in achieving a ceasefire. What they ended up learning through this process was that any basis for lasting peace required them to adopt and promote life-affirming values whose broad application could change the realities of their communities. A contingent of those involved in the truce movement came to realize that becoming peacemakers required their involvement in social change. It is this contingent that I continued to work with for over ten years.

THE STATE OF CIVIL RIGHTS

The form and face of the movement has changed over the forty years since the mid-1960s to the present. Whereas activism at the hey-day of the movement was on the ground, it steadily moved toward institutionalization in subsequent years. The emergent groups and organizations for support of the movement became intermediaries over time, brokers between the community and the sources of social, political, and economic power. These were groups like the Crusade for Justice, the SCLC, and the National Council of La Raza. Litigation organizations, such as the NAACP Legal Defense and Education Fund, the Mexican American Legal Defense and Educational Fund (MALDEF), and the Asian Pacific American Legal Center (APALC) became protectors of hard-fought gains rather than aggressive advocates of movement advancement. Sometime after the moral conscience and organizing orientation of Dr. King, Malcolm X, and César Chávez left us, organizational leaders from public interest groups and nonprofits became the voices of civil rights, followed in turn by elected officials playing this role. I trace the drainage of life and vibrancy of the movement to this evolution.

I see the movement as presently being exhausted. The vision is not sufficiently radical or far-reaching to address what I believe to be the twenty-first-century agenda. The social-change agenda of today will need to be revolutionary if we hope to end extreme poverty in our generation. After ending domestic apartheid in its first iteration, the second phase of the civil rights movement in many ways got aborted. I paraphrase Dr. King who once said that "agreeing to end brutality is not the same as achieving brotherhood, any more than agreeing to end segregation was not the same as achieving equality." In an essay penned before he died, Dr. King spoke of the second phase of the civil rights revolution being the realization of equality, not just pledging allegiance to the concept of equality. The essay challenged us to strive for a higher standard of justice and fairness, bringing an end to legalized white privilege. He knew that achieving such a true standard of equality and justice would require a radical reconfiguration of the American political and economic systems. The concepts and imperatives set forth by Dr. King in these parting words set the framework for what remains to be done in civil rights today.

Achieving equality does not necessarily mean ending capitalism. But it will require completely redesigning the machinery that distributes educational, economic, and other essential resources and opportunities. This means rebuilding the staircase to upward mobility. If we are going to get poor blacks, Latinos, Native Americans, whites, and other low-income people to the American table, a grassroots groundswell must be created within and across these communities. What really happened to the civil rights movement that we haven't owned up to is that those of us who benefited settled for just a few being let into the room to sit at the table. What remains sadly true still today is that the bottom third of black and Latino America languishes in the darkness of poverty. The civil rights agenda of the past two decades has been woefully insufficient to address the problem, partly on account of having lost its focus on the poor. I venture to say that if Dr. King were alive today, he wouldn't be at social fund-raisers, hanging out with celebrities, or chumming around with the Congressional Black Caucus. He would be side by side organizing with those that the movement has left behind. This is the mandate and future of human and civil rights work.

THE COMMUNITY PEACE MOVEMENT—GROUND ZERO

We have allowed poor communities by our collective neglect to descend into such a level of deprivation that the situation may be reaching a point of no return for some. National disregard for poor families and especially of our youth has allowed harmful pathologies to sink deep roots. I see the activists in groups like Barrios Unidos, Unity One, and Common Ground, who were once part of the pathological gang or street culture but who have since transformed their lives, as important bridges back to health for those they serve. These leaders recognized that the violent gang or street culture was leading them toward death and destruction. They learned new ways (or recaptured old ways) of living, and now they are trying to reclaim and restore those in need around them. Such leaders have used the true expressions of culture to teach healthy manhood and womanhood, as well as family and community responsibility; reclaiming and preparing young men and women to be forces of construction and not destruction.

One of the unique roles of Barrios Unidos is that it works effectively with an element of the community that needs to be constructively dismantled, that is, the culture of destruction and violence embedded in gangs and the code of the streets. The faux cultural codes of community, sexist gender roles, belonging, honor, respect, and loyalty that guides the gang culture—and glorifies violence—all need to be changed from within the community itself. Those who have lived by these codes and accords, people who understand them and have chosen a new way, are the ones with the moral authority and credibility to change them. Barrios Unidos starts with the personal and individual transformation of its own people. Replacing false culture with the life-affirming values of their Latino and indigenous heritage, Barrios Unidos provides a scarce path for young people caught up in the madness to transform themselves with the love and support of people who understand their experience. The young folks see themselves in Nane Alejándrez, O.T. Quintero, and the other organizers, teachers, counselors, and peer leaders that comprise the Barrios Unidos leadership circle.

Barrios Unidos represents a community transformation model that is organic to and that emerges from the experience of the people they serve. By introducing young people to their true identity, self-worth, humanity, and purpose, Barrios Unidos creates a bridge back to their rightful place in family, community, and society. The constructive dismantling of the culture of destruction that has taken root in poor black and Latino communities is essential to mounting any social revolution within those communities. It is easy to suppress people who don't love or respect themselves because they will fight and kill one another. History has shown that the conditions of poverty are fertile ground for the cultures of destruction to thrive. Barrios Unidos represents a way out of nihilism, destructiveness, and self-hatred, offering a remedy rooted in the contemporary application of ancient cultural values, traditions, and heritage. This is why the organization's work is so terribly important and timely.

THE PRIORITY FOR CIVIL RIGHTS

One of the lessons of the Los Angeles riots is that we can expect only a minimal response by government and corporate America to address the root causes of such social rage and discontent. The economic development initiatives that occurred afterward mostly benefited the middle- and lower-middle class. There were also piecemeal reforms in police policy and practice but, ultimately, little if anything changed for the poor. It is almost as if there is some canned political response to these episodic civic explosions that occur every ten to fifteen years. The powers that be visit for photo ops, make some empty promises, drop 1 or 2 billion dollars on the usual suspects, and then go back to business as usual. There is simply no urgency in America's public or private power centers to end the poverty that drives community violence.

Similarly, if you looked at the civil rights movement today, you would think our number one priority should be getting more kids of color into the prestigious Berkeley campus of the University of California. To be honest, I don't believe that the civil rights, public-interest, or progressive sector presently has a radical or galvanizing vision for either social or systems change. Addressing this vacuum is admittedly daunting. For instance, impact litigation, work that I have been directly a part of at the Advancement Project, has leveraged some $15 billion to help transform systems that serve the poor, such as schools, law enforcement departments, and public transportation agencies. I am proud of our work but I also know that moving $15 billion toward poverty issues is a drop in the bucket, considering that it would take something like a $2 trillion investment just to start making a real difference.

As beneficial as my field of work is—meaning litigation, legal defense, education, and policy advocacy—it is not big or powerful enough to deliver the more fundamental civil rights reforms America needs. The legal and policy arm of the movement is a critical component but it cannot by itself achieve the kind of radical systems change America needs to eliminate poverty. Many of the clients that groups like the Advancement Project serve will never achieve upward mobility out of poverty. The communities I represent, and the children and families that Barrios Unidos serves, are born in the middle of a minefield. Meanwhile, kids in Beverly Hills are reared on a lush polo field, their middle-class counterparts on a well-maintained soccer field.

No children of the richest nation on earth should be born in a minefield. Changing this reality can only come about by radically transforming the social, political, and economic systems that create and sustain poverty. The political will to command such a social-change agenda will require an unprecedented coalition movement that cuts across race, class, culture, and political affiliation. None of these circumstances or coalition prospects presently exists.

REVIVING THE MOVEMENT

The natural extension of community peace work is dealing with issues of justice and equity. The corollary issues with civil rights are many and include broad reform imperatives related to the justice system, law enforcement, and education, as well as the promotion of social and economic investment in community development, youth, and families. That is why those of us in the more established institutional tiers of the civil rights community need to reprioritize our work to support efforts emerging from organic movement-building within the poorest communities. The youth and adult activists who emerge out of such communities are the ones who are going to lead the unfinished work of civil rights. These types of value-driven community-building and leadership development entities are the only hope of preparing people (and especially our young) to rise up in a sustained nonviolent movement. The work of Barrios Unidos is preparing the type of intergenerational community leadership that will become the new credible voices of the poor.

On the civil rights front we must take a huge conceptual leap forward and bring together the best social theory with the hard realities of economics and politics. A sustained nonviolent grassroots revolution led by the poor and supported by a mass multicultural and multi-class coalition stands the best chance of redirecting the heart of the nation to the moral imperative to end poverty. However, because it is inevitable that ending poverty will require some redistribution of wealth, we need a restructuring formula that is politically feasible. To this end, the middle class and the wealthy will need to see it in their interest to end poverty for any successful effort to take place. It is incumbent on those concerned with justice and equality to develop a platform and action agenda that can receive support across class and partisan lines. The key is developing a viable change framework that harnesses democratic principles and the power of capitalism through outcomes-driven social investment strategies. Creating a plan around which a social movement can be built will take the creative genius of the best social, economic, legal, and political minds of this nation.

We are talking about the creation of a true democracy, as well as a new model of capitalism. The first part of this vision requires the establishment of a truly participatory multiracial and multi-class democracy. The second part involves fashioning a value-driven, twenty-first-century global economy that is more equitable, human-centered, and socially responsible. This next phase of achieving equality and civil rights for the poor may take a decade, two, or even more to see through. Therefore, sustained progress will require a real partnership and symmetry between the heart of the movement—poor people and grassroots communities—and the legs of the movement—diverse community institutions, networks, and civic structures—and the mind of the movement—the academic, legal, philanthropic, and creative infrastructure. When all is said and done, the prospect of achieving greater equality and justice in America is impossible without such a broad-based, value-driven social movement aimed at revolutionary change.

Manuel Pastor

Manuel Pastor is professor of Latin American/Latino Studies and codirector of the Center for Justice, Tolerance and Community at the University of California at Santa Cruz. The son of immigrant parents, Pastor was born in New York and grew up in Los Angeles. His father came to the United States in the 1930s from Cuba and earned his U.S. citizenship by joining the army and fighting in Europe. Pastor was exposed to the importance of social movements and public policy by his father's experience in active union membership and as a beneficiary of the G.I. Bill. He began both his academic career track and his activism while studying economics during the 1970s. During these years, he earned an undergraduate degree at the University of California at Santa Cruz, as well as master's and doctorate degrees at the University of Massachusetts, Amherst. As a college student, Pastor became actively involved in United Farm Workers organizing around the boycott of nonunion agricultural products and Gallo wines. While a student organizer working in Santa Cruz and San Jose, California, Pastor met César Chávez. The farmworker leader's influence had transformative personal and political impacts on the aspiring scholar. Throughout his academic career, Pastor has effectively combined his passion for academic research with effective leadership and activism in the areas of economic, community, and environmental justice. While serving as a professor at Occidental College in Los Angeles, Pastor actively convened Latino, African American, and Asian Pacific American urban planners and community leaders to advance shared economic development aims. The group eventually formalized as the New Majority Task Force, which convened to promote alternative economic development strategies designed to address growing wealth and income disparities in Southern California. In his most recent book, coauthored with civil rights leaders Stewart Kwoh and Angela Glover Blackwell, *Searching for the Uncommon, Common Ground: New Dimensions on Race in America*, Pastor and his colleagues advance provocative and insightful arguments for interracial solidarity as the pathway to achieving greater justice, equality, and democracy in America.

It is a pleasure and honor to be included among the group of people that have been invited to offer some insights into the work of Barrios Unidos and the possible direction of the civil rights struggle today. My work and identity is very much the product of social movements, beginning with the experience of my parents. I am the proud son of immigrants who came to this land for a better life. My father came from Cuba in the 1930s and attained his U.S. citizenship by joining the Army and fighting in Europe. He was also a union member and took the work of the labor movement very seriously. It was impressed upon me at an early age that the opportunities my family took advantage of to get ahead were not solely due to our hard work and initiative, but also due to the social movements that made these opportunities possible.

In my father's case, he benefited from both the labor movement and the Veterans' Rights Movement that produced the passage of the G.I. Bill. This federal program provided veterans of the armed forces resources to advance educationally and economically. There he was, a war veteran with a mere sixth-grade education, returning to school with the aid of his G.I. benefits to learn in a community college about electricity and air-conditioning repair, both of which helped him advance from being a janitor to more skilled employment. These achievements were certainly a reflection of his *ganas* (desire), but they were also a direct result of the movement. My dad made certain that I understood the G.I. Bill's role in putting in place new rights and benefits that, combined with his union membership, created opportunities he may otherwise have never had. By the time I went to college in the early 1970s, I was acutely aware that I owed my opportunities to these movements and the doors being opened by civil rights. A sense of debt and responsibility to social movements was thus bred into me during my youth.

My first forays into civil rights work came early in my college career when I got involved as a student organizer with the United Farm Workers (UFW) during 1973–1974. This was an era during which it was important for progressive people in urban areas to support the farmworker-inspired consumer boycott of nonunion agricultural products. Like many young Latino students, I was drawn immediately into organizing in support of the UFW call to boycott Gallo wines. I began organizing on the U.C. Santa Cruz campus and also spent time in San Jose, California, with urban organizers working to support farmworkers. This was where I found my political chops and consolidated the political values to which I would give voice throughout my ensuing career. It was a time when political, cultural, and spiritual elements in my life were coming together and allowing me to feel whole.

It was during this period as a student organizer with the UFW that I had the opportunity to meet César Chávez. Meeting César was a tremendously transformative experience in so many ways. I felt like I was in the presence of a saint, someone who had tremendous faith, values, vision, strength, and courage. César was a man who was able to act on his convictions with a powerful sense of peace and love that always seemed to build community. I share this experience because it helped to define the way I understand, internalize, and approach my civil rights work to this day. Civil rights activism must do more than advance political causes and objectives upon which we agree. César appealed to our fundamental sense of connection to each other, our common humanity with other people, our shared commitment to justice and peace, and our desire to advance as a community. Many of these underlying values are central to the work of Barrios Unidos and what I believe civil rights organizations and grassroots efforts should embody.

The combination of exposure to the importance of social movements in my upbringing, the experience of involvement with the UFW struggle as a student organizer, and my interest in research inevitably led me to a career as an academic in the fields of economics and community development. My personal and political affinity with the values and guiding principles of civil rights has converged with my calling to produce new bodies of knowledge in close collaboration with community organizations. One of the most transformational things to occur in the progressive movement has been the creative combination of research and activism to achieve social change. The progressive movement has always been driven by great values and ideals. The challenge has been that more moderate perspectives don't always see progressive ideas as very pragmatic. An important role of value-driven, culturally sensitive research is to show that things like responsible environmentalism, providing accessible universal health `care, decent affordable housing, restorative justice approaches, and living wage standards are not just solid aims morally, but also ideas that make pragmatic sense. Research can also be an important bridge for informed debate and consensus-building across race, culture, class, and institutional lines.

LESSONS AND ACCOMPLISHMENTS OF CIVIL RIGHTS

One of the biggest effects of the late twentieth-century civil rights movement in America, especially among the poor, was that it instilled a new sense of possibility. Important changes in social conventions and public policy buoyed this positive sense. When we think about social movements, it is important to consider how norms, values, and social standards that inform peoples' conduct are affected. The realities of economics and social justice have not caught up to these changes. There were monumental gains for poor blacks and Latinos— as well as for women—in terms of new voting rights protections, legal desegregation, and affirmative action. The key area the movement fell short on, however, was on the attainment of full economic empowerment and equal educational opportunity, both of which are critical to true advancement of the poor.

The civil rights movement was able to articulate its message in terms of universal values and language. This is to say that while the initial impulse of the movement was lifting up the rights of oppressed African Americans in the South, its language was really vested in basic human rights and democracy and a vision of what America was supposed to be about. One of the lessons is that the more we can talk about our values in a way that is common—that is, in a way that crosses boundaries and helps to create and sustain alliances—the more likely we are to build a broader movement with real staying power. In a book that I coauthored with Angela Glover Blackwell and Stewart Kwoh, entitled *Searching for the Uncommon Common Ground*, we talk about this strategy in referring to universal and particular needs, issues, and goals of civil rights for poor blacks and Latinos. For instance, achieving educational equity and economic self-reliance might be seen as a universal goal for both communities while immigration, land rights, and language issues might be considered a particular need of Latinos. The key to effective future coalition-building that advances civil rights for everyone rests with framing both universal and particular interests in the context of common values that have mass appeal across lines of race, culture, and class.

The civil rights movement set up a new perspective and set of values upon which we continue to build today. The area of immigration reform and the treatment of immigrants, for example, were positively affected because of the unmasking of racism inherent in American policy and practice in other areas. There was a very racist nature to U.S. immigration law and policies and a bias toward northern Europeans that was challenged and changed due to new values that emerged from the movement. Stewart Kwoh of the Asian Pacific American Legal Center points out that changes in the 1965 Immigration Act grew out of the effects of the Civil Rights Act and opened doors previously closed by Asian exclusions, based exclusively on racism. These common values that emerged from the movement to counter racism and discrimination and promote justice and equity are the foundation for contemporary multicultural and multiethnic approaches to coalition work and community-building.

ADVANCING THE AGENDA OF CIVIL RIGHTS—COMBINING RESEARCH AND ACTIVISM

Dating back to my work as a college professor at Occidental College in Los Angeles, I participated in the convening of Latino, African American and Asian Pacific American urban planners and community leaders around issues of community development and economic equity. The group was called the New Majority Task Force (NMTF). We came together to think about new economic strategies to deal with the growing economic divide. The Los Angeles civil unrest put to the test the depth of our commitment to common values that underlie multiracial and multicultural coalition work to advance justice. It was a powerful testimony that in the aftermath of the racial unrest, the vast majority of NMTF participants continued to coalesce even more deliberately, notwithstanding resulting tensions and divisions within the group. In addition to its multicultural vision, the group was noteworthy for launching some cutting-edge research initiatives on alternative economic strategies focused on how to better link communities and regional economies.

The efforts to include community participation and voice in research goes against conventional wisdom in the academic community, the belief being that such a relationship often compromises scientific integrity. My experience has been that when you tie in closely with community organizers and leaders, the common sense they bring to bear often results in more insightful and practical research questions. Some of the best research I've done is in collaboration with or in response to the insights raised by community leaders and organizations that live on the ground. We brought these principles of community collaborative research to the Center for Justice, Tolerance and Community (CJTC) at the University of California, Santa Cruz, founded in 2000. The research center is focused on social justice and produces new knowledge guided by the principles of rigor, relevance, and reach.

The CJTC strives to conduct the highest quality of scientific research possible that is relevant to current policy issues such as environmental protection, labor rights, and fair trade. We try to have a broad reach into community, working side-by-side with advocates to advance informed civic participation on critical policy matters. The CJTC establishes a base for students and researchers committed to civil rights and social justice issues. Our approach to research is facilitating collaboration across various areas of expertise in a border-crossing way—that is, not confined to a single issue. The goal is to provide a space for synergy between different fields of interest and constituencies such as environmental justice, gay and lesbian concerns, community development, and Latino studies. We try to build bridges between these fields and constituencies with a common vision for social justice. Most of our efforts are geared to bringing researchers together with community leaders and other diverse stakeholders to strengthen advocacy and community activism for change.

Addressing the intractable issue of poverty will require fundamental changes to the social, economic, and political structures in this
country over a sustained period of time. Important universal values
will necessarily guide the movement, bind diverse coalitions, and
hopefully generate the political will to achieve still-needed change.
The framework to realize the kind of democracy and economy that is
consistent with our highest values will inevitably also need to draw on
new bodies of knowledge across various disciplines. I believe that
combining our highest values and intelligence in nation-building or
community-building allows us to do both the right thing and the smart
thing. For us to wage a successful war on poverty, all arms of the civil
rights movement will need to work collaboratively: the grassroots sector, community organizations, labor groups, minority business associ-
ations, philanthropy, the legal and policy communities, and academic
researchers.

CONTEMPORARY FRONTS—EXPANDING OUR VIEW OF CIVIL RIGHTS

In the book *Searching for the Uncommon Common Ground,* we
deal with many of the more traditional civil rights issues, such as voting, political empowerment, and education. At the same time, we necessarily wanted to speak to some of the newly evolving fronts of the
movement. There is so much to consider in the restructuring of our
economy that relates to the eradication of poverty and a more equitable distribution of wealth. A key emerging issue that we identify is
sprawl. One of the trends that has recently taken root in the United
States is a set of public policies that have encouraged suburbanization.
This trend has drained resources from the central cities, and, as time
has gone on, it has also drained older suburbs located closest to the
cities. The issue of sprawl refers to the steady outlying development
of new communities into open land, posing serious consequences for
the overall well-being of entire regions.

The consumption of open space has negative effects on nature and
a sense of balance with the environment (e.g., pollution, displaced
wildlife, and disruption of important ecosystems). The price of the
suburban American dream is often multi-worker households, long
commutes, and social isolation. The disconnection created by sprawl

also strains family stability and fractures social support systems, civic life, political identification, and community functioning. Economic opportunities are reduced for those left in the urban core and diffused overall by hindering beneficial regional economic integration. The expense of linking increasingly remote developments to the existing infrastructure of core urban centers further exhausts limited public resources. What research has identified is that if we really want to do something about poverty pockets concentrated in the central city areas, the processes of sprawl need to be reversed. We need to explore policies that redirect resources and opportunities to central urban and adjacent suburban areas and restore ties that characterize a healthy civil society.

The emerging issue of *environmental justice* is also very important as a civil rights matter because it encapsulates and corresponds with other challenges being faced in poor communities. A cynical view of civil rights might characterize the present struggle as shuffling chairs on the Titanic. If you conceive of civil rights as trying to mitigate the impacts on minority populations of society's least desirable jobs, poorest performing schools, and most toxic waste dumps, this is a pretty limited notion of justice. In fact, resisting this thinking can actually lead to new approaches that would help clean up the whole environment and benefit everyone. However, we must contend with the continuing reality that opportunities in poor communities are still too often relegated to such options as building prisons or building much-needed new schools on toxic waste sites. The growing prevalence of sprawl, inner-city decay, and contaminated industrial sites contributes significantly to the challenge of balancing justice and opportunity concerns. Research is showing that we still live in an economy and with a regulatory system that generates a disproportionate distribution of environmental health hazards in poor communities of color. In the face of inequality and latent discrimination, environmental justice emerges as an increasingly important organizing front.

Ultimately, there remain many other critically important issue areas that demand civil rights attention, such as the digital divide, immigrant policy, and criminal justice reform. The *digital divide* issue has direct implications for both educational and economic advancement of the poor. The digital economy, with the value it places on skills and social networks, is contributing to a widening gap in economic fortunes by class and race. Competing in the modern economy requires a higher level of technological fluency, yet the opportunities to acquire these skills are unevenly available. Bridging this digital divide is important to advancement of the poor but also to improving the economic viability of the larger society.

Another important focal area should be the development of a more humane and effective *immigrant policy*. A distinction should be made between immigration and immigrant policy. Immigration policy focuses on determining who is admitted, in what numbers, from what nations, and so forth. Immigrant policy focuses on how to best integrate immigrant populations that reside here into the civic and economic life of America. An important aspect of this would be facilitating access to educational resources for children of immigrants, who are typically United States born. Education considerations should include providing culturally fluent transitional language and academic instruction in preschool, elementary, and secondary school programs. Community colleges could and often do play the role that settlement houses played for the integration of European immigrants in the nineteenth century. Providing immigrant families with increased access to comprehensive human services, such as health care, childcare, job training, and transportation is critical. Other institutions and organizations, such as unions, community-based nonprofits, and legal centers, provide additional platforms from which to support the economic, social, and political empowerment of immigrants.

Equally important is making significant reforms in the *criminal justice system* for both youths and adults. America has one of the highest rates of imprisonment in the world. The present system has effectively taken many African Americans and Latinos outside of society and permanently disenfranchised them from voting and any prospect of economic success. In turn, this has created serious long-term harm to their families and communities, which encourage a further downward spiral of still additional cycles of juvenile and criminal activity. There is a racial bias in the criminal justice system, which is borne out by research, that shows disproportionately harsh sentencing and levels of incarceration of blacks and Latinos versus those levied on whites for the same criminal offenses. The drug economy and patterns of criminal enforcement in poor versus suburban communities also contributes to disproportionate representation among people of color in the nation's courts, jails, juvenile detention centers, and prisons. Changing these disturbing trends in criminal justice and law enforcement will require political will and a fundamental rethinking of current strategies that focus on punishment in place of alternatives that combine prevention, rehabilitation, and reentry.

What we say in the book *Searching for the Uncommon Common Ground* is that there are old and outstanding issues we must continue to pay attention to in civil rights, such as voting access and political empowerment, equitable and accessible education, and discrimination protections. At the same time, there are many issues that don't usually get thought of as civil rights concerns, but that turn out to be essential to overcoming the barriers of poverty and the remnants of structural discrimination in society. The whole issue of working with the young who have experienced various forms of violence in their lives, with people who are in prisons and juvenile detention facilities, with community residents doing the work of building peace in violence-torn and otherwise distressed communities—this work is entirely consistent with our notion of the new civil rights agenda. Barrios Unidos is key to this new front in the struggle for civil rights in America.

Even though Barrios Unidos grew out of the movement, I'm not sure that thirty years ago its work would have been defined as civil rights. Groups that were rooted in community, working with young people and gangs, reconciling community violence while trying to figure out alternative community development strategies were uncommon hybrids. I'm not sure that many outside of the most insightful within the early Chicano movement would have called this civil rights work. From my perspective, Barrios Unidos really captures the essence of the values of civil rights and of the important cultural revolution that took place within the movement. More importantly, the organization continues to serve members of the community who were left behind. If Barrios Unidos was not recognized as part of the civil rights movement in the past, it certainly is today. In fact, I see that the

Barrios Unidos organization provides a powerful model for civil rights advancement, one that is particularly suited to working with youth and allied constituencies.

THE ROLE OF BARRIOS UNIDOS AND THE COMMUNITY PEACE MOVEMENT

Barrios Unidos preserves many of the gifts and legacies of the Chicano experience within civil rights. Of course, aspects of the cultural revolution that took place for Latinos within the movement have been recently expanded to embrace the experiences of Central Americans, Cubans, Dominicans, Puerto Ricans, and others in the context of today's increasingly Latino-dominant America. The issue of culture is an important factor in giving the United States' rapidly expanding Latino population a sense of agency to move the civil rights agenda forward. Early on in the United States, it was anticipated by many that civil rights would eventually accomplish a melting pot society in which diverse groups could participate equally by adopting a homogeneous assimilated identity. Many still today see multicultural aspirations to reclaim particular identities as separatist or an obstruction to building coalitions or a broader sense of common identity. I do not agree. Barrios Unidos is a great example of this cultural dimension being central to empowerment. By re-instilling pride in heritage and cultural values, the approach enables people to realize their human potential and contribute to their family, community, and broader society.

CONCLUSIONS

In my capacity with the Center for Justice, Tolerance and Community at the University of California, Santa Cruz, I have had the opportunity to partner with Barrios Unidos on several interethnic initiatives and international forums. The group's strong emphasis on *cultura* and spirit always creates an environment of trust and commonality among participants. When we remember the pride that Latino people felt in the farmworkers' movement, to see *gente* standing up for themselves and being a force of positive change in the world, we understand that these experiences mark a restoration of our dignity and self-respect, which has been damaged by generations of oppression and discrimination. The way Barrios Unidos does its work and the role it plays is an extension of the best traditions of the movement.

The Barrios Unidos way is an affirmation, a rediscovery, and a collective nod to self-determination—key ingredients of community empowerment and progress going forward.

The cultural and spiritual elements of Barrios Unidos's work are essential to community-building, organizing for change, and the progressive movement in general. The progressive movement has been concerned about the Christian right wing and the use of spiritual values as moralizing. This concern has somewhat inhibited the progressive side from using the power of spiritual values to advance social-change objectives of its own. As a consequence, some may see the progressive front as becoming soulless and overly secular in orientation. We must remember that spiritual values were a driving force of the civil rights movement. What motivates us is not some hard analysis of power structures, or inequality, or even visions of the perfect society, but rather a profound sense of our humanity and the possibility inherent in each human being. The ecumenical spiritual approach taken by Barrios Unidos is really faith-based work at its best, because it is centered on a life-affirming sense of responsibility for the individual, the community, and the larger society. It is increasingly clear to me that this sort of approach is what will ultimately animate and revitalize the progressive movement in America.

In closing, I want to leave with the message we stress in *Searching for the Uncommon Common Ground* and that is so beautifully exemplified in the work of Barrios Unidos. That message is that the movement will not advance without multiracial coalition-building and without preparing and empowering culturally versed interracial leaders. We need to prepare and nurture leaders who can lead and serve across lines of race, culture, and class. In these changing times when the nation's populations grow increasingly diverse and no one racial group is a true majority, there is no substitute for drawing on the highest values of our culture, democracy, and humanity to find common ground. This demands that we reconcile our individual and collective historical experiences in America as a people with honesty and respect. It means that we must be prepared to face hard questions that address issues of privilege or deprivation based on racial and other factors. It means that we must squarely face the most critical issues of the day, such as lingering poverty, and resolve to make changes. To meet all of these challenges, finally, we will need to visualize and map a course for creating a national culture that truly values, benefits, and incorporates everyone.

Part V
Author's Observations, Conclusions, and Thoughts About the Future

Sustaining the Movement

Some see things as they are and ask, why? I dream things that never were and ask, why not?

Robert F. Kennedy

Despite the progress America has achieved in recent decades to dismantle legally sanctioned racism, discrimination, and apartheid, we have only begun as a nation to reconcile the failures of our past in relation to power, equality, and justice. For still too many Americans, the achievement of civil equality, has not translated into economic equity or even fairness. The role of race in determining privilege and/or deprivation remains an especially fundamental variable by which we must measure the state of American democracy and society in the early twenty-first century. Although the root causes of interpersonal, community, and societal violence are manifold, ultimately civil peace is only possible and sustainable by realizing certain American ideals. Principal among these must be the attainment of racial justice and the eradication of poverty in poor communities of color and elsewhere.

The achievement of such core ideas of American democracy in turn requires a new poor people's campaign with a far-reaching vision, goals, and a change agenda. Recent immigrant rights organizing efforts across the nation may establish the necessary platform upon which to base such a campaign. Such efforts have reignited public awareness of the possibility of change through civic engagement and the potential of mass-organizing efforts to inform needed policy reforms in U.S. law, education, health care, housing, public finance, and foreign affairs.

American social history reveals the hard reality that the larger goals of equality and justice are achieved through major transformations of social, political, and economic systems. These transformations typically require the building of coalitions that cut across lines of race, class, culture, creed, and partisan politics. The logistical requirements of advancing such a mass social movement are many, to be sure. The essential ingredients include effective organizing; leadership and communications that draw on the collective resources of influential individuals, grassroots community organizations, and civic groups; legal, research, and policy institutions; and progressive philanthropies.

Organizations like BU are essential participants and leaders in the prospective galvanization of a modern social-change movement in America. By serving as an authentic bridge between grassroots multicultural communities in need and society's most influential leaders and institutions and by combining conventional practices with effective alternative approaches to lift up society's most disenfranchised youths and families, groups like BU essentially model on a micro-scale what our society needs to do more effectively on a macro-level. In this connection, BU's future vitality—and the viability of groups like it all across the land—will likely have much to do with the nation's civic and democratic health in the years to come. This is especially the case when considering the sweep of demographic change that most credible experts agree will transform American society into a majority-minority culture in the years shortly after 2050. In this emerging context, the work of BU and other advocates in the community peace movement will no doubt significantly inform the sort of nation the United States ultimately becomes in the decades ahead.

SANTA CRUZ BARRIOS UNIDOS: LOOKING BACK, LOOKING FORWARD

The evolving work of groups like Barrios Unidos that bridge historically disconnected work in community violence prevention, youth development, community-building, and civil rights has arguably never been more important. In California alone, between January 2000 and December 2003, more than 3,500 young people between the ages of twelve and twenty-six died from intentional firearm injuries. By the publication of this book in 2007, thousands more will have succumbed to interpersonal violence in the communities and prisons of America.

As we have learned from the Columbine High School tragedy and hundreds of subsequent shooting incidents in American schools, workplaces, and homes, violence is not the sole domain of the nation's urban centers or poor communities of color. But there can be no question that extreme poverty of the sort that disproportionately besets U.S. communities of color is a source and root cause of its own strain of extreme violence. Recent public health research demonstrates that environmental factors associated with poverty contribute to cultural alienation, the disintegration of family, and the breakdown of essential community and social support structures. These conditions in turn cultivate educational underachievement, unemployment, and substance abuse—all of the conditions that give rise to gangs, interpersonal street violence, and other maladjusted or antisocial behaviors. Violence, likened to a social disease, has reached epidemic levels in this country. The culture and history of violence that permeates all walks of life in America is increasingly exacerbated by oppressive social conditions of poverty linked to racial injustice, discrimination, and inequality. And yet we know that even the most extreme forms of interpersonal violence can be prevented and cured.

The multidimensional approach employed by BU centers on the medicinal power of culture and spiritual expression to bring healing, health, and well-being to people and communities living in the throes of chronic violence and poverty. As BU strives to build and sustain its institutional model for the future, it will necessarily draw on the fundamental lessons learned from its now thirty years of experience in the field. At the same time, along with allied violence prevention leaders and experts, BU will necessarily need to consider new strategies to expand its reach and impact in the future.

At the core of BU's planning for the future is the concept of sustaining the organization's work in the form of an endowed institute that will ultimately be able to self-support an expansive range of current and prospective BU programs. The grand vision will certainly require a level of prowess and success that few U.S. grassroots groups have achieved in recent years. Yet, BU leaders believe that they have begun to attain the necessary knowledge and acumen to work toward making their vision a reality. Their commitment to this belief is at the heart of BU's prospects for continued success in the years to come as a leader in America's growing community peace movement.

To conclude this publication, I offer two important final sections: first, a broad summary of BU's next-phase challenges as an organization based on lessons learned and recent developments in the national violence prevention field; and, second, some reflections on potential opportunities for BU and the U.S. community peace movement looking to the future. These closing segments are intended to help put in overall context what Barrios Unidos's work can teach us about effective violence prevention and community-building involving traditionally hard-to-serve groups and how leading organizations like BU may need to direct—or in some cases redirect—their sights in key aspects of their next generation development.

MANAGING GROWTH AND SUSTAINABILITY: LESSONS LEARNED, EMERGING IMPERATIVES

The founding leaders of BU were not seasoned nonprofit professional managers, but rather activists and organizers. They had to learn about the requirements of institutional stewardship as they pushed forward to advance BU's organizational aims. Initially, they knew little or nothing about policy, financial management, grant administration, or property acquisition. Until fairly late in BU's evolution, its principals did little to document or catalog their accumulated knowledge. Rather, like most emerging grassroots nonprofit leaders, they focused on the many immediate challenges before them and addressed the mechanics of governance and administration only as necessary along the way. All of this had to change as the organization matured and began to interface with major public and private institutions that required a more standardized professional approach. Turning this corner toward institutional maturity required the organization to undertake a difficult twelve-month period of critical self-reflection, strategic planning, and reorganization. This process called upon BU leaders to think concretely and comprehensively for the first time about organizational lessons learned in key areas of their work. In many cases, the most important lessons stemmed from periods and circumstances involving BU's greatest challenges.

FUNDING AND RESOURCE DEVELOPMENT

During early 2004, Santa Cruz Barrios Unidos experienced a serious financial crisis that momentarily threatened its organizational viability. This is not uncommon for nonprofit organizations that have experienced periods of accelerated growth over a short period of time. The issues giving rise to BU's nonprofit incorporation, the perseverance of its leadership, and unprecedented funding opportunities created by the social context of the times all made possible a rapid ascension of Barrios Unidos as an organization in a relatively short period of time after 1993. Particularly key to this dynamic was BU's heavy dependency on a single funding source, The California Wellness Foundation, for much of its core operating budget. BU benefited immensely from the Foundation's forward-looking ten-year unrestricted core funding commitment from its inception as a nonprofit corporation. Although the organization had relatively good success in ensuing years diversifying its income base, transitioning from the TCWF funding relationship was not a smooth process for BU.

In the first place, BU leaders did not anticipate profound shifts that were reshaping the surrounding funding environment as TCWF began to wind down its long-term commitments to groups like BU. When the Foundation's core funding to the organization ended in 2003, public and private grant support of community violence prevention work from other sources was insufficient to cover the gap.* Also, in the aftermath of the 2001 terrorist attacks on America and ensuing military engagements overseas, public and private support of progressive groups began to wane as the attention of critical funding sources turned to other interests and priorities. Even many of the nation's most seasoned and long-established public advocacy nonprofits experienced challenges to their stability in the months following September 11. These developments severely disadvantaged newer grant-dependent organizations like BU, whose work was inherently progressive, antiviolence-oriented, and thus fundamentally opposed to post-9/11 U.S. policy.

BU found its way through this difficult epoch using a combination of cost-cutting and new revenue-generating strategies, relying especially on entrepreneurial ventures that provide unrestricted budg-

---

*In the ensuing years, The California Wellness Foundation has continued to support select violence prevention activities. Among major additional private funders since 2003, only The California Endowment and the David and Lucile Packard Foundation have maintained a significant funding interest in the California field.

etary resources in support of operational development. Still, BU and similar organizations in the community violence prevention arena face serious ongoing sustainability challenges.

In the absence of more dedicated private funding for violence prevention, establishing a clear relationship between violence prevention work and other philanthropic priorities (in education, youth and child development, health, family preservation, community-building, and economic development) has become an essential resource development strategy for groups like Barrios Unidos. To make this relationship clearer, such groups have collaborated with important institutional allies, including organizations like the Washington-based Institute for Community Peace and the National Centers for Disease Control. Together, such groups have partnered to advocate for and lift up new research that establishes the case for philanthropic and federal investments in allied fields that centrally involve community violence prevention activities. Complementary efforts to leverage greater state government investments and resource deployments are sorely needed as well. A recent effort that created a statewide violence prevention authority in Illinois could provide a model for California and other states to generate increased and more integrated public spending in support of promising local violence prevention strategies.

THE REORGANIZATION: ACHIEVING MATURITY AS A NONPROFIT

In recent years, the imperative to achieve financial viability and sustainability in the nation's increasingly tight external resource environment has driven a process of reflection and strategic decision-making by BU's staff and board. Such work has been designed to help BU realize a next phase of organizational development that can lead to BU's institutionalization and ultimate financial self-sufficiency. This next section highlights BU's resulting reorganization challenges and long-term business vision focusing on issues related to staffing, sustainability, and enterprise development.

STAFF DEVELOPMENT AND RETENTION

Maintaining a movement culture has been difficult for BU principals to balance as the organization has grown in size and the demands on senior staff have changed. As the organization has evolved into a million-dollar enterprise, its executives have found their time to lead, plan, and envision increasingly mitigated by the demands of management, organizational development, finance, research, fund development, and grant reporting. In the organization's early days, BU executives effectively operated without considerable hierarchy, often sharing and trading institutional roles based on shifting circumstances and needs. Today, BU founders are having to face a much less fluid and more formal work structure. Their bandwidth for serendipity and informality has been substantially reduced.

BU's founding leaders have begun to move the organization toward decidedly greater professionalism in order to meet the inherent responsibilities that have developed before them as a result of growth in organizational programs and assets. While it is still common for seasoned staff to work occasionally across program areas, BU's steady expansion has required its executive team to implement a more standardized form of service delivery. The current approach increasingly calls upon managers and senior staff to concentrate on one or another of the organization's now impressive number of specialty program areas, including youth education and training, communications technology, preschool and childcare service, housing development, and small business incubation.

The philosophical tendency of BU leaders to resist adopting "an agency mentality" has created inevitable tensions and dilemmas within the organization. Going forward, it will be essential to BU's success that its leadership further professionalize organizational staff, programs, and back-office systems; maintaining relevance and competitive advantage in the current nonprofit management environment will demand no less. But maintaining the cultural authenticity and historical soul of the BU movement will also be a nonnegotiable element of institutional progress going forward. Combining these often competing imperatives will present ongoing challenges to BU leaders.

A steady influx of new leaders, organizers, and community workers into BU offers continuing opportunities to maintain a larger footprint in the grassroots communities the organization most directly serves. However, achieving stability and high-level professional capacity is inherently difficult in the nonprofit sector, especially where the preponderance of staff is from grassroots backgrounds that invariably compel the most talented and successful to quickly pursue better-paid opportunities, while leaving behind committed but often less professionally seasoned individuals. The problem is exacerbated for BU by the fact that it has experienced past difficulty incorporating professionals and consultants from outside of its grassroots community centers of gravity. Typically, such "experts" have lacked the cultural competence required to work effectively with BU's core constituents. Gratefully for the organization, BU has experienced unique success retaining key staff members over the years who have grown in their professional capacities; it has also attracted a small permanent stable of outside consultants who have proven both a good cultural fit and a discernable organizational asset. These factors have combined to spare Barrios Unidos from the worst possible circumstances relative to staff competence and turnover issues.

As BU's founding circle of organizational executives ages, it becomes possible to anticipate their eventual retirement years, hence the opportunity and the imperative to develop next-generation leadership and a succession strategy. Through BU strategic planning work, organizational principals have begun to factor in these contingencies. The organization's long-range vision to institutionalize BU around a central focus on human and community development will further provide incentives to develop and place capable grassroots professionals as key next-generation staff members. The BU strategic plan, in fact, calls for the creation of comprehensive recruitment, employment preparation, skills training and staff development programs as a core priority for achieving this aspect of the organization's evolving mission. Beyond building its own staff capacity, the envisioned BU Institute of the future will focus on nurturing students, young leaders, activists, organizers, and community peace workers through the broader application of its education curriculum, including support for new internship, fellowship, and professional apprenticeship programs.

The lingering barrier to bringing such programs on line sooner than later, not surprisingly, is funding. New programs on the scale envisioned by BU in the areas of leadership development and community and human resource investment could surpass the $500,000 per year level and would likely require three to five years of ongoing support to gain meaningful traction for an entity like BU. Here again, questions and challenges of sustainability loom significantly for BU leaders looking to the organization's next stage of evolution.

SUSTAINABILITY

In 2001, The California Wellness Foundation (TCWF) developed a monograph on the key elements necessary to achieve nonprofit organizational sustainability. According to TCWF experts, based on their collective grant-making experience, organizations that have maintained integrity and efficacy over time are those that most readily achieve sustainability. In addition, according to the TCWF report, several specific factors tend to inform the sustainability of these organizations. The element of *spirit*—the enduring energy, inspiration, and commitment of leadership, staff, and volunteers in relation to organizational mission—turns out to be one of these. The closely connected ability to effectively articulate, teach, and model core *values* turns out to be another key ingredient of sustainability. A third core element of long-term organizational success and endurance, *niche*, relates to sound analysis and decision-making about the organization's best and highest uses of available assets, its most appropriate core constituencies, and its optimal role in the field. A fourth and final factor identified in the monograph, *capacity*, speaks to the competency and effectiveness of the organization, including its leadership, programs, and systems.

BU fares well across TCWF's various criteria for nonprofit organizational sustainability, which accounts for its proven ability not only to survive over the years, but also to weather the invariable storms that it has encountered along the way.

The 2004 fiscal crisis that beset BU required a significant, temporary staff downsizing, the development of an emergency financial plan, and a structural reorganization. Rather than deplete the organization's capital investments in the Soquel Avenue property in Santa Cruz through a risky refinancing package, BU leaders made a disciplined decision to preserve long-term organizational principal in this critically important asset. Since that time, BU staff leadership has worked diligently with board members to bolster the longer-term prospects for continued and improved organizational viability through efforts to build board governance capacity, streamline management and financial systems, and shore up resource development (with a focus on diversifying institutional funding sources).

The expanding focus of Barrios Unidos leaders on building and sustaining the organization as a viable nonprofit bode well for BU's future success. Additional strides in this area will help to ensure the organization's continuing capacity to advance leading program and advocacy efforts that fulfill its core mission to empower at-risk youth and families of color in California and elsewhere. Critically important aspects of BU's prospects for sustainability and continuing impacts along these lines will be the organization's success in fulfilling its community and economic development goals as outlined in the César Chávez Peace Plan, a long-range set of BU goals and commitments specifically intended to consolidate the organization (and movement) in a self-sustaining social-change institute framework.

THE BARRIO ENTERPRISE ZONE AND THE CÉSAR CHÁVEZ PEACE PLAN
When the leaders of Barrios Unidos began to consider developing a Barrio Enterprise Zone (BEZ) in Santa Cruz, they pursued exploratory conversations with experts at the University of California, Santa Cruz and several local community development corporations. These consultations helped BU leaders modify their early ideas about the BEZ and informally advance their thinking about how best to work toward making the now-improved potential project concepts a reality. After developing the concepts still further internally and then addressing the unanticipated fiscal challenges of 2004, BU secured an important grant from the David and Lucile Packard Foundation to support allied organizational development activities, as well as formal planning and feasibility work on the BEZ project. Based on this work, Santa Cruz Barrios Unidos recently began to explore possible partnerships with several private firms to build a mixed-use program, production, operations, and residential facility on the Soquel property.

The leading proposal for BU's first BEZ envisions a 57,400 square-foot development that would replace all the existing structures that house BU operations, as well as several small businesses, BU Productions, and three residential units. Constructed in place of these structures would be a cluster of new buildings. This new configuration would include 35,000 square feet of office, program, meeting, retail, and small business space. It would also involve a major increase in the site's available residential space. The proposed new development would furthermore include 9,000 square feet of working space for BU programs and administration. The BEZ plan currently anticipates the construction of forty new residential units, on-site parking, and exterior plazas that would accommodate various commercial enterprises and community events. The BEZ's realization will bring BU closer to the fulfillment of its founders' dream to effectively implement the core elements of the César Chávez Peace Plan, which emphasizes institutional self-sufficiency and the forging of a more sustainable community peace movement.

ADVANCING THE COMMUNITY PEACE MOVEMENT

The core constituents that BU represents and serves have been essentially forgotten in the broader arenas of recent American politics, economy, and culture. In the process they have been left with very few legitimate ways to realize the American Dream. Instead, their innate possibilities to contribute and to thrive have been mired and mitigated by the worst aspects of gangs, criminality, community violence, broken homes, drugs and addiction, unemployment, and below-poverty-level family incomes.

Over the past quarter century, U.S. political and civil rights retrenchment in relation to the issues has profoundly inhibited the advancement of social justice. These factors have substantially enfeebled the movements of the 1960s and 1970s that began to make a positive mark in communities of color. Now, in the wake of recent impressive mobilizations around immigrant and workers rights in California and other states, it appears that a reawakened movement for much-needed social change may be at hand. An important opportunity for movement-building in America seems to be upon us.

BU and its allied groups in the area of community peace occupy a critical position in facilitating movement revitalization. Insofar as the focal points of BU's mission are concerned, working with poor Latino youth and families to promote popular education and skills development, civic leadership, community-building, and political mobilization efforts in such areas as family preservation, educational rights, economic self-reliance, and restorative justice are essential battlegrounds. BU, and other groups like it, operate on the front lines of social change. The organization helps to advance movement-building in two especially important areas: developing progressive grassroots leadership and building organizing capacity in poor communities.

Developing New Movement Leaders

The late Corky Gonzales, the iconic Chicano movement leader of the 1960s and 1970s, was critically important to defining the fundamental values of the Chicano and BU movements. On several occasions over the years, Gonzales visited BU leaders, providing support and encouragement for their work. He never stopped reminding Chicano advocates of all backgrounds and affiliations that the key to ultimate success in the movement was the involvement and meaningful leadership of young people. Gonzales's Crusade for Justice gave the BU community peace movement both philosophical and organizational frameworks it still follows to this day in the pursuit of community self-determination and political empowerment. At the heart of all of BU's work is Gonzales's epic poem, *I am Joaquín*, which lifted up the voice of our collective souls as Raza and helped to define *Chicanismo* in America. In the spirit of honoring and advancing Corky Gonzales's legacy, BU leaders are fundamentally committed to developing a new generation of Chicano and Latino social justice advocates. Realizing this goal is a central rationale for BU's drive to reinvent the organization as a multilevel institute in its next generation of work.

A primary goal of the BU Institute model is to more effectively structure the organization's various program, educational, community-building and human development strategies around social change. In addition, BU intends to enhance its research, development, training, technical assistance, and dissemination capacities under the BU Institute's auspices. The idea is to create a cultural and spiritual center for learning and political action for the community peace movement. Training and leadership development curricula and intergenerational program modalities will be developed and refined in various key areas. These will include alternative academic instruction; interethnic, nonviolence organizing; conflict resolution and mediation; violence prevention; planning and organizational competencies; communications and multimedia technologies; and mobilization and advocacy strategy. As a community-based academy, the BU Institute will offer internships, multilevel fellowships, residency programs, and field placements to better prepare and support a critical mass of inter-generational community leaders. Working in this way, BU can support the development and preparation of new leaders who are organic to the communities that BU serves in the various locales where its chapters are located. The varying institute-related education, training, and leadership initiatives envisioned by BU principals share the goal of preparing value-driven, highly skilled, lifelong activists and community advocates. The vision is to nurture and mobilize legions of peace warriors to lead timely new campaigns for social justice in Chicano/Latino and other disenfranchised communities during the years to come.

The Institute will train emerging barrio leaders in social and political organizing, economic policy analysis, community research, advocacy, and communications. It will develop and support grassroots campaigns to address violence and social justice concerns facing the poor and the young. And, it will engage public and private leaders in dialog intended to encourage legal and policy reforms leading to more favorable conditions for Chicano and other poor communities. Through these efforts, BU will strive, when called upon for support, to substantially augment grassroots capacity to seek and secure increased justice and opportunity in barrios across the United States.

BU's efforts to advance social justice gains for its barrio constituencies and allies will build, in turn, on local infrastructure investments: namely, increased capacity-building and technical assistance for BU chapters.

COMMUNITY CAPACITY-BUILDING AND SUPPORT—LOCAL CHAPTERS

In the past, BU leaders have focused their energies on establishing and incubating local BU chapters. But with little financial wherewithal to professionally support the BU vision and model outside of Santa Cruz, the organization has necessarily depended on grassroots organizing efforts or smaller scale programs to extend its reach. This approach has not been without success. Operating under the auspices of other nonprofit entities, several local chapters have gone on to self-incorporate and contribute complementary work in youth and community development, community peace movement-building, and related policy advocacy. All of these groups have struggled, however, to achieve the scale and stability of the Santa Cruz headquarters organization. While their work is important and continues to contribute to improvements in barrio life, BU affiliates have lacked the benefits of deep headquarters support and sustained coordination. Instead, sporadic or uneven interventions at BU biannual convenings, informal mentoring by BU national staff, and/or occasional targeted support interventions have been the vehicles through which BU affiliates have necessarily developed. It is important to note that, with the exception of a chapter capacity-building grant from the David and Lucile Packard Foundation, BU has received few resources to provide such support services to requesting communities in California. Historically, assistance to chapter affiliate communities has fallen on the shoulders of senior BU staff and leaders supported by volunteer efforts and limited discretionary resources.

On balance, this has led to considerable inconsistency in the viability of BU's organizational network. Over the years, for example, the network has ebbed and flowed in composition from a high of twenty-seven affiliate organizational sites to a low of fourteen. Such fluidity in the BU organizational base has inherently prevented Barrios Unidos from maximizing its overall impact on the issues most central to its mission and priorities. Recognizing the inherent problems created by this situation, BU leaders have prioritized field capacity-building as a next-phase focus for the organization. Consequently, the BU César Chávez Plan places a high priority on field-focused capacity-building efforts over the next several years.

One of the central strategies in discussion to ignite BU affiliate capacity in the near term is to develop an annual series of BU congresses. The envisioned congresses would involve all site leaders in team-based capacity-building and mutual support activities. A major concentration would be organizational development and alignment. More intensive field-building of this sort among BU affiliates, with the support of core headquarters staff and development specialists, would greatly increase BU's collective network viability and advocacy wherewithal.

SETTING A POLITICAL AGENDA BASED ON CORE SOCIAL OBJECTIVES

Barrios Unidos supporters have recently expressed the strong desire for BU to evolve in the aforementioned directions quickly, in order to graduate to the next level of institutional stature necessary to lead a more targeted and strategic political agenda—one that would galvanize Chicano/Latino youth and communities to further unite in the face of growing anti-Hispanic and anti-immigrant sentiment in the United States. Such an agenda would logically advance specific social objectives and policy goals for the community peace movement. Past organizational activity has occasionally modeled what this sort of work can look like. For example, in the late 1990s BU leaders and allies coalesced to compel California legislators to pass Assembly Bill 963, the California Gang, Crime and Violence Prevention Partnership Program. With this important new legislation, the State of California provided $3 million in new revenues for violence prevention activities in communities where BU chapters are located. A more formalized network and shared policy agenda, encompassed in the California Coalition of BU, was activated as a result to monitor and assist in the legislation's implementation. Similar campaigns (some of which are already in their incipiency or ripe for development) could be advanced by BU in any of the following policy arenas.

CRIMINAL AND JUVENILE JUSTICE REFORM

There exists a real window of opportunity to advance progressive juvenile justice reform with imminent proposals surfacing to restructure the California Youth Authority. After a series of recent incidents, including a brutal videotaped beating of juvenile inmates, state and federal investigations have resulted from public outrage over the deplorable conditions of the California youth and adult prison systems. Spurred to respond, Governor Arnold Schwarzenegger has announced his support of legislative efforts to reform the state juvenile corrections system. The governor and others want to renew the original intent of California's comprehensive juvenile corrections law enacted in 1941, to emphasize rehabilitation rather than punishment. After a steady dose of failures in the system, the California public has begun to question overzealous zero-tolerance practices and the efficacy of supportive hard-line policies that have led to a 70 percent rate of recidivism. For the first time in two decades, therefore, Californians appear to be open to a more restorative approach. BU could play an important role in helping state officials identify innovative reform strategies that would more productively prepare incarcerated youth for reentry into communities and society.

There are presently some 170,000 adults and youths incarcerated in California's prisons, jails, and youth authority facilities. The draconian policy environment that has prevailed over the past two decades allowed tens of thousands of minors to enter the adult criminal justice system each year. Data from the state's largest court jurisdictions reveal that 82 percent of juvenile cases filed under adult court involve young people of color. Progressive state legislators, such as Gloria Romero (D-Los Angeles), chair of the senate's prison oversight committee, have seized the opportunity to demand far-reaching reforms and funding reallocations that significantly increase the prospects of at-risk youth benefiting from quality education, training, counseling, mental health treatment, community support partnerships, and other extensive reentry investment programs.

The California Youth Authority (CYA) houses inmates, ages twelve to twenty-five, in eight prisons and two camps. Recognizing the need to reform the state's juvenile justice system in key areas, including inmate access to basic services and restorative programs, BU has joined with allied advocacy, policy, and legal groups to challenge existing approaches and explore alternative justice models. BU's partners in this work include the Community Justice Network for Youth (CJNY), Books Not Bars, the Youth Law Center, and the Center for Juvenile and Criminal Justice. Litigation by the Youth Law Center, and sustained community advocacy and mobilization by BU and other key groups, has kept pressure on policy makers to make necessary changes. These efforts are now paying off. Recent legal victories and negotiations by the Youth Law Center, for example, have secured court-compelled CYA reforms in the provision of mental health services to incarcerated juveniles (most of them Latinos and other young people of color). Implementing these changes will now require careful community monitoring and sustained engagement on the issues.

As a result of work along these lines, BU is now an integral participant on various public and private reform bodies, including standing committees, forums, and review boards of state legislators, the California Department of Corrections, and the state attorney general's office. Such participation and consultation helps BU to inform the development and integration of community-based interventions in official reform decision-making. BU leaders are now supporting important supplemental CYA reform efforts by piloting culturally based reentry programs in two northern California facilities for possible system-wide replication. Further and more specifically targeted intervention activities by BU leaders and grassroots constituents could build on these recent gains and help to advance other system-wide reforms still needed but not yet achieved.

EXPANDING MODELS IN COMMUNITY SUPPORT, EDUCATION, AND PUBLIC-PRIVATE PARTNERSHIP

BU also stands poised to contribute to campaigns that address the continuing "mis-administration" of justice in America through community, public information, and cooperative innovations that advance comprehensive reforms in the field. The need for such work is paramount. The "get tough" policies of recent years that many public officials and institutions have supported continue to fail and victimize poor people, without significantly reducing crime, preventing community violence, reducing homicide, or creating a heightened sense of public safety. Prison and jail populations have tripled in the past twenty-five years, but the conundrum presented by gang warfare in America continues to grow. With only 5 percent of the world's population, the United States incarcerates approximately one out of every four prisoners in the industrialized world. Yet U.S. rates of gun violence and homicide remain the highest in the industrialized world. Even despite drops in crime rates nationally, America experienced a 50 percent rise in gang-related homicides between 1999 and 2003. These data should clearly suggest to most Americans that the draconian and inhumane approaches to the administration of justice, law enforcement, and corrections during recent years have run their course. New and different approaches are needed.

The Barrios Unidos organization has developed important alternatives that promise better results for at-risk youth and society at large. One of BU's most important program models, which could be developed at a more significant level or scale in the future, is the Barrios Unidos Prison Project.

PRISON INTERVENTIONS: THE BARRIOS UNIDOS PRISON PROJECT

The Barrios Unidos Prison Project combines education, cultural and spiritual ceremony, peace promotion, leadership development, cross-sector partnerships, and advocacy. The project uses these strategies to promote inmate reconciliation and improvements in correctional policies and practices. In this work BU enlists private leaders from the media and other sectors in efforts to maintain a substantive bridge between rehabilitating individuals in selected correctional institutions and their families and communities. The Tracy Dual Vocational Institute and the Solano and Soledad prisons have been core sites for the BU Prison Project.

Prison Project volunteers also frequently play an important ambassadorial role in communicating the interests and needs of incarcerated individuals to the authorities that house them. *Cultura* and healing are once again central elements in BU's approach to this work. Deep involvement of family and community members in restorative program activities is a key characteristic of the program, which involves dozens of prominent artists, writers, poets, scholars, political figures, and civil rights movement leaders. Particularly notable program contributors have included well-known performing artists, such as José "Dr. Loco" Cuellar, Harry Belafonte, Mike Farrell, and Danny Glover, as well as United Farm Workers cofounder Dolores Huerta.

BU founder Nane Alejándrez has explained the significance of these and other artists' and civic leaders' program participation in the following terms:

> We know that it is important to bring *cultura*, education, fellowship, and spiritual ceremony to those who are locked up to help preserve and sustain their humanity and connection with their communities. Bringing the spiritual message through leading public figures is an especially important element in encouraging reconciliation and peace, while at the same time working to make institutional change within prisons. In the long term it gives us credibility and traction for advocacy on the inside and the outside.

Through this work, BU has effectively coordinated with Latino, African American, and Native American inmates at various California penal institutions to support education and cultural programs. Such programs have included powwows, sweat lodges, and *danza* ceremonies, which BU has undertaken with the partnering support of spiritual elders and such groups as Izkalli. This work in turn has made discernable inroads into reducing tensions between Sureños and Norteños and between Latino and African American inmates at Tracy prison. Each year, BU provides support to the prison's Latino and African American cultural organizing committees to plan large Cinco de Mayo and Juneteenth cultural events. An important galvanizing aspect of these celebrations has been their promotion of cross-cutting political interests and intercultural engagements on social justice concerns that connect brown and black people in America.

In promoting an understanding of the commonality of cultural values, social experiences, and struggles in America among its pan-Latino constituents and between the brown and black inmate populations, BU hopes to plant the seeds of a new solidarity that has been lost or forgotten on both sides of these historically destructive intracommunity and inter-community divisions. On occasion, the results of these educational and cultural exchanges have been noteworthy beyond the prison's walls. To the delight of inmates, for example, Dolores Huerta gave a rousing speech on critical prison-reform issues during one Cinco de Mayo celebration that led then-California Governor Pete Wilson to ban the labor leader from future visits to the facility during his term. Human rights activist and actor Danny Glover later spoke at a Juneteenth celebration at Tracy. His experience there with African American and Latino inmates redoubled Glover's already staunch public support for prison reform and ending the death penalty in the period that followed his visit.

A widely successful art exhibit held in 2003 at the Santa Cruz Barrios Unidos site generated significant public attention and community understanding regarding the experiences of thousands of Chicanos and Latinos incarcerated across the United States. The exhibit showed works produced by inmates incarcerated in California's Pelican Bay State Prison under the thematic banner, "A View from the SHU: The Human Face of Those Labeled the Worst of the Worst." Featured were eighty-five works created by twenty-seven prisoners. The collection and showing, cosponsored with the advocacy organization Bar None, underscored the need for prison reform and youth deterrence from lifestyles that pave the way to prison. The art presented at the showing embraced the beauty of Latino culture and spirituality, the complex history and heritage of Chicanos and other *Indios*, the inhumanity of mass incarceration, social conditions in barrios that breed crime and violence, and messages of reconciliation, hope, and humanity.

The exhibit was complemented by educational speakers on issues including the negative impacts of "three strikes" sentencing laws on poor communities of color, the inhumane conditions in many California prisons and youth detention facilities, and the devastating long-term impact of adjudicating and incarcerating youth in adult prisons. In his introduction to the exhibit and its public education message, BU's Nane Alejándrez commented:

> For too many young people, there is a misguided notion that incarceration is a rite of passage to manhood on the streets. We want to change this vicious cycle. This is why Barrios Unidos works to maintain family and community ties with our incarcerated brothers and sisters, understanding that without such human contact, they will be hardened beyond redemption. The political pendulum in America has swung too far towards absolute punishment and all but abandoned

the values of human redemption and reconciliation. Given this philosophical bent, the justice and prison systems have become agents of complete dehumanization and criminalization for people who, with the right kind of support, could pay their debts to society and return to be productive members of their communities. . . . We provide community support to rehabilitation and education efforts and enlist inmates to spread the message of peace. . . . We work with them to help us to deglamorize incarceration with young homeboys and homegirls on the inside and out on the streets. Our hope is to bring them back into a positive role in the community and to prevent the young from making the same mistakes. The use of the arts, cultural exchange activities, and education, as well as spiritual ceremony in prisons and juvenile facilities have been powerful tools for us. As a civil rights issue, the unequal application of justice and mass incarceration for Latinos and African Americans is a critical battlefront for both of our communities.

BU programs in adult and juvenile detention centers seek to prepare inmates to be self-advocates on the inside and agents of activism and change within the larger community upon their release. While advocacy for specific institutional and policy reforms is central to all of these endeavors, the process of promoting more comprehensive reconciliation and restorative justice models is equally important to the work.

In California, BU has worked effectively with hundreds of advocacy organizations to promote policy education and institutional reforms. These partnerships have enabled BU to prepare its constituents and allies for effective and informed advocacy as part of a larger reform movement infrastructure. Through the development of the Barrios Unidos Institute concept and the promotion of important policy-reform proposals in the field, BU has begun to consider opportunities to extend this work to the national level in collaboration with an expanding network of community peace activists. BU's standing to pursue such work would not lack precedent. In California, since the late 1990s, for instance, BU has aggressively supported broad grassroots dissemination and policy advocacy of a seminal report by the National Criminal Justice Commission (NCJC) through its various chapters and partner organizations in the Wellness Foundation-supported Violence Prevention Initiative.

Proposals and analysis contained in the NCJC report are among the most thoughtful ever developed on the issues. The NCJC recommendations continue to resonate among many of the most progressive thinkers and advocates in the national criminal justice reform field. Several state policy entities, such as the Little Hoover Commission in California, have developed similar reports and recommendations with BU's encouragement and qualified endorsement. Bolstering BU's capacity to bring increased public and policy-maker attention to such work as a key function of the BU Institute would be an important contribution to offer the national community peace movement during the years to come.

INCREASING INVESTMENT IN VIOLENCE PREVENTION

Another important social and institutional objective for BU to pursue in the years ahead is greater investment in violence prevention, model development, and field-building. Many observers and supporters agree that the BU violence prevention model is one of the best organizational representations of the public health community action frameworks in America. BU's *cultura*-based public health model cuts across a broad spectrum of disciplines including the fields of youth development, violence prevention/intervention, and offender rehabilitation and reentry. BU has strengthened its movement and *cultura*-based strategies by building on evolving public health concepts of violence as a disease and established community development principles.

There is still much that Barrios Unidos can do to advance the beneficial application of its core concepts and principles within youth advocacy, funding, and policy circles at the statewide level in California and nationally. Recent years have presented a compelling need for new and updated legislation around which dynamic advocacy can broadly move public opinion in directions consistent with the views of BU leaders and their field allies. A campaign to establish a California violence prevention authority may be particularly timely and can serve as a launching pad to seize this opportunity. Such an entity can play a major role in encouraging policy and resource coordination on the issues, as well as increased support of violence prevention concepts in the nation's most populous state.

A 1995 report issued by the California Attorney General's Policy Council on Violence Prevention provides an excellent and still-relevant framework to guide such a proposed violence prevention authority. Entitled *A Vision of Hope,* the report sets out seven key strategies to inform coordinated public and private funding of community-based initiatives and more strategic public policy to prevent violence. Summarizing generally, the Policy Council proposals were as follows:

- Strengthen individuals, families, and communities
- Support locally initiated and community-controlled efforts
- Deliver family-focused, community-centered services
- Emphasize balanced prevention and intervention approaches
- Develop comprehensive, integrated plans to change the physical and social environments that produce violence
- Facilitate collaboration and more integrated resource allocations in the field
- Establish outcomes benchmarks for community health-related improvements

Through the broader expansion of its work, BU would be in a unique strategic position to advance community-building principles, such as those outlined above. In the process the organization could dramatically increase the prospects for nationwide violence prevention and community peace work. Mobilizing BU chapters, the VPI network, and allies in the criminal and social justice fields both within and outside of California, BU would be powerfully situated to advance the cause of minority community-building and peace as an achievable national objective. Potential partners for a national campaign of this sort would include such groups as the Institute for Community Peace, the National Crime Prevention Council, the Open Society Institute, the Youth Law Center, the Children's Defense Fund, the Center for Community Change, and the Aspen Institute, among others.

ADVANCING COMMUNITY PEACE AND CIVIL RIGHTS: WHAT NOW?

The 2004 presidential election made barely a mention of prevention in relation to crime or violence issues. Neither incumbent President George Bush nor challenger John Kerry seriously contemplated changes in social policy or investments to end poverty or prevent violence. The words poor, poverty, and prevention were scarcely uttered during the campaign. In fact, throughout the campaign, both candidates spoke as if there were no class of Americans existing below the middle-income level or outside the spectrum of special-interest voting blocks. The truth, however, is that some 36 million people—including 13 million children—live in poverty in America today. Millions more Americans constitute the nation's working poor, who survive only delicately just above the poverty line. Sadly, these individuals and families are increasingly invisible in public discussion and debate.

The California governor's special recall election that replaced law-and-order conservative Democrat Grey Davis with live-action-figure Republican Arnold Schwarzenegger was no more illuminating in addressing issues related either to violence or to poverty in the state. Gross state budget deficits and disinvestments in education and social services have starkly marked the past several years of governance in California. Democrats and Republicans alike have conspired to create this crisis in California politics.

The leadership and trends that shape national and state policy increasingly beg the question, is there any hope? Where are the candidates who represent the poor, the dispossessed, and the young among us? Where are the organized movements of poor people and progressives that are needed to compel the major political parties and their candidates to act?

One encouraging response to these questions occurred recently in Los Angeles, providing an important new chapter in Chicano history: the election of Antonio Villaraigosa, a Mexican American, as mayor of Los Angeles. Villaraigosa's election in 2005 made him the city's first Latino chief executive since 1872. His election is a monumental step for Latinos in California and nationally. In many ways Villaraigosa is a larger-than-life role model for the young constituents of Barrios Unidos. Born in East Los Angeles, he grew up in relative poverty, raised by his mother in a single-parent household. By his own admission, he knew the streets and experienced early trouble with neighborhood violence before being expelled from high school. Villaraigosa completed his diploma at night school before attending community college; he eventually received a bachelor's degree from the University of California at Los Angeles. While at college Villaraigosa was a student activist. He became involved in protests to stop the Vietnam War and efforts to advance minority and farmworker rights. He would eventually find his professional niche as an advocate of labor, education, and progressive justice causes for many years before beginning his career in politics in the California state legislature, on the Los Angeles city council, and now as mayor of America's second-largest city.

Although Villaraigosa did not run specifically on violence prevention or community development issues as cornerstones of his election platform, he has been a consistent champion of poor communities, workers, and education throughout his career. And he is an authentic product of the barrio. Given his voting record to date and his proven commitment to progressive social policy issues, it would appear that poor and working-class residents of Los Angeles now have a leader of unprecedented potential in city hall. It remains to be seen what this homeboy-made-good will do with his newfound power and position.

One of Villaraigosa's early campaign ideas was to establish an office of violence prevention as part of his administration. As a leader, the new mayor has proven to be both an able advocate for Latino issues and a true multicultural leader who strives to achieve the greater good. Balancing these interests will be imperative as Los Angeles faces increasing incidents of interracial tension between black and Latino youth in public schools and escalating violence on the streets. There have been too many instances in recent years in which African Americans and Latinos have failed to find common ground. To stem these tensions, it is essential that Villaraigosa succeed in finding new solutions to old problems by bringing people together on issues of common interest. An office of community violence prevention would be an important investment in civic bridge-building.

One hopes for more leadership in California such as that represented by the new Los Angeles mayor, leadership that is both humbly rooted in multicultural communities and mindful simultaneously of the need to find common cause across historical identity-group divides. But even the most promising and successful political leaders cannot hope to lead going forward without the supportive assent and watchful eye of active, informed, and empowered constituents. Elected officials and institutional leaders can do very little when it comes to engineering meaningful social change without a mandate or the real presence of a tangible political will. Every monumental civil rights achievement that has found its way into American law and policy has resulted from mass social mandates. The sledgehammer of reform is people power.

Sadly, in our current historical context, there is a particularly discernable lull in the sense of responsibility for or accountability to the poor by most institutions of power in this nation. The emerging grassroots movement for immigrant rights in America is a clear indicator of the problem. Humble, law-abiding immigrant workers and their families, subjected to shortsighted and reactionary policy proposals, have found no option but to take to the streets in defense of their fundamental human rights, as well as their many uncompensated benefits to the U.S. economy and culture. Recent moves in Congress to develop comprehensive immigration reform with some provision for the legalization rights of longstanding noncitizen residents have come in response to progressive advocacy by immigrant rights organizers and immigrants themselves, rather than through initiatives originated by political leaders.

There is too little urgency in public sentiment to connect the values of democracy to the moral imperative of reaching some level of social, political, and economic equity in contemporary America. The integrity and viability of democratic governance hangs in the balance. It is a right and responsibility of the people to find a better way. Social movements lead to social change because they connect people to a higher moral purpose. In America, the higher purpose for all of us should be fully realizing the inalienable ideals and rights of democracy for the benefit of all. Severe imbalances between civil equality and economic equity in our society today attest to a moral and substantive breach in democratic practice. The extraordinarily high rates of poverty among blacks, Latinos, Asian immigrants and refugees, and Native

Americans powerfully reflect deepening injustice. Most Americans—people of goodwill and fairness—understand and accept these realities. But what will it take for us as a society to tackle the root causes and forces that have sustained the presence of poverty and racial inequality in America?

Perhaps the time has come to join our hearts and minds in an inclusive process of soul searching, honesty, healing, and reconciliation. At issue is not the creation of more hollow legislative mandates or dates of commemoration, but rather a national dialogue that strengthens the human fabric of our democracy by acknowledging the failures and mistakes of our past and the lingering imperfections of our present society. There was no such process in the aftermath of the conquest of indigenous people nor in the aftermath of slavery or Jim Crow segregation. History suggests that we have paid dearly as a society for our inability to face and heal the wounds of these darker passages in the American journey. A comprehensive, participatory, inclusive, and healing national discourse on the dark side of U.S. history and its reconciliation would help us to repair long-standing ruptures in our social fabric that still to this day prevent us from being fully one America.

ACHIEVING TRUE AMERICAN DEMOCRACY: TRUTH AND RECONCILIATION

Reconciliation cannot occur without honesty, and healing cannot occur without forgiveness. People need to accept poverty, racism, injustice, and discrimination as their responsibility, not for the purpose of blame but for the purpose of change.

Dolores Huerta

It is impossible to create a deeper understanding of the underlying tenets of BU's work without engaging history. At its core, the work of BU is about truth and reconciliation. The quest for democracy—freedom, equality, justice, and voice—in America inevitably requires an honest confrontation with aspects of our history that are inherently uncomfortable. These include, among other things, oppression, discrimination, inequality, and violence. Certain pivotal historical experiences define the nature of the relationships that all racial groups in America today have with one another and the nation we all now call home. Historical instances that undermine our claims to democracy include the conquest and genocide of sovereign native populations, the dispossession of Mexican lands in the Southwest, the institution of slavery and Jim Crow laws, the Japanese internment of World War II, Asian American exclusion and segregation throughout the nineteenth and early twentieth centuries, and the formal and informal discrimination of Jews, Irish Americans, and other ethnic whites along the way. With the exception of congressional approval of reparations to Japanese American families subjected to internment during World War II, there has yet to be a public accounting that adequately reconciles any of these occurrences to the contemporary realities of race, privilege, and deprivation in America.

Moving forward in a way that truly heals and addresses the vestiges of this tragic history requires honest discourse and conscious reconciliation. At President Clinton's first inaugural address, the poet Maya Angelou said, "History, despite its wretched pain, cannot be unlived but, if faced with courage, need not be lived again." Throughout the years, the core constituents of BU—youth, youth organizers, students, parents, elders, teachers, community leaders, clergy, academics, and civil rights advocates—have come to appreciate the power of spiritual and community engagement. They have come to understand the essential role of self-reflection, intellectual honesty, and forgiveness in personal, familial, and communal healing. Many, therefore, have come to support the notion of advancing formal public dialogs on the still unaddressed demons of U.S. history as they pertain to persistent social inequities.

In recent years, leaders in the nation of South Africa effectively employed a national truth and reconciliation commission that enabled historically divided white and black citizens of that country to surface, face, and publicly resolve long-standing institutional divides based on race. The process effectively enabled South Africans to make remarkable community- and nation-building progress as their country transitioned from a white- to a black-controlled governance structure.

Drawing on the South African experience, many BU and allied minority, youth, community, and civic leaders have recently considered supporting a value-driven truth and reconciliation process to address still unresolved institutional inequities that bear on community violence and injustice across the United States. Various notions have surfaced about what such a process might entail, but there has been virtual unanimity about its potential to heal lingering racial animosities that lie at the root of violence and social inequality in America, while creating the redemptive space to strengthen our democracy. Proponents of the idea thus see it not as punitive, but rather as healing and reflective—an honest reckoning of where we have been as a nation and an opportunity to reach some mutual accord about where we want to go from here.

Beyond the healing potential and prospective benefits to American society of engaging in such work, Harry Belafonte has offered the following observations related to the ethical and practical rationales for pursuing it:

> It is critical to understand the history of oppression in America. It is in understanding the anatomy, physiology, psychology, philosophy, and historical application of oppression that it can be dismantled in the present and prevented in the future. To acquire a true sense of self and of collective identity in what is now America, children and adults of color should have an honest accounting and understanding of their historical experience. In a nation built on violent conquest and social, economic, political, and cultural domination by one group over all others, there is 500 years to account for in the light of absolute honesty. There is a scar on the collective soul of oppressed people. Forgiveness is among the highest human virtues. Before there can be atonement, absolution, redemption, and forgiveness, there needs to be truth. Reconciliation between people can occur only after standing face-to-face in the light of truth and the redemptive power of love. To prevent the recurrence of our past failures to live up to the higher values and principles of democracy, we need to collectively face the precepts, motivations, and beliefs that allow these horrific violations to happen. Without truth and reconciliation there is a hidden cancer in America that cannot be cured by half-measures or by masking symptoms.

In June 2006, President George Bush briefed the nation on his findings during a surprise visit to Iraq to assess progress in the "war on terror" and the status of nation-building efforts in that country. The president lauded the plans of the new Iraqi prime minister and the recently elected government to undergo a nationwide truth and reconciliation process intended to confront the unaddressed events of history that stand as a source of profound sectarian violence and roadblocks to civil peace. The process of national reconciliation, as President Bush reported, is essential to establishing a foundation for lasting harmony and democracy in Iraq. Proponents of a truth and reconciliation process in our country should be encouraged. America can send a powerful message to the world as to the integrity of our own democracy if we lead by example and examine the historical sources of our own national divides. Who knows? Perhaps one day the United Nations can promote and support an international movement of truth and reconciliation to inform world development and equitable relations among nations, while ameliorating war and breaches of sovereignty.

The beauty of liberation and justice movements around the world is that they tend to feed one another over time. Gandhi gave the gift of nonviolence to Dr. Martin Luther King, Jr. and César Chávez. Nelson Mandela built on the lessons of the American civil rights movement to end apartheid in South Africa. Now Mandela and Bishop Desmond Tutu have provided the world with the gift and lessons of the Truth and Reconciliation Commission in South Africa. As BU leaders and allies see it, a truth and reconciliation effort in America could build logically on the processes and mandates that have guided prior, government-sponsored efforts along these lines, first in South Africa and, more recently, in Guatemala. A U.S. Truth and Reconciliation Commission (TRC), however, could be crafted as a privately financed undertaking (to ensure its independence) under federal governmental mandate (to secure its legal and societal gravitas). The mandate could be enacted for a two-to-three-year period and include a protocol for investigating and reporting on specific violations of civil and human rights. Based on this work, the commission could develop informed recommendations for dismantling laws and practices that support structural inequality and violence in America. Conceivably, the proposed commission could be organized in the following way:

- Secure financial support from private institutions and individuals
- Enlist a highly qualified, multidisciplinary professional support staff
- Consist of a diverse cadre of commissioners, building on the strong involvement of civil society leaders, reputable academicians, and respected representatives of historically oppressed communities
- Hold fact-finding conferences, forums, hearings, and roundtables nationally, with strong local input and participation
- Issue and widely disseminate multilingual quarterly, annual, and final reports with plenary documentation submitted to Congress, all state legislatures, and the Library of Congress

The envisioned commission's final report would include key historical accounts of unjust policies and practices in America and their lessons, an assessment on the state of American democracy, recommended corrective social measures intended to strengthen multicultural opportunity and civic participation in the United States, and a vision statement for strengthening American democracy in the years to come.

The TRC's final report and attendant archival information would establish a shared historical record and road map for encouraging more equitable future public policy in areas ranging from poverty and justice to violence and democratic participation. The report would additionally serve as an authoritative source in the development of multidisciplinary social studies and civics curricula for publicly funded schools and colleges in ways that would help to encourage a more socially aware and informed next generation of Americans.

CONCLUSION

In the window of history during which this book was commissioned, researched, and finally completed, there has been a terrorist attack on American soil, the declaration of a new war, and three catastrophic hurricanes that have captured the attention, energy, resources, and compassion of our government and the American public. The worst of these storms was given the name Hurricane Katrina. It has been recorded as the most devastating natural disaster in modern American history. The overall devastation to life and property in the Gulf Coast region was horrific and heart-wrenching. What also made Katrina so terrible and appalling, however, was the deep and wide-spread presence of abject poverty and racial inequality that it unveiled. The images broadcast across the nation were irrefutable as thousands upon thousands of poor African America families were left stranded, starving and abandoned in the communities surrounding New Orleans. With Hurricane Katrina, America got a firsthand snap-shot of the deep decay and misery that still faces the poor living in our ghettos and barrios on a daily basis. The disaster revealed a level of disparity that has been too easily masked in recent years by the neon lights of commerce, political rhetoric, and romanticized notions of America. Americans of all backgrounds should be concerned about the implications of our national path in the early twenty-first century.

During only the past decade, we have lost precious ground in civil rights, witnessing a virtual gutting of social policies aimed at advancing the quality of life for the nation's poor. Hard-won legal protections and civil liberties have been steadily deteriorating under the reign of conservative political leaders. Indeed, U.S. rights and justice leaders are facing unprecedented new challenges threatening to further turn back the clock. A prevailing mind-set of fear and siege is being exploited to justify the siphoning of public resources to a war of narrow economic interest abroad and a xenophobic police state at home. The concentration of conservative power in the White House, the Congress, and the federal judiciary pose real threats to democracy.

The recent passing of iconic social justice figures of the twentieth century, such as Corky Gonzales, Coretta Scott King, Rosa Parks, James Foreman, and Bert Corona, marks the symbolic passing of the torch for protecting and advancing U.S. civil rights to progressive leaders who have benefited from their life's work. Established Latino leaders in California and other parts of the western United States are heavily affected by these developments. The historic leadership of both the Chicano civil rights and BU movements is graying, and the time has come for a new wave of principled and capable leaders to emerge. The young people who participated in the historic 1968 East Los Angeles student walkouts are now fifty years of age or older. It is essential to the future success of the struggle that the lessons, experiences, and knowledge of our social justice history be passed on to a next wave of leaders. Arguably, the need for new leadership has never been greater in the nation's barrios.

The current immigrant rights struggle for justice in America establishes a framework for a new social justice movement to emerge in Latino communities across the nation. This next stage of change will require the best and brightest minds of the coming generation of young Latino men and women. Many young Latino leaders have risen to take up the cause and put life back into the *movimiento*. Still, too many have not. The war in Iraq, cast first as a response to terrorism, then as a battle to promote democracy, has been exposed as a product of misinformation and lies by the White House to justify invasion. The war has now cost several thousand American lives. Many of our soldiers killed in action have been poor young men and women of color. Many have been Latinos. Yet, the antiwar movement just barely registers as a whisper in our communities.

Minority students continue to experience unacceptably high rates of failure in inner-city schools, and in Los Angeles race riots between black and brown students have become an increasingly more common occurrence in recent years. Yet no multiracial student coalitions involving Latino youth leaders have materialized to protest with their black counterparts against the underlying circumstances that produce these problems and condemn too many of them to lives of marginality and incarceration. Young students of color are less likely to get into a college or university than at any time in our contemporary history, yet affirmative action has been allowed to die a quiet death in California. When will people of color, particularly Latinos and African Americans, join one another (and other poor and marginalized people in this country) to challenge the common plights of our communities?

While writing this book I was able to discuss the tragedy of September 11 and the subsequent wars in Afghanistan and Iraq with literally hundreds of youth and community leaders from poor neighborhoods in California and other places. A surprising commonality emerged from my conversations with these individuals, all of whom shared an intimacy with poverty and violence, but only a few of whom shared a common geographical experience. Although emphatic condemnation of the barbaric attacks on New York and Washington was universal, my conversations produced a simultaneous sense of understanding (particularly from more politically and historically versed informants) as to the deeply rooted hatred toward America that exists today in many oppressed countries. The vast majority of these commentators clearly expressed their patriotism and support for the American way of life. But they were consistently able to comprehend from their own experience and knowledge of U.S. history how the failures and hypocrisy of American policy at home and abroad had produced such violence. As one young poet of Native American heritage expressed to me,

> If you are on the wrong side of American history and privilege, it is very hard to forgive the wrongs your people have suffered. It takes our highest and most profound beliefs in the Creator and in the ultimate good of humanity to be reconciled to one's oppressors and to believe in what is now called America. I wept at the horrific sight of the burning twin towers not only because of the unjust loss of innocent life, but because I know the love and faith it takes to fight such destructive hate within me owing to the past atrocities on, and the present circumstances of, my people. Although I have chosen a path of peace, I know that history unresolved and injustice unremedied will give rise to rebellion if not violence, again and again.

The lessons and contributions of BU to the human family in America underscores that truth and reconciliation are both possible and necessary. The potential for achieving healing and peace pertains to the individual, the family, the community, and the larger society as a whole. Dr. Robert Franklin, in a speech at an Institute for Community Peace conference, prescribed the medicine of moral literacy to restore virtue and renewal to American civil society. Moral literacy, as he defined it, is learning and passing on the redemptive lessons of history and culture as the fundamental basis of instruction to our children. In America, a truth and reconciliation process would allow for a cleansing that we have never undergone as a nation. The process would yield a living testimony that could undergird the continuing vitality of our Constitution and Bill of Rights. It would produce an inclusive and definitive articulation of our highest ideals and aspirations as a nation. It would establish the basis for a new and authentic social contract.

The offering of BU to the world is the transformative power of *La Cultura Cura*, or, as BU observer and California Tomorrow capacity-building director Rubén Lizardo has helped to reframe it for this publication, *Cultura es Cura*: culture is the cure. Indeed, BU's work with multicultural youth and communities reveals that culture is transformational. The transformation entails reconnecting people to the beauty of their humanity. It involves lifting up the life-affirming values of family, community, and society that flow from the inheritance of traditional culture. And, finally, it deals with providing a foundation for self-love and respect of others. Paramount to the reconciliation process practiced by BU is providing young people with an honest account of history and a base of knowledge for understanding their origins, their common experiences, and their rightful place in the human family.

A fundamental lesson of the BU story is that within every culture there exists the universal imperative to fulfill each individual's human potential while achieving collective harmony. *E Pluribus Unum*—out of many we become one. If America is to heal and reach the moral ascendancy to which it has always aspired, it must be made whole by trusting in the power of its pluralism. It must believe in the growing diversity and potential of its people. This is the essence of true democracy. This is the essence of Barrios Unidos. *¡Sí, Se Puede! ¡Gracias, Tata Dios!*

Appendix
Selected Poems: *Palabras de amor, justicia y paz*

Flor del Barrio

Querida Flor del Barrio, from where do you come?
De sangre indígena, corazón sagrado,
Sanctified spirit, flourishing in a garden of pain.
The poverty and desperation that oppresses our children,
Cannot contain the dignity the Creator has placed in their hearts.

Tender Flor del Barrio, show me how to care.
Your tender hands like the petals of a rose,
Reach out with each new day towards the sun,
Nurturing the frail, celebrating love, and affirming life.
In infinite beauty, you breathe the pain of others,
Your resolve to serve heartened by their tears.

Wounded Flor del Barrio, how graceful should we bleed?
You've known the pain of cruelty, addiction, and neglect,
You wear human frailty like a thorny crown upon your head.
Where is that place of stillness where the Creator soothes our soul?
To conceal or reveal our scars to others, what makes us understood?

Resilient Flor del Barrio, how do warriors survive?
Do you wither in the longing of your own solace?
Knowing the moon rises that even the sun may rest.
Have you found yourself a sanctuary, have you made yourself a home?
Bringing hope, teaching forbearance to the broken and forlorn,
Where do you find your peace?

Radiant Flor del Barrio, refusing to be muted.
Nuestro barrio, suffering and thriving in the shadow of opulence and
    human indifference.
A divine light in a poisoned land, your love and conviction illuminate
    the darkness.
There are others like you—embrace, respect, and encourage them.
There are those that came before—honor, learn from, and account for them.
There are those that will follow—nurture, nourish, and prune them.

Mystic Flor del Barrio, of what do you dream?
The transformation of this garden of pain is not beyond our grasp.
To live as the Creator intended,
Nuestro barrio, a paradise filled with the laughter of emancipation.
A place where our elders sunset in peace and with dignity.
Where our children blossom with the taste of love, justice, and discovery
    as their daily bread.
Our barrio, a place where we are one with the earth, with one another,
    and with the Creator.

Frank de Jesús Acosta
(Para JGS)

A Prayer for Nane

Peace warrior, called to bring to an end the madness in our barrios
The blood of our ancestors flows strong and true through a loving heart
Once a tortured soul in the belly of the beast
The beckoning of *carga* seared your consciousness
The endless search for false flight dimmed your light if only for a time
Seeking to destroy the *corazón* that beats in the center of our *movimiento pro paz*

Campesino, pachuco, tecato, hermano, padre, buen hijo, street and Saigon soldier
These are all jackets you have worn on the journey to redemption
Like smoke and ash you have risen and fallen with the sun and the moon
Risen and fallen with every prayer, victory, human failing, and broken promise
With every young life you have lifted up to a more noble life
A mother's prayer has been answered, a desperate promise has been kept

Just as the children you have chosen to love and reclaim
You know what it is to thirst for love and hunger for belonging
Filling the emptiness with poison as false prophets built a hollow home for the lost
But the truth will not abandon its children as another peace warrior is born
Culture, spirit, and the living power of an ancient past rose up within you
To unite our fractured barrios, creating a circle of healing where none is left behind

The faith of one who has loved you in darkness and light
Sister Jenny has been in your essence since before your first breath
El amor de tu sagrada madre, hermanas de sangre y de espíritu
The woman nation encircles you now as your strength and your hope
The brotherhood, spirits of the unborn, hearts of our children, and wisdom of the elders
Together with our ancestors, surround you in the circle of love your life has forged

Peace warrior, born by the loving hand of Tata Dios to guide the way to
our true selves
Like the morning star to the sojourner, your love has brought light to the lost
We pray for you now in this moment of need
That the poison that afflicts you may be no more
A testimony to the power of the old ways, the medicine Creator has given us
In unity with the four directions, we enfold you now in the sacred hoop
of life
All my relations

Frank de Jesús Acosta
(To my carnal Nane, *con todo amor y respeto*
Gracias, Tata Dios, The cancer is gone)

Reina Azteca

The sacred blood of ancient kings and queens runs through your veins,
Sangre indígena binds you to all creation on mother earth.
There is healing in your tenderness and power in your faith,
La Virgen de Guadalupe and Tonantzin are alive in your acts of love and
  mercy.

La reina azteca, on your lips a never ending prayer for the children.
The four winds lifting up your hopes to heaven on the wings of the eagle.
You are called to walk in a sacred manner as a witness to the presence of God,
As woman warrior, priestess, prophet, wife, mother, and sister you guide us.

Mi reina morena, the brown nation will not survive without your
  courage.
The suffering of a barrio in decay is the playground for our children.
Your thorny crown reminds us that pain is the pasture of redemption.
Teach us to walk once again as a loving *familia* with dignity, respect,
  and grace.

Mi reina azteca, heart flowing with the blood of a once glorious nation.
The faith within you binds heaven and earth in a great circle of spirits.
I lay my life at your feet and place my heart in your hands,
Walking at your side to fulfill the prophecy that Aztlán99 will once again
  rise.

To the woman nation

Frank de Jesús Acosta

Of a Child and Mother

The love of a child and a blessed mother
Nothing sweeter in God's creation
A love that can save and bind a nation

I saw the little one burst out of his skin
For the chance to dance, to laugh, to sing
The child's spirit fills the room to keep the old ones true

Child presses a cheek to his mother's hand
Earth and heaven merge with flesh, blood, and spirit
A perfect moment when we dwell in the heart of God

The love of a child and a blessed mother
These are the eyes with which we should see the world
Tomorrow, through my mother's heart, I will see only sisters and brothers

Frank de Jesús Acosta
(Para Little John of God)

Sometimes A Man Comes

Sometimes a man comes whose song is deep heartbeat;
Sometimes such a man breaks the bounds of self-made imprisonment of drugs and alcohol and the madness we call "the life."
Sometimes a man like this becomes a hurting body of the hurting soul, yet whose healing is in a word, who has seen his body crucified on the cross of the hypodermic needle and *locura*, and still dreams;
Sometimes, but not always, such a man finds his lights, whose passion is caring, whose wisdom is a blazing spear, and who has turned the darkness scarring his essence into a path we can all follow;
Sometimes a man comes who holds the deepest cries in his eyes and sacrifices what no one else will dare for peace;
Sometimes we are truly alive for the presence of such a man, such a woman, such a human being, for when the Creator has given a great task;
Sometimes such a person is our blessing way, our purifying waters, engulfed in Earth Mother's enchanted tears; we are fuller, more complete, for the love of such a man.
Sometimes a man comes whose life is a seed for the spring of our humanity, who turned an enemy into a friend, who reached out to this humble poet in his darkest need and said, carnal; who loved all our children as if they were his own, including my son draped in the same cloth;
Sometimes, but not always, we are truly honored by the presence of such a man, such a woman, such a human being.
In the spirit of this man, this Fire Keeper, we will always be strong.

Tu carnal siempre,
Chicome Tochtli/Luis Rodríguez
(For Walter Guzmán, The Fire Keeper)

Chicana

Chicana
You make
Men machos
With hearts of gold
Chicana
You alone
Make the sun
Set in the east,
Water run uphill . . .
Chicana
You make
Man's dreams
Man's realities . . .
Chicana
Te doy el grito
de mi corazón
Te doy el mundo
por tu amor . . .
Chicana
Mona Lisa
Of the universe, The magic carpet rides
You alone possess
And you
Chicana
And
Only you
Can give
Life beauty
And
Death reason

Magdaleno Rose Avila, a.k.a. "Juan Valdez"

Nuestro sueño—Our Dream

our dream
late at night in the barrio
listening to one more
police siren . . .
we searched the moon
for a way
out
for a way
in . . .
we searched for peace
and found the doors closed
some boarded up with permanent plywood of rejection
we knew that *la raza*
wanted something more
expected something better . . .
late at night we looked up to brother moon
and began to burn our sage
to bless our song
to beat our drum
to build a house for all our dreams
and we thought of *la raza*
we thought of *los cholos*
los pintos
we thought of us all
we thought of mañana
wanting to make it better than yesterday
we wanted to stop the violence
from the guns
from the fists
from the eyes
from the heart
we wanted to heal
of the wounds
of the minds
of the hearts

we wanted to give them . . .
to give them hope
where there was despair
to give them love
where there was hate
to give them more
when there was less
we ran the race
more than once
we embraced mother earth
and she loved us back
she gave us rain
and sun for all our dreams to grow
with which to bear their fruit
we gave to the barrio
and it gave back to us
and we reached beyond our house
to help other villages be strong
we built a wind of hope
we built a house of remember for any one
any where
and we let them share our dream
a dream built on
drumbeats
heartbeats
and remember.

Magdaleno Rose Avila
(for Barrios Unidos)

Mi Barrio, My Hood

Mi barrio is home
My hood is home
It's all we have
     These days
The ways of our ancestors
       Have been forgotten
They've become the old songs of old people
But the old people believed
In faith and in confession
And forgiveness and the
       Honor of our children
And our children are
Now and not later
Mi barrio is home
My hood is home
Together they become one world

My brother you prayed for me
And I in turn prayed for you
And now we are one
Mi barrio, my hood
     Ashe!

               Kwabena Antoine Nixon

When the Ice Breaks

Have you ever been beaten
Beaten banged broke
    Abandoned
Tied bound and gagged
And dragged in the mud wallowing in your memories
While wishing you could turn back the hands of time
    Have you ever felt
    Betrayed belittled
    Withered wrinkled
    Restless
    Defenseless
    Self-less . . . helpless
    No self-esteem
Have you ever felt that . . . God
Should be spelled dog
    Have you ever
    Dropped stopped laid
Prayed for the sun to come out tomorrow
    Have you ever
Listened to the sound
Beautiful bluebirds singing Sunday songs of sweetness
    That makes the dew drop to the earth
    Have you ever
    Hugged your mother
    Loved your brother
    Kissed your sister
    Kissed your daughter
Have you ever smiled at danger
    Held your heart
Cried like Niagara Falls
Have you ever wiped the sun from your face
    And knew God
        Gives
        Light
    And life and love and
        Happiness

Kwabena Antoine Nixon

The Spirit of America

Ain't it our blood that separates the white on that flag
aint America really our motherland
but dont mommaland look like a hag
I wont say land of the free
Im saying home of the brave
cause it was the home of slaves
in God we trust
she never declared our independence
so prayers and spirituals became a must
we would rather be African
because we cant define being American
Why would we rather be African unless the truth is
that we are American
we creep up on human beings
stealing the souls from their emotional continents
we rape ideas
a racist towards skin complexion
because of internal fears
we set up economic establishments
to nurture a silent greed
we appear to be more like America
with the dream of Africa being a desperate need
just beyond the paradise smoke
imagine the perfection
Utopia
the dreamy land of Africa
the fertile crust of creation
with the shape of mountains beyond the will of words
and African kings walked with African queens
taking care of African children
building African traditions
listening to African music
eating African foods
watching beautiful African dance
enjoying African customs

raising African civilizations
and African kings
and African queens...
but what about African screams
the tears of little girls beneath
the penetration of a two-hundred-pound king
the molestation of children
because an African is mentally sick
what about African blood
those spears that gorged out eyeballs
and split skulls in half
an African tribe floating
in a pool of blood is dead
while the African tribe that conquers moves ahead
What about those African wars, African jealousy,
African crimes, African punishments, African violence,
African greed, African anger, African rage,
and African pain
what about African pain...
we would rather be African
because we cant define being American
I wonder
how much of that kinte cloth
is representing African art
how many people are actually hiding
their true souls beneath African clothes
cause Africa is so great
So what is America?
She is a spirit of hope
that presses on through time
and only by Gods will
she allowed Jesus to become mine
Aint it our blood that separates

Brandon Morton

The View From the Edge Of Hope

For so long
Dreams have scattered before the night
Leaving my vision naked
A pattern conceived along
The miles of fear
An emptiness that grows near
As focus fights for its freedom
To be clear
And before my eyes
The road has come to a split
A fork set into the heart of destiny
A direction of choice
For now my soul can only stand bent
Searching beyond purpose
For the voice
From the waste of this life
My soul is given rest
I sit me down on the rim of hope
And dangle my feet over its edges
It feels good to be here
And the breeze I feel is somehow familiar
Ive known it once before
But never like this
The smell of hope fills more than my nose
It wraps me like a blanket
And gets all in my clothes
Ive always wanted to be here
I mean
By my choice
Because I wanted to
Because it was good for me
The view from hope
Is beyond anything Ive ever known
But it is not beyond me
I see the rhythm and pace of life

Moving in a concert of creation
I see the give and take
Of night and day
Working together to mold the notion of time
I see the ritual dance
Of life and death
Moving slowly
Deliberately
And from where I sit
It is a beautiful dance
And there is nothing to fear
And out of the corner of my eye
I catch a glimpse of a familiar face
No longer matted with pain
And loosed from the strings of darkness
Far beneath the dangle of my feet
I catch a glimpse of me
I call down to myself
But I will not answer
I am ignoring myself
I hear me calling me
But I will not answer
And all at once I look up
While I am still looking down
And we smile at one another
What a beautiful sight
What a beautiful god
To allow the two halves of myself
The one who waits and wants
And the one who wants and waits for nothing
To finally meet
To reassure each other
Of the miracle of hope
I wish you could feel
What I feel
I wish you could see

What I see
And the marvelous thing about god
Is you can
You can come out of your closet
Of fear
You can shake yourself free
From the weight of the lie
You can
But do you want to?
I didnt always want to
I didnt always know how
There is a view from the edge of hope
That you have got to see
It is a view of you at a better place
At a better time
Theres more than enough room for the both of us
Have a seat
Take off your shoes
And wait for the miracle called you to pass by
Once you see
You will never be the same.

Brandon Morton

A Chicano Manual on How to Handle Gringos
José Angel Gutiérrez
2003, 240 pages, Trade Paperback
ISBN 978-1-55885-396-6, $12.95

A Gringo Manual on How to Handle Mexicans
José Angel Gutiérrez
2001, 160 pages, Trade Paperback
ISBN 978-1-55885-326-3, $12.95

The American GI Forum In Pursuit of the Dream, 1948-1983
Henry A. J. Ramos
1998, 224 pages
Clothbound,
ISBN 978-1-55885-261-7, $24.95
Trade Paperback,
ISBN 978-1-55885-262-4, $14.95

Black Cuban, Black American: A Memoir
Evelio Grillo
Introduction by
Kenya Dworkin-Mendez
2000, 224 pages, Trade Paperback
ISBN 978-1-55885-293-8, $13.95

La Causa: Civil Rights, Social Justice and the Struggle for Equality in the Midwest
Edited by Gilberto Cárdenas
2004, 176 pages, Clothbound
ISBN 978-1-55885-425-3, $28.95

Chicano! The History of the Mexican American Civil Rights Movement
F. Arturo Rosales
1997, 304 pages, Trade Paperback
ISBN 978-1-55885-201-3, $24.95

Colored Men" and "Hombres Aquí" *Hernandez v. Texas* and the Emergence of Mexican-American Lawyering
Michael A. Olivas, Editor
2006, 352 pages, Clothbound
ISBN 978-1-55885-476-5, $44.95

Dictionary of Latino Civil Rights History
F. Arturo Rosales
2006, 528 pages, Clothbound
ISBN 978-155885-347-8, $69.95

Enriqueta Vasquez and the Chicano Movement: Writings from *El Grito del Norte*
Lorena Oropeza and Dionne Espinoza, Editors
2006, 320 pages, Trade Paperback
ISBN 978-1-55885-479-6, $16.95

Eyewitness: A Filmmaker's Memoir of the Chicano Movement
Jesús Treviño
2001, 400 pages, Trade Paperback
ISBN 978-1-55885-349-2, $15.95

Hector P. García: In Relentless Pursuit of Justice
Ignacio M. García
2002, 416 pages, Clothbound
ISBN 978-1-55885-387-4, $26.95

The Life and Times of Willie Velásquez Su Voto es Su Voz
Juan A. Sepúlveda, Jr.
2005, 398 pages, Trade Paperback
ISBN 978-1-55885-402-4, $16.95

The Making of a Civil Rights Leader: José Angel Gutiérrez
José Angel Gutiérrez
2005, 160 pages, Trade Paperback
ISBN 978-1-55885-451-2, $9.95
Ages 11 and up

Memoir of a Visionary: Antonia Pantoja
Antonia Pantoja
Foreword by Henry A.J. Ramos
2002, 218 pages, Trade Paperback
ISBN 978-1-55885-385-0, $14.95

Message to Aztlán
Rodolfo "Corky" Gonzales
Foreword by Rodolfo F. Acuña
Edited, with an Introduction, by
Antonio Esquibel
2001, 256 pages, Trade Paperback
ISBN 978-1-55885-331-7, $14.95

The Struggle for the Health and Legal Protection of Farm Workers: El Cortito
Maurice Jourdane
2005, 192 pages, Trade Paperback
ISBN 978-1-55885-423-9, $16.95

Testimonio: A Documentary History of the Mexican-American Struggle for Civil Rights
F. Arturo Rosales
2000, 448 pages, Trade Paperback
ISBN 978-1-55885-299-0, $22.95

They Called Me "King Tiger" My Struggle for the Land and Our Rights
Reies López Tijerina
English translation by
José Ángel Gutiérrez
2000, 256 pages, Trade Paperback
ISBN 978-1-55885-302-7, $14.95

We Won't Back Down Severita Lara's Rise from Student Leader to Mayor
José Angel Gutiérrez
2005, 160 pages, Trade Paperback
ISBN 978-1-55885-459-8, $9.95